The Family Ranch

T0168574

The Family Ranch

LAND, CHILDREN, AND TRADITION
IN THE AMERICAN WEST

Linda Hussa

PHOTOGRAPHS BY
Madeleine Graham Blake

UNIVERSITY OF NEVADA PRESS
RENO & LAS VEGAS

University of Nevada Press, Reno, Nevada 89557 USA
Copyright © 2009 by Linda Hussa
Photographs copyright © 2009 by Madeleine Graham Blake
All rights reserved
Manufactured in the United States of America
Design by Kathleen Szawiola

Library of Congress Cataloging-in-Publication Data

Hussa, Linda.
   The family ranch : land, children, and tradition
in the American West / text by Linda Hussa ; photographs by
Madeleine Graham Blake. — 1st ed.
      p.   cm.
   Includes bibliographical references and index.
   ISBN 978-0-87417-771-8 (hardcover : alk. paper)
   1. Ranch life—West (U.S.) 2. Ranchers—West (U.S.) 3. Family—West
(U.S.) I. Blake, Madeleine Graham, 1948– II. Title.
   F596.H88 2009
   306.850978'091734—dc22   2008043554

The paper used in this book is a recycled stock made from 30 percent post-
consumer waste materials, certified by FSC, and meets the requirements
of American National Standard for Information Sciences—Permanence
of Paper for Printed Library Materials, ANSI/NISO Z39.48-1992 (R2002).
Binding materials were selected for strength and durability.

Credit: "Anthem" by Buck Ramsey is from *Buck Ramsey's Grass: With Essays
on His Life and Work.* © 2005 Scott Braucher and Bette Ramsey, Texas Tech
University Press, 800-832-4042. Reprinted with permission.

Frontispiece: Visalia and Charley Hammond

University of Nevada Press Paperback Edition, 2010
19   18   17   16   15   14   13   12   11   10
5   4   3   2   1

ISBN-13: 978-0-87417-819-7 (pbk.: alk. paper)

To our mothers and fathers, our husbands, our children

Contents

Preface, ix

Acknowledgments, xix

Introduction, xxi

The Stoddart Family | CROOKED CREEK RANCH 1

 Eminent Domain and Land Use: Cattle Free in '93 22

The Tyson Family: | TYSON QUARTER HORSE RANCH 31

 Entrepreneurs: The Emerging Rural Marketplace 50

The Hammond Family | TJ QUARTER CIRCLE RANCH 73

 Advantages of Being Ranch Raised: Ginger Graham
 and Jessica Hemphill 93

The McKay Family | WALKING BOX RANCH 109

 The Public Trust: Missing Water 137

The Harper Family | LITTLE HUMBOLDT RANCH 161

 Planning for Succession: Handing It Over 187

The Walker Family | DUCK VALLEY, SHOSHONE RESERVATION, OWYHEE 205

 The Hope and the Promise: Working Together 226

Preface

> *"When you've reached the edge of an abyss, the only progressive move*
> *you can make is to turn around and step forward."*
> —ANONYMOUS

T his book is about ranch families in the rural West today. Remarkable stories arise when these parents, their children, ranch work, and nature come together for a lifetime. Modern America offers few other situations where the family enterprise continues to thrive as it does on ranches like these. Entire families work together for the success of the common enterprise. Parenting includes passing on to the children the skills, values, and traditions that have held the ranching community together—in every state, in every region, in every country—for generations, because they work.

The book is also about the challenges of maintaining the family ranch as viable and the ways independent ranchers meet those challenges. Although ranching protocol has not changed over time, ranching in the modern world has gotten a great deal more complex. Regulations governing grazing and water rights, taxes, and inheritance laws, as well as the challenge of providing education for children on ranches that may be a hundred miles or more from the nearest school, escalating operational costs, and markets that respond more to international politics than local supply and demand threaten their unique way of life.

I know of no other industry that turns totally within the concentric circles of family and community. Company towns build up around mining and timber sites, but none immerse the whole family, including children, in the day-in, day-out, year-round work like ranching. Even their clothing, developed for out-of-doors rough use in winter or summer, is a signature look.

Films, documentaries, and the media tend to emphasize stereotypes when depicting people of the land. In order to find unique yet authentic families, I polled ranchers, cattle buyers, and farm advisors around the Great Basin, and talked with the staff at the Western Folklife Center. Their list of recommendations was astounding. The families I've chosen to focus on represent scores of others who etch their presence on the land in clear terms. They are as different as wildflowers: the members of four of the families are biologically related, while those of two others are linked by adoption; one is a single mom, and one is a single father. Yet they all accept the challenge of tending and growing a small business, despite the odds, and in doing so they bring their children along. I wish all of those recommended could have been included. In spirit and commitment, they are here. Any generalization made on these pages is based on a personal perspective shaped over a lifetime of working and playing with ranching families, and I hope it will be taken in that spirit.

PARENTS IN THE WEST make use of tools present in the physical world outside the classroom: Going out on horseback replaces recess; learning where to be to turn the wild cow is companion to splitting fractions; assessing the feed and the condition of the cattle is economics; helping with irrigation is mathematics, geology, understanding contours of the land, and the exercise of practical application; sending a loop to settle swiftly on a calf at a branding is the finesse and teamwork of sports; the responsibility of caring for animals—seeing birth, trying to hold off death—are undertakings of a serious nature. All of these lessons build self-esteem.

These parents nurture and care for their children with tenderness, marveling, forgiveness, compassion, and trust, making sacrifices to give them a life in and with nature. Within that context they encourage their children's thinking outside the *self* by connecting them to the welfare of animals, land, water, and the community of neighbors. Carrying thought forward to action requires planning beyond *self,* contributing to their development as responsible, productive citizens—the very qualities of a leader.

Indeed, this book shows, above all, that the children of ranching families have time and space and silence in which to explore and grow their own ideas, to figure out how things work. Combined with their practical experience, they develop common sense, good judgment, and independent thinking. At home, there may be a school set up in an extra room, or a studio with modeling clay and colored pencils, or a shop with a plasma welder and a pile of banded pipe. Children range in age from infants to college-age young adults. The thing they have in common is a right to a sane and caring future.

THIS BOOK began in 2004 when I heard the story of Joyce and Joe McKay, ranchers in eastern Oregon, who had adopted six Haitian children from halfway around the world. In doing so they reached across lines not commonly crossed in the rural West.

In the heart of conservative ranch country, Joyce McKay grew up in a house where black faces were daily companions. Her father, Julian Arrien, subscribed to *Ebony* magazine and, among other newspapers and magazines, he set *Ebony* out for his children to read. It may have been an unusual choice for an immigrant Basque sheepman, but Julian kept an open door to new people and ideas.

Joe McKay and his brothers and sisters shared their space and the food on the table with displaced kids from the area. Joe's parents willingly took in any orphaned or left-behind child. The McKay home nearly levitated with the thump of energy generated by their generosity.

When Joyce and Joe married, this generosity and openness became a part of their union.

When an article featuring the McKay family—and their adoption and rearing of six Haitian children on their ranch—ran in the *Western Horseman* magazine, reader response was unprecedented. The public wanted to know more about working ranch families. That launched the idea for this book.

As luck would have it, a second extraordinary ranching family, the Stoddarts, moved to our ranch. They had three children at that time, with a fourth born a year later. These children were on horseback with their mother, Tami, from the age of two weeks.

Joyce was handed the world in print by her father. Tami had a mentor, too. Her grandmother Marge Isaacs passed away long before Tami was born. On a trip home, Tami's father gave her the journals and papers of her Grandmother Isaacs. One of her journals contains a letter written forty-five years ago to the president of *Ebony* Publications. Her words are the essence of what binds these families together.

Rte. 1 Box 279
Clackamas, Ore
Aug 24, 1961

Ebony Publications
Mr. Johnson, Pres

Dear Sir,

In the little community of Rock Creek, Oregon, where I have lived most of my life and am now raising my family, there have never been any Negro neighbors. Therefore most of the children in the community have never had the opportunity of having any colored friends.

One of our best friends is a wonderful Negro gentleman named Charles King, who lives in Phoenix, Ariz. On his last visit to us a very amusing incident occurred.

One evening we were all gathered in the living room reminiscing about the "good old days" when we were children. Charles mentioned that when he was a boy in Cleveland during the Depression he and the kids in his neighborhood used to chew tar as a substitute for chewing gum. I was amazed, as I had never heard of such a thing. "Where did you get the tar?" I asked. "We peeled it off the street." He said. "In six or seven years we had that street very nearly peeled clean."

My husband remembered that he, too, had chewed tar as a boy.

Charles went on to say "It was very good—good for the teeth too. It made the teeth real white. I liked the taste, too. In fact, I used to swallow the juice."

With a real serious look on his face, my husband placed his suntanned arm along side of Charles' darker colored one. "Well, that accounts for the difference in color. You swallowed *more* juice!"

We all had a good laugh, but my eight-year-old daughter took this very seriously. The next day my little girl and her friend came in from play with black stains over their hands and beneath their fingernails. They held out both arms to show me and looking sadly up into my face, my little girl said, "We tried it, Mom. We ate the tar and it didn't work!"

We were amused but our hearts were touched by two little tar babies who saw so much love in our friend they wanted to look just like him. This kind of love imagines no color barrier but reaches out in response to that which is real within everyone and loves a person for what he really is.

What can an average person like myself do to be of help in promoting good racial relationships? I am not very well informed, so I am subscribing to your magazine and would welcome any suggestions you may have.

With a sincere desire for a peaceful world where all men truly have the same privileges and dwell together in love, I am,

Sincerely yours,
Marge Isaacs
(Mrs. Lewis Isaacs)

In addition to the McKays and the Stoddarts, this book contains the stories of other families:

Gail Tyson, a single woman who adopted an eighteen-year-old daughter. They work together on the Tyson Quarter Horse Ranch.
Carl Hammond, a single dad with two grown children and one daughter in junior high, who binds his family with the art of his ranching heritage.
The Harper Family, who ranch on the historic Little Humboldt Ranch.
The Walker Family, who ranch on the Duck Valley Shoshone reservation.

These are more than just stories, however. These interviews reveal something essential about child-rearing in the rural West today. They teach us that ranching families who contribute good citizens and multitalented youngsters to society are a culture in decline. The myriad challenges that face the small family ranch threaten the survival of the traditional ranching culture and the values that define it. These families—and others like them—have an important role: they are the bookmarks holding the West open for the rest of us.

Many of the children on these pages are doing the work of adults with competency and responsibility. That is possible because they have learned the consequences of carelessness, and their teachers are parents whom they love and who love them. They develop a balanced view of their parents' work, understanding why things break down, or fail, or don't go as planned. But they also witness pride in success. As junior partners in the family company, ranch children develop around realistic expectations, making observations based on their actual experience. They may even initiate a solution to a problem or suggest an alternative plan. Contributing to the welfare of the family ranch is a heady achievement for these young men and women, and it is a lesson that will carry them through difficult teenage years.

Today most urban children live with the aid—or distraction—of their own cell phones. Music is a constant companion thanks to iTune headphones; cars have DVD players for backseat passengers as a source of entertainment; text messaging means that children are never out of touch with their friends.

Ranch kids are not isolated into a world of their peers where their tastes, thoughts, values, habits, and attitudes are influenced by the whim of the most dominant child, by what is *popular,* by what they can *buy,* or feel shame for the things their parents *cannot afford.* Kids who see their parents join in a system of helping their neighbors with spring or fall cow work understand that the big crews will also show up at their place. Everyone benefits from sharing the load. It's as close as our modern culture gets to the country tradition of barn-raising, and puts the young generation in the mind-set of cooperation and friendship. In addition, they are always in contact with, and learning from, adults. *Elders* are more than a familiar and respected part of the adult community: They are friends who have time to spend with youngsters during the work ranchers share; they are friends whose advice and stories are pertinent to the children's learning. It is common for ranch children to approach adults with out-stretched hands and express genuine pleasure in the greeting. As a party to the camaraderie and encouragement of these adults, they develop confidence and the strength of character to trust their own values.

These families live at a distance from the opportunities available in towns and cities, but the advantage lies in the control parents have to welcome appropriate, beneficial, fun information, and to screen out the inappropriate. The children have connected, united lives where they understand the impacts of their decisions. This kind of parenting, a comprehensive plan with an application that will span nearly two decades, is less likely to be overturned by the temptation of a momentary risk.

I have observed that these children are already influencing the behavior and goals of others. Theirs is a lifetime achievement. They began forming the answers to some of life's questions quite literally at their mother's breast where earth's rhythm becomes the beat they long for in the place they revere. The West cannot escape the pressures of development, mining, and urbanization. Neither politicians nor business will fight for its future. Families must orchestrate the movement back from the abyss, and together we can step forward.

When families such as these gather, conversations will likely turn to issues that impact their lives. The essays interlaced with the profiles of the families represent the concerns of all people of the arid West. Ranches may be set far apart around the West, but ranching families are tightly spooled around issues that affect their future.

"Eminent Domain and Land Use: Cattle Free in '93." With good reason, a majority of ranchers in the West rely on grazing leases on government lands: one-third of the United States is under the control of the government; half of those lands are west of the Continental Divide. Half of California and 87 percent of Nevada are public lands. Eminent domain is not a new concept; however, news reports make it clear that the rules guiding acquisition have changed, and the law is often open to interpretation in the courtroom.

"Entrepreneurs: The Emerging Rural Marketplace." A segment of the population has discovered "slow food," the art of growing, of preparation, and the dining experience. It may not be for everyone, but those who believe *their bodies are what they eat* are willing to pay for high-quality food. David and Julie Evans and Wendy and John Taggart are ranchers who are designing their products to serve those philosophies.

Advantages of Being Raised Ranch: Ginger Graham and Jessica Hemphill." A surprising number of high-profile people have grown up on the back of a horse and give credit for their development to the time they spent in the saddle. What they gleaned from the experience prepared them to succeed elsewhere. These two women, raised a generation apart and at opposite ends of their careers, give us insight into *the value of time and space and silence in the arms of nature.*

"The Public Trust: Missing Water." Two old sayings surface in the arid West: "Whiskey is for drinking; water is for fighting over." This one also, "Water rolls downhill to money." In the Great Basin, the average annual precipitation is between four and ten inches. Yet the population of the West is growing at a rate that threatens to eliminate the resources necessary to support life. The greed that led to the *drying up* of Owens Valley, California, in order to *green-up* Los Angeles is recurring in other parts of the West to the disadvantage of California, Arizona, New Mexico, Nevada, and Utah—the driest states in the nation.

"Planning for Succession: Handing It Over." Who has time for paperwork? Apparently not a lot of ranchers. Yet providing for your children and for the land is the ultimate duty of responsible parenting and land stewardship. This guide to legal terms and procedures make the process of accomplishing financial equity less painful.

"The Hope and the Promise: Working Together" reminds us that solutions to vexing problems such as fair distribution of water, the authority of eminent domain, and federal land management can come from our own experience and effort. In the end, strength comes from doing the right thing for the right reasons.

BUT GETTING BACK TO THE KIDS: As you may have guessed, these kids are adorable and sweet and funny, but they are also clever and resourceful and gentle.

Visalia Hammond plays the piano. Joe Harper plays the bagpipes. Tilly

Walker can kick a football fifty-three yards. Gabe McKay can run like the wind. Isabel Stoddart is a poet. Anna Rose McKay wants to be a veterinarian. Elsie Anna Stoddart likes horned toads. Charley Hammond is both artist and mechanic. Cedar Tyson taught her pet hen to do tricks. Joan McKay tells the best stories. Grace Stoddart lost both boots while chasing an ornery cow in a two-thousand-acre field and found them again. Gloria Hammond designs jewelry. Clare McKay has a perfect Cockney accent. Reuben Stoddart was slimed by a leprechaun. Kyon Walker is an expert on dinosaurs. Sam Harper is an expert cinch maker. Rusty Walker is majoring in art. Luke McKay is quiet and thoughtful, Martin McKay is an action hero, and they both ride steers in the rodeo.

All the children have their own horses. Some have two or more. They all have learned the prevailing winds, the indigenous trees, and where the beautiful rocks at their feet came from. They are familiar with the birds that migrate through their region, they know the edible plants in the area, and when the deer rut and when the fawns are born. They know the native grasses and which way is north. They can find their way home from any place on their ranch. Each child is totally individual, yet their experiences are so in-step, and they're so agreeable, they could change houses at night and it might be weeks before the parents caught on that they had the wrong kids. These ranch families, for all their similarities and differences, represent the best of the modern rural West. They embody a deep sense of responsibility to the land and to the human community around them, and they reflect a sense of the fundamental importance of the family unit and of the vital role of children within this exquisite universe of land and livestock, family enterprise, and extended community. The parents see their role not only as overseers of the ranch unit but as their children's most important teachers. Child rearing on these ranches includes passing on the values and skills that are fundamental to the western community.

I hope you will enjoy getting to know these parents and children and how they are preserving the western way of life.

Acknowledgments

I am grateful to Madeleine Blake for her collaboration. Seldom does the opportunity come along to share an experience as rich as the making of this book. She and I offer sincere thanks to the many people who supported the ideas explored on these pages:

To those six families who are the foundation of this book, we are indebted. They are people who have scant leisure time to welcome strangers into their homes, yet they generously made time to explore their thoughts on ranching and rearing children in a ranch environment.

And to the many people who gave information and perspective for the essays, clarified and expanded on their opinions, and encouraged with new questions, our thanks.

Essential to us was our friend and project manager Carole Anne Fisher, who began working with us shortly after the inception of the book. We are deeply in debt to Carole for promoting the project and raising funds to provide us with travel and work expenses. We thank Carole for her encouragement, and seeing to every detail in an astute and businesslike manner to make the book a reality. The project would have been impossible without her. We were blessed to have her optimism, good humor, directive suggestions, and her resplendent cocina.

And to acquisitions editor Margaret Dalrymple, who recognized the value in this book from the outset, thanks for her continued support through the publishing process.

To Sara Vélez Mallea, my thanks for her editorial expertise, wisdom, and guidance.

There are several important organizations in our region devoted to celebrating traditional western history and lifestyles, and we are honored to have their support and grateful for their contribution to this project: the Favell Museum, the Great Basin Institute, the High Desert Museum, and the Western Folklife Center.

Friends of the project whose generosity made this work possible include Laurie Curtis, Pete and Gloria Fundis, Howard Ellman, Frank and Ginger King, Ned and Marilyn Livingston, Bill and Barbara Thornton, Palmer and Lynn Traynham, and Dick and Nancy Wendt.

There were many people with a deep interest in America's West who offered their time, experience, and creativity to provide invaluable support: Bill and Sheri Burke, Hal Cannon, Carolyn Dufurrena, Lee Juillerat, Marita Kunkel, Pat McMillan, Wally McRea, Peter Pisarczyk, Stefanie Pisarczyk, Laura Pritchett, Taki Telonidis, Forrest Rodgers, Charlie Seeman, Katie Hussa Tims, Ray Decker, Bobby Ray, Mary and Jim Richert, and Jack Welpott.

For the use of the poetry of Buck Ramsey, we are grateful to Bette Ramsey and Texas Tech University Press.

Finally, a special note of gratitude for their boundless encouragement, patience, and understanding: Tupper Ansel Blake, Bob Fisher, and John Hussa.

The true beneficiaries of this project are Madeleine, Carole, and myself. The everlasting joy is in the journey. Thank you all, and dear readers as well, for recognizing the value of western ranchlands and the families who protect them.

In the mid-1950s, a family we knew well took my parents and me to see the ranch they recently bought near Calistoga in Northern California. The purchase was initiated by their interest in the house, which I was told had been designed by Frank Lloyd Wright. It seemed to rise out of the steep terraced hillside as bedrock might if it were squeezed enough. It was shaped like a settled v, and each room of the three levels embraced a view of gold baked hills and monstrous oaks that held deep green shade within. The Yellow Jacket Ranch was isolated far above the valley floor on the side of Horse Mountain. With range all the way to the top, it had undisputed water rights.

The manager took us on a tour of the ranch that included a look at the cattle, horse barn, a two-cow milking parlor, chicken house, garden and orchard inside a twelve-foot deer-proof fence, a root cellar, and finally, a small building set over the creek flowing through deep woods of oak, laurel, and madrone. As a fifteen-year-old, I stood in that small room hearing the eternal rush of water beneath my feet, looking at machinery I was told was a water-powered generator. The manager pushed his hat back on his head and, as if still amazed, said, "This ranch is completely self-sufficient."

His words rested within me. Perhaps it was the look in his eyes of utter satisfaction. The animal in us is capable of recognizing things we must remember for our survival, and his respect for self-sufficiency settled into my being.

Urbanization in this country has encouraged a system where others keep us warm and fed. Because our houses have been built on top of the fertile soil and we are too busy to plant and harvest our own gardens, we expect our local grocer to offer a choice of the foods from the world market-place: fresh—every—single—day. Although we ought to demand that our local government deliver to us potable water at our tap, we have been conditioned to *buy* bottled water. Because cities and suburbs have become unsafe places to our raise children, we drive expensive cars powered by costly fuel that pollutes our environment to commute hours each way to work just to get them out of undesirable neighborhoods. The irony is that by providing them safety, they are deprived of time with us. We have crafted other gods and lost title to the frontier. It's a matter of evolution.

Who does the future belong to? I believe it will belong to those who commit their lives to finding answers to the difficult questions that affect the future of our environment and its nonrenewable resources. It will belong to those who devote their attention to finding solutions that benefit future generations. It will belong to those who can sustain life. It will belong to those who recognize that devotion of a kind that passes between parent and child—*mothering*—can be applied to every relationship humans have with nature.

RANCHERS are often characterized in stereotype as the monosyllabic country hick with a passel of backward kids, narrow of vision, uneducated, unsophisticated. How then, do we explain the success of the following ranch-raised people? Hard work, fresh air, healthy food, and nature's peaceful partnership helped them rise to the top and gave them the platform from which to influence the thinking of several generations.

JUSTICE SANDRA DAY O'CONNOR remembers "horse" was among her first words. She was the first woman in our history appointed to the U.S. Supreme Court. When she retired in 2005 after twenty-four years of service, Justice O'Connor left behind a reputation for rendering decisions that were carefully deliberated and fairly reached. She never wavered from the belief that the Supreme Court's role in American society was to interpret the law, not to legislate. In her dignified manner Justice O'Connor has been a role model for all Americans, saying, "Society as a whole benefits immeasurably from a climate in which all persons, regardless of race or gender, may have the opportunity to earn respect, responsibility, advancement, and remuneration based on ability."

In their book *Lazy B: Growing Up on a Cattle Ranch in the American Southwest*, Justice O'Connor and her brother, H. Alan Day, wrote about the ways they and their sister were brought up:

> We know that our characters were shaped by our experiences there. The value system we learned was simple and unsophisticated and the product of necessity. What counted was competence and the ability to do whatever was required to maintain the ranch operation in good working order. Verbal skills were less important than the ability to know and understand how things work in the physical world. Personal qualities of honesty, dependability, competence, and good humor were valued most. . . . We like to think we benefited in many ways from our ranching experiences, that openness, generosity, and independence were ingrained in each of us. If so, it is due to the life created for us by our parents on that island called the Lazy B.[1]

AT THE YOUNG AGE of thirty-five, Jeff Bezos, founder and CEO of Amazon. com, was named *Time* magazine's 1999 Person of the Year. He gives much of the credit for his extraordinary success in business to the summers he spent on his grandparents' ranch in Texas. His grandfather, "Pop," added another layer to his parents' guidance, teaching him that isolation could lead him to higher ambitions and adventures he hadn't yet dreamed.

Every summer until Bezos was about sixteen he traveled to his grandparents' ranch in Cotulla, just north of Laredo. The physical demands of the ranch were a healthy change from his book world at home. He learned to ride horses, drive cattle, brand and castrate calves, fix windmills, and drive Pop's '62 Scout. He and Pop fixed a D6 Caterpillar tractor using nothing but a stack of manuals that were as tall as he was. "You have to have a lot of patience on a ranch in the middle of nowhere," Bezos noted.

His grandfather was a model for the value in having two unrelated careers, aerospace and raising beef. He believed that if you understand the function of every minute element of your business and you are prepared to work and wait through the hard times, you can succeed at anything.

Of the time he worked beside his grandfather, Bezos said, "Ranchers . . . learn how to be very self-reliant. . . . My grandfather did all of his own veterinary care on the cattle. To repair the D6 Caterpillar bulldozer when it broke we would build cranes to lift the gears out. This is just a very common sort of thing that folks in far away places do. . . . It was a great experience."

"Everyone always says that parenting is not a popularity contest," Bezos said. "I think that grand-parenting is. My grandfather taught me that it is harder to be kind than it is to be clever. That has always stuck with me. People think of liberty or freedom as being happiness, but it's not. Those very smart people who wrote 'Life, liberty, and the *pursuit* of happiness' had it right."[2]

DAVE BRUBECK'S importance to American jazz is unmistakable. The Dave Brubeck Quartet, headlined by Brubeck and alto saxophonist Paul Desmond, helped to reawaken public interest in jazz after World War II. Their innovative composition "Time Out," released in 1959, was a tour de force. Brubeck was the first jazz musician to earn a cover of *Time* magazine, which heralded him as the leader of "the birth of a new kind of jazz age in the U.S."

One might think that a jazz musician of Brubeck's stature would have to have grown up in the neighborhoods of Harlem or Bourbon Street. But Brubeck was born in Concord, California, in 1920 and raised on a cattle ranch at the base of Mount Diablo in the San Francisco East Bay. His rancher father and world-class pianist mother provided the ingredients that led him and his two brothers to create unique musical compositions. When he wasn't riding with his father he was composing his own musical signatures on the parlor piano. Dave was eleven when his father sold the homeplace and took a job running a large ranch in the foothills of the Sierras near Ione, California. Dave loved life on the ranch, the horses and the daily work.

"I grew up on a 45,000-acre cattle ranch. And my dad was the manager," Brubeck said. "If he owned it, I wouldn't be talking to you now. I said, 'Ma, you've got two musicians [his two brothers]. I want to be a rancher.'"

To him, ranch work that might be boring to some provided the foundation for many of his most famous jazz compositions. "In the beginning, I just thought differently than other people and I was alone a lot growing up," he said. "I'd always be thinking musically when I had jobs to pump water or ride horseback. I'd lie there under the gasoline motor that was vibrating and I'm singing rhythms against that. . . . I was always singing rhythms against the horse. If he was trotting I'd sing in a different rhythm, if he was walking a different rhythm, if he was galloping. . . . So I'd get these different rhythms going against the horse's gait. The sounds of my horse's hooves were the music I would write."[3]

IF RENOWNED SILVERSMITH Ricarda McCleary Clause wasn't shopping with her mother on Union Street in San Francisco, she was riding with her father on their Spring Creek Ranch in northern Nevada, tending their cattle, or at the workbench he built for her alongside his in the shop. He gave her a toolbox of her own and his love of ranch life and books. Her mother showed her the beauty of carved ivory, pearls, silks, art, and books. Together they presented the idea that she could make pretty and useful things. When she was in grammar school her parents divorced, and she was sent to boarding school where she struggled for many years. "If the nuns at the school had known to give me something to do with my hands," she said, "it would have been easier."

Ricarda is a self-taught silversmith. Her objects d'art in the form of jewelry, bits, and spurs are highly sought after. Her lifework began at her bench in the ranch shop learning to create with her set of tools. Ideas come to her in the twilight hours just before dawn when she remembers the layer of amber willow limbs above log rafters in an old cabin, or it's the one-dimensional design of a pine cone smashed in the street, or two fish passing in a stream that appear able to pass air through their gills. People admire her work without knowing the origin of the elements that make it unique.

She cuts silver in the intricate and complex designs of her childhood days on their desert ranch in Nevada.

ALL OF THESE PEOPLE packed the great quiet and everyday touching nature with them on their journey. Are they an anomaly—a handful of people out of place in our company? Did they reach their destinies regardless of their birthplace? Or because of it? Was there some ingredient that let them know they had more to give the world? Were they complete, so full of the rightness of their rearing that they were able to reach back to the door standing open and go on again, leaving in increments of one step? In the perfection of rhythms and routine is there the knowledge that going forward is possible without losing anything behind, freeing them to seek a way to offer that wholeness to others through music, service, beauty, justice? While for others—home is enough. What would they say to us who chose to stay?

Perhaps they would say mothering is the act of rearing in the gentlest of terms, expansive and generous. But it comes at a price: work will occupy the life and be the fiddleback curve of its infallible design. The smallest child holds a bottle for an orphaned lamb or calf or foal. Milk flows with a motion of giving forth locked in the infant memory. The foundation of caring is born of those elementary chores leading early on to a sense of purpose, and pride. Children grasp the concept that they are a part of something and are made sturdy by the connection.

They would say—Let the lessons advance. The value of the process is that the building of self-confidence happens while doing a sometimes tedious but necessary job. The field they plow, harrow, disc, seed, and, finally, harvest is an investment in themselves, both in a sense of business and humanity. Their lives grow around production, and they are reared with responsibility outside of their own desires. Those empowering, strengthening lessons are learned under the loving eye of parents.

Ranch families assume that the West is the perfect place to be a parent. They live at a distance from one another by choice and necessity, and thereby accept the challenges of solitude where imagination is unlocked and ideas have room to form. Isolation purifies the development of character in a classroom of quiet horizons. Entertainment in infinite variations comes, for the most part, from within. The parameters developed from nature's energy and vastness and seasons provide a map to follow, on the same track with nature.

I think back to the man who designed a practical way of living around the art of the Frank Lloyd Wright house, and realize that the practical elements these parents invest into mothering their children becomes the art of a whole life. Self-sufficiency is difficult to attain, but paramount and worthy of the effort.

IN THE FACE of these challenges to think of the West as a place to raise kids is a small idea. The families collected here, and many others, care for the land in a way that only those who are invested can care, by history in and love of a place. Their commitment comes from their deep understanding and appreciation for their home land. Their payoff is the family unity of purpose, the shared work and responsibility, the ever-present learning and teaching, the rewards and challenges of productivity.

The West depends on handing it over. The way these parents raise their children is an integral part of how they care for the land. Without this kind of mothering dynamic, we lose the West.

Notes

1. Sandra Day O'Connor and H. Alan Day, *Lazy B: Growing Up on a Cattle Ranch in the American Southwest* (New York: Random House, 2002); Evan Thomas and Stuart Taylor Jr., "Queen of the Center," *Newsweek,* July 11, 2005.

2. 1999 person of the year—Jeff Bezos, December 27, 1999, http://www.time.com/time/magazine/article/0,9171,992927,00.html. Jeff Bezos, interview, Academy of Achievement, May 4, 2001, http://www.achievement.org/autodoc/page/bezoint-1.

3. "Rediscovering Dave Brubeck," with Hedrick Smith, "The Ranch Years," http://www.pbs.org/brubeck/theMan/theRanchYears.htm (accessed April 18, 2007); personal correspondence.

The Family Ranch

The Stoddart Family

CROOKED CREEK RANCH

Isabel, Reuben, and Grace Stoddart

Reuben Stoddart is a yearling. He is sitting on a horse, propped on the swells of the saddle with his back pressed against his father's body. This elevated seat is familiar territory. He's been riding almost daily since he was two weeks old. One wonders what it is like to learn the world from the back of a horse.

It's spring branding time on the Crooked Creek Ranch, and Reuben is watching the ropers sail loops to snare calves quietly from the rodear. Dave Stoddart is letting his horse take a breather, holding Reuben while his wife Tami ropes. He said what happened next took him by surprise. Reuben lifted his hand as if he had a rope in it and, mimicking what he was watching, rotated his wrist to send his imaginary loop toward an imaginary calf. No one said, "Hey, Reuben, let's twirl our hand like the ropers are and pretend to catch a calf." Somewhere in his mind he collected an image and translated its action into physical reality.

A year later Reuben was in the living room one snowy day trying to rope his rocking horse. The loop fell short time after time. Dave could see frustration building in his son, so he said, "Hey Reuben, let me build that loop for you." He slid the hondo down the rope to make a small loop and handed it to Reuben. One swing and Reuben let the loop fly. As if by magic, it settled around the horse's neck. Reuben walked forward, took his rope off the horse, and beamed, "Well! That makes me happy."

BEYOND the Stoddart house there are horses in corrals. A mare in a round pen pulls strands of long hay out of a manger. She is three—halter broke, gentle, feet trimmed regularly, routine health care, and turned out with the mare band. Basically, life has been good. Today, she meets Dave for the first time. With a halter over his arm, he opens the gate and steps in. He looks at her the way a fellow might look at a girl on their first date—admiring her form and wondering what's cooking inside her head.

He moves quietly around the mare without approaching her. She turns her head and looks at him with curiosity. Soon she follows his movement, bending to see what he's up to, drawn as if a string is tied between them. He leads her mind to seek him. In the beginning, he doesn't care if she turns into the fence or toward him, just so he gets a change from side to side.

The mare will learn that she can move away freely, and that helps develop her thinking toward what he is doing. Then he will start asking her to hang in there a little bit. When he stops her, he steps back and takes the pressure off. "Pretty quick," he said, "she will look for that place where there's no pressure. And then pretty quick, that place where there's no pressure is where I am."

It's a natural instinct for a horse to go into pressure. Put a horse in a corral and try to stop him. He will put his head up and try to go over it. Put a snaffle bit in his mouth and try to get his head down—his head will go up. Try to get him to put his head up and it will go down. "They go against the pressure," he said, "so I teach them to *yield* to pressure."

Dave tries to trick them by causing what they want to do to be the right idea. "It might seem backward," he said, "but you reward them by taking the pressure off and then they've got it." As Dave talked, he coiled and uncoiled the soft rope. His eyes never left the mare, hoping for a glimpse of interest he can follow to her mind.

These are the ideas of a man who trains horses to be useful partners in the business of ranch work. He develops a regimen for each horse and stays flexible, letting the horse dictate progress. "When I run up against brick walls, I go back to the things that worked, clear back to something elementary to remind them, *you can yield here.*"

He applies the same patient thinking to his children.

DAVE WAS RAISED in the third generation of the Stoddart family on Crooked Creek Ranch in eastern Oregon. He has met a good many horses on the unbroken ground of the partnership between horse and man. He says he learns as much as he teaches. In his home country, four inches of rain is the norm. It takes a lot of acres to satisfy the appetite of a cow, and daylong outside riding provides time to work through the layers of a horse's intelligence.

The Stoddarts' Crooked Creek Ranch is tucked between Steens Mountain and the Owyhee River in a north-south drift. It is high desert country, surrounded by other historic ranches that also trace their beginning back to the first half of the 1800s: the Alvord, the White Horse, the Kunney, and Mann Lake. The Crooked Creek range is thirty miles wide and seventy miles long, inside one perimeter fence with no cross fencing. The Crooked Creek cattle are always at home except when they ignore drift fences and wander. Then, true to tradition in the ranching business, the country is gathered for branding or working out calves of a weanable age, and rodears are held. The word *rodear* is taken from the Spanish *rodero,* meaning to gather to work. Riders hold the cattle, or horses, in a loose bunch, and one at a time, a representative from each ranch separates out their cattle according to the brand and drives them home.

Holding rodear, riding through dry cows on winter feed, or checking on calving cows is quiet work for young horses like Dave's three-year-old mare. The action, the challenge of gathering or moving cattle, breathes new energy into a tired horse, like catnip to a kitten.

DAVE AND HIS WIFE, Tami, have four children. Coming at you on horseback between their parents is the future of the ranch, the only grandchildren so far. Isabel is nine, Grace is six, Reuben just turned three, all on their own horses. Two-month-old Elise Anna is snug in a front pouch inside Tami's coat.

The economic value of a ranch is in the feed it produces and the livestock it supports. Ranch life is generally not extravagant; it's a job, often a difficult

Dave roping a calf out of the rodear

job, tedious, demanding of time and energy and exquisite attention. There's no 401(k) retirement package, but there should be. The only payoff comes when/if the ranch is sold. When that happens, every increment of progress the family has worked to create is sacrificed.

IN APRIL OF 2005, Dave pulls the truck and trailer into a vista point above the waterfalls of Fall River Canyon. The Stoddarts are returning from the Californios, an event celebrating the vaquero tradition of working horses and cattle. Dave's six-year-old ranch gelding was the high-selling horse, going for more than fifteen thousand dollars. Memories of a ride in the spotlights and the applause, and the check in his pocket, ease the long drive home.

When the truck and stock trailer roll to a stop, doors open and kids and dogs cascade out in burst of energy that mimics the waterfall in the canyon below, active, unending, and beautiful. They run and explore and squeal with laughter, gathering pinecones, picking tiny lavender asters before they gather back together.

Dave, Reuben, and Merlin Rupp, a grandfatherly family friend, sit on the rock wall overlooking the canyon high above the drama of the plunging waterfall. Isabel is learning slight-of-hand tricks. With the excitement of a magician with a trick up her sleeve, the clear blue eyes of childhood lock on Merlin, rendering him immobile. If Merlin catches a glimpse of silver as her fingers slip behind his ear, he says nothing.

"Ta-da! Magic!" Isabel sings to her audience as she draws a quarter from Merlin's ear. He gasps his surprise as a reward for her neon smile. Grace, the magician's helper, giggles. Merlin asks Isabel if she can do that again. She can and does, and then, smiling shyly, slips the magic coin into the pocket of her jeans, patting it as it slides to the bottom. In her eyes, and Grace's, is a look of triumph.

Merlin was the buckaroo boss on Don Miller's Rock Creek Ranch and the Double-O in eastern Oregon when fifteen-year-old Dave hired on. Buckarooing for Miller meant Dave would have to ride horses with a reputation for being tough. At that point in his life, Dave thought he was every bit as tough as they were.

Merlin spent his working life on the best ranches in the Great Basin, bringing young men like Dave along. His goal was to get the work done and keep the boys from getting killed. He and Dave have been as close as friends can be for twenty years. Now he's bringing along the next generation.

Off to one side, Tami and Isabel are engaged in a conspiracy to master a new trick. Tami drapes a chain over Isabel's thumb and index finger and slips a brass ring up the loop of chain from the bottom. When she drops the brass ring, the edge is supposed to graze Isabel's third finger and flip over so it hangs on the chain without falling. Mother and daughter are nose to nose when the brass ring slides from Tami's grip. It misses Isabel's third finger and falls, spinning onto the pavement. Tami's laugh, quick as the sliding ring, flips Isabel's disappointment into a smile. "Well, that didn't turn out like we thought, did it?"

By Tami joining in the effort, Isabel is not criticized, nor does she feel the weight of those sighing words "try again." Isabel drapes the chain on her fingers and focuses on the timing. The second attempt works perfectly. The ring grazes her third finger, flips, and holds halfway down the chain—magically.

Later, Tami said, "Isabel is competitive, and yet if she fails, she's quick to give up. Tami tries to be funny with her mistakes if she drops an egg on the kitchen floor or spills something, so the children, especially Isabel, will see that everybody makes mistakes, and it's not devastating if she tips over a cup of milk. Sometimes Tami sees a look on Isabel's face and instantly knows what she's feeling. "It's hard for me to let her sort it out," Tami said. "I want to rush to the rescue. Afterward she'll come to me and we'll talk about it, when she's ready."

Tami builds Isabel's confidence by closing off the escape route. From the coin appearing out of nowhere and the brass ring holding on the chain, praise builds her will to try. Magic tricks, working with horses, or school lessons are all the same—Tami makes learning fun. Her encouragement and confidence help the children progress toward a sense of achievement. Coin to brass ring to the long list of efforts in a lifetime, it's all a matter of attitude. As Tami teaches her children rudimentary reading and math, she also tries to equip them with a balanced sense of themselves. Fear of failure walls away the will to try new things and a hope of accomplishment. Each step forward gives them a tighter hold on their own abilities.

TAMI HAS PERSONAL EXPERIENCE with the effort of building confidence. She was raised one of eight children in a suburb of Portland, Oregon. Like many young girls, she was fond of horses. With very little help, she raised a colt and broke him to ride. That horse carried her to a lifetime of working with horses. Initiation into ranch life with a family devoted to the vaquero tradition was in her stars. She met Rosie Stoddart at a colt-starting clinic held at the Bell A Ranch in Burns. The first thing she saw when she drove into the ranch yard was a fair-haired young woman bent over with a horse's hind foot braced on her knees, driving nails to hold the shoe in place.

"A woman putting shoes on her horse, *that* had my attention," Tami said. Rosie's oldest brother, Dave, showed up later. Tami had heard about Dave and Rosie Stoddart being *the real deal* ranchers, working with colts, feeding with a team, building reatas, and she admits to having "a certain curiosity."

At the end of the day, Dave sent his two dogs Snip and Shade to put a cow out of a corral. The dogs worked as a team, aggressive but *listening* to him, controlled and focused. "I was in awe," Tami said. As the participants all walked to the house for supper, Dave and Tami were the last two going through the gate. She got up the courage to say that she enjoyed seeing his dogs work the cow, and he stopped and began talking about his dogs. Then he said, "Wait a minute." He took his coat off, laid it outside the gate on the ground for his dog Snip, and said, "She hasn't been too many places, and when we're someplace she's not sure of, I leave something of mine for her to lay on, so she'll know where I am." That was her first interaction with Dave.

Rosie invited Tami out to Crooked Creek to help them gather the cattle in the fall. Tami was initiated into gathering the many square miles of desert country by professionals.

"Crooked Creek Ranch is perfect," Tami said, "It's unique in that there aren't fences. The riding is different and the cattle are a hardy bunch. Dave's family bred that into them. They're self-sufficient, they know the range, and they have to have some wits about them. They can't be just a cow that's used to somebody putting them here or there. They have to be a *thinker-cow.*"

Riding the open country of Crooked Creek Ranch kept Dave interested in horses. There was always something to do, to see. It was never the same. The light can make an ordinary day spectacular in the desert, even in the middle of the winter. His dad would have a project, and off they would go across the country—Rosie, their brother Dobe, and him, eight or ten hours, freezing their fingers off, little kids, just miserable. "Every day you're just pretty certain you're gonna die," he said. "We'd get home and Mom would fix some hot chocolate or something. We'd thaw out and find out we were going to live. Then the next day—'Well, where we goin' today?'"

Summertime, it was always hot, and they never had enough water. "Mom

Lunch break at a Crooked Creek branding

sewed up these little quart bleach jugs in a pant leg, and we'd hang 'em around our saddle horn," Dave said. "They'd last till about ten o'clock and then no water the rest of the day. 'Oh! We're going to die.' We were right there again the next day. I think it's the same thing for horses when they're wrangled out of the pasture every morning. It's a cowboy thing. Everybody loves that morning. Everybody hates it midafternoon. Any old cowboy or buckaroo you talk to, they all live for that morning."

WHEN DAVE was fifteen he packed his bedroll and left home. Maybe the cause was restlessness, or a family conflict. He didn't want to wade the mire of family politics just to find out that the ranch he'd been born to and the work he'd been doing would get him nothing in the future—that all he was working for and could expect to get in the end was wages. He went to work for Don Miller in Catlow Valley, on the Rock Creek Ranch and the Double O, widely known for their unpampered horse string and buckaroo boss, Merlin Rupp.

"I got the opportunity to ride some really tough horses at Miller's," Stoddart said. "The way we used to start horses at Rock Creek, we just roped them and tied them up and tied up a hind leg, sacked them out, got a saddle on them, and then they got some dummy like me to get on them and go for a bronc ride. It mostly turned out okay."

Dave never set out looking for a wreck, but every morning it was a battle for survival. "Every day, 'cause those horses were really tough and they were really cranky," he said. "There were some that could buck pretty hard, and dang sure all of them could buck some. If you could get on, you could probably ride most of them. But it was an *on the ground thing*. You had to hobble them and tie a leg up, or tie a hind leg to the hobbles, because some of those horses could run and buck as well with a leg tied up as without."

The horses were wrangled every morning, and the day horses were roped out. At Miller's they didn't use halters; they put a snaffle bit right on the horse. "If your horse was real tough, somebody would help you hobble them. You got your saddle on and you stood around and waited for everybody else to be ready to go. That was how you warmed your horse up. Meanwhile, he stood there thinking about what he was going to do.

"Being a short-legged guy, I couldn't get on those horses real easy, so I'd ride them right out of the hobbles. To do that, I'd get on and off while they were still hobbled a few times, and then loosen the hobbles, step on them and GO! Invariably, they'd go to bucking or stampede. But if you ever got the opportunity to do that, it's *very thrilling*."

WHEN TAMI AND DAVE MARRIED, they hoped to have a place of their own. Crooked Creek is their ideal. They went back to work at the ranch for a few years after Isabel was born, and they lived at Rye Grass, a cow camp on the north end of the ranch. In time the honeymoon with the family ended.

"It was a life you only find in books," Tami said as her hands turned imaginary pages. "That country is spectacular, and it can be brutal. But it's very satisfying work and you work hard. Of course, Dave has always been so gracious to invite us along into his work, and to bring our kids along so that we're a unit doing our life, mothering and doing our work, carrying on as a family."

On a ranch you are constantly going from one set of dynamics to another, depending on the season and the job. Riding is something that happens every day, all year long. "When Isabel was a baby, I was highly offended if anyone even suggested that I not go," Tami said. "I didn't miss a day, whether it was feeding or riding. She was happy to be wherever we were. When Gracie came along it was the same, and when Reuben came along nothing really changed except that we were saddling four horses, Dave's, the two girls,' and mine with Reuben. Sometimes the days can be pretty cold and long, but the kids were happier doing that than if we were in the house all day. If the weather was really awful, we adjusted to staying home. If we're stuck in the house, they get crabby and cranky, but if we saddle up and go, all that changes instantly."

Tami looked down and rested her lips on Elise's hair a moment, then lifted her chin. "You never know if you're making the right decision."

DAVE GREW UP working cattle in a rodear, holding the cattle in a loose herd while they are worked outside with no fences whatsoever. As riders cover each section of the range, they gather the cattle out in the open, wherever the cow boss decides. Riders hold the perimeter of the bunch. In turn, they ride near the cattle, rope a calf, and take it to the branding fire. The shots are thrown from the outside to keep the cattle mothered-up. "It's especially important for the cattle to stay mothered-up when you've got strays in the bunch," Dave said. "You have to be sure which cow the calf belongs to before you brand it. So, the long shot that comes from out of nowhere and settles quietly is the most efficient. My idea of the tradition of the reata is that everything is slow and easy."

For children, gathering is recess, freedom, and scattered thoughts. They move across hills, seeing cattle hurrying ahead of riders far into the distance. Rodear is the classroom, the beginning of the apprenticeship. They help hold the cattle to keep them from breaking out or straying while the crew sorts or brands. At a distance from the action, kids typically become bored or lost in daydreams by midmorning. Those with desire keep sharp, observing the cattle, the way the ropers position their horses, how they handle the cattle once they are roped, where the wrecks happen, and why they don't. Like Reuben, they copy what they see; their small hands trace the air, sending imagined loops to their mark.

The older kids take a turn working on the ground, tending the fire, setting ropes, carrying the iron. And they itch to mark and castrate and brand before they are asked to perform those jobs. Around the fire they hear the old men's gossip, the silence of criticism, and the praise. It is a well thought out plan of initiation.

No one courts the child's attention. But know it or not, those children are becoming a part of the vaquero tradition. The accumulated lessons run through to the heart blood of old Spanish men who lived their lives around two things—the partner-horse and the cow. Over patient years each child will absorb the whisper of the reata running on the horn and the excitement of the good loop. Every task learned is one step closer to being asked to rope. They live for the day the grandfather says, "Go get your horse."

WITHIN THE WORKDAY at Crooked Creek, conflicts arose between the generations. There was no one person who was *the boss;* goals or decisions were amended or scrapped entirely. Tami and Dave were in limbo waiting for his dad or his aunt to make up their minds. There was no solid footing or place of peace. Finally, it was the pervasive negativity that drove Tami and Dave to make the decision to leave the ranch. "It was our hardest decision, but Dave and I believe that our job, and the children's job, is to do our work and be kind," Tami said. "To stay, we would have had to surrender our way of parenting. So we left. We had to think about the kids, too. It was hard to maintain a positive attitude. We constantly had to bolster ourselves. It got to a point where we were really having a hard time doing that."

They followed Dave's dream to train good ranch horses, like the one he sold at the Californios. They rented a place in Cedarville, a ranching community on the western edge of the Great Basin, and the horses started coming. Dave's reputation for honesty and hard work preceded him.

"I think we have to remember something," Tami said. "We don't have to be in a certain place to teach the children what we want to teach them. And where we are now, with Dave training horses, has been a particularly important step. Because where he's been, his gift and skill haven't been allowed to really blossom. He's always been accountable to a boss and limited by the demands of his work."

Dave has little regard for time when he works with a horse. Tami admits to sometimes getting aggravated with that aspect of her husband, but at the same time, she respects his particular way of seeing a specific task. "I don't want him to change that," Tami said. "He's purely in the moment and working through *feel*. Not thinking, 'I've spent twenty minutes on this and I need to go do something else.' No. He cultivates the thing that needs cultivating at that moment, whether it's with a horse or one of the kids. To operate on the energy, to totally immerse yourself in what's happening, that is the true *feel*, and it's crucial for success. He does not go into a training session with a firm idea of what he is going to teach the colt today. That would defeat the purpose of training; then the schedule dictates the agenda, not the horse's, or child's, state of mind or timing or development."

Their goal is to make sure that if the children want to carry on with ranching, they can do that. At this point it's a necessity for them. They crave that interaction with the animals and the land, and their horses. Tami and Dave encourage their interest. It goes beyond the obvious. It is how they interpret the experiences of life. Nearly every event is tied to things they have learned while working with the cattle or with their horses. When a situation presents itself, like Elsie Anna's birth, they compare it to the birthing of calves or puppies, because that's their nearest experience.

Isabel and Grace had a different start than Reuben and Elsie, having been present during calving all their lives. They have seen birth and death.

Elsie Anna

Isabel was six and Grace was three when Reuben was born, and they knew how babies were born. It didn't startle them. They didn't worry. Their experiences were ones Reuben didn't have.

"Reuben didn't understand how the baby was going to get out," Tami said. "When we came home from the hospital with Elsie, he lifted my shirt and looked at my belly, looked at the baby, lifted my shirt and looked at the baby. He didn't have the same kind of idea that his sisters did. Before, when we talked about her being born, he thought that she would come out the belly button. And he said, 'She's gonna have to get Dad's pocketknife and cut a door, and you're really gonna be mad.'

"I asked him, 'Do you really think she's going have to cut her way out?'

"'Yup,' he said. He didn't have the experience that the girls did. Even though it's calving, it's a universal event."

ISABEL WAS READY to begin first grade when they lived at Crooked Creek, but the nearest school was in Burns, Oregon, ninety miles away. Tami had been homeschooled through high school and was comfortable with the process, as many ranch parents are. She could not conceive of making her young daughter face a three-hour bus trip night and morning, especially in the winter. At home, she would gain valuable class time and take part in the activities of home life. Tami found support from the neighboring ranch wives; they compared and shared information. They seemed to her more committed to their children's education than mothers who send the children off in the dark and don't see them again until suppertime. In her role as teacher, Tami enjoys designing the lessons to the specific needs of the girls and formulating her own approach to subjects. The schoolroom is in the kitchen, but she tries not to cook or wash clothes or take phone calls during class time, in order to maintain the character of the classroom. Every morning, after a hot breakfast, Isabel and Grace come to their desks with faces washed, hair combed, and dressed for school.

Ranch families living at a distance from town and school are faced with difficult decisions about the education of their children. When the subject of homeschooling comes up with friends and others who don't understand

Tami's wish to homeschool, Tami pleads that distance is the deciding factor, especially during winter weather. In reality, homeschooling goes hand and hand with what she and Dave wanted for their family, which was for their children to be an integral part of what they do. "Not to quit what we do to get the children in school," Tami said, "but to incorporate their schooling in our lives, to be hands-on with their education, is just perfect for us."

The uninitiated child, the one who has been carefully raised, with kindness and encouragement, can be exposed to behavior, language, and attitudes in public school that the parents do not condone. Then, discipline is required to set them back on the right track, and once those undesirable things are learned, they are difficult to unlearn.

"Institutional learning is a good choice for those who choose it," Tami said. "We never condemn anyone for their choices, but we wanted to try homeschooling."

Dave approaches each young horse with an open mind. He believes that the colt teaches as much as it learns, and each one learns differently. The teacher's job is to figure out the best way for the individual. Tami has found the same is true of Isabel and Grace. She gives a great deal of thought to how she presents information and gauges their response to discover the success of her approach.

"They learn differently, and their personalities are different, too," Tami said. "And Reuben learns differently, which is neat to see. I'm constantly juggling to make the information more available to each one. It's important that I keep them engaged and curious. If that means that right in the middle of everything we grab our coats and walk down to the tree where the hawk's nest is, or check to see how the alfalfa looks after it was nipped by frost, or listen at the badger's holes and trace his tracks in the dirt, that's what we do."

There is the concern that homeschooled children may be too isolated, that they may miss out on learning social skills. Tami remembers her own shyness but doesn't feel that it was to her detriment.

"Our kids seem to interact pretty well with other kids and especially well with adults. Isabel is expressing some interest in 4-H, and both girls have signed up for soccer. As they grow older, I think that we can incorporate social interaction in other ways. It doesn't have to be restricted to a school-room environment. I think that in isolation, kids can learn a great deal about themselves."

Tami has studied many methods of teaching: no books and only practical applications as the focal points of math, reading, history, social studies, or the use of textbooks and incorporating the environment in the lessons.

"If they express an interest in a given subject, we can explore that to their satisfaction," Tami said. "As a teacher, I must stay focused on the *plan*. I can easily get scattered without that discipline. Dave has been very involved in their study of science and math, and they respond enthusiastically to him as a teacher. The schoolroom has become a family project."

Dave also involves them in starting their colts. Under Dave's close eye, Reuben participates, learning how to be safe when moving around horses. "They think about something besides themselves, and every little step for-ward with their colts develops their confidence," he said.

"They'll have their whole lives to socialize," Tami said, "and they will go into that situation with a firm grip on their values. There's a difference between surviving and thriving," Tami said. "They can go to school and sur-vive, or they can thrive. It's always been our goal that they thrive."

AFTER MOVING TO CEDARVILLE, Tami and Dave joined a church in order to introduce the children to spiritual guidance and to make new ac-quaintances and friends. Grace and Isabel, pressed shoulder to shoulder, clung to their father and mother with unadorned expressions of awe as the minister and the congregation greeted them warmly. Other little girls smiled and waved. As the choir led the congregation in singing "Amazing Grace," Grace's eyes widened. She listened. Again and again she looked at Isabel and her parents. At the end of the song she asked her mother, "Why are they singing my name all the time?"

Grace knew God. When she stepped her horse across the creeks, she saw waters passing from the snowbanks under the mountain to feed the dry meadows far below in the valley without understanding the benevolence of

Mealtime prayer

water. She saw the miracle of the glistening envelope of life work from the cow and rip open to let the calf slide out. Sometimes she saw a still body and learned of death. Once, she found a baby robin in the litter of leaves, all beak and bones and large eyes under the blue membrane not yet split for vision. Watching her mother's careful hands, she learned the excitement of the fleshy bird for crumbles of cooked egg—the very substance of his life— and saw it rise up in him in an open beak begging for sound and touch and food. She filled his box with soft cloth to ease his resting and watched as he progressed from pinfeathers to glossy plumes, from clumsy trembling to sturdiness. She drew aside the bit of cloth that kept him warm at night to let the broken light of morning warm him, and she felt the glory of the sun. One day, perched on her finger in his feathered fullness, his long beak pecking at her braid, head tipped to gather sounds, he moth-fluttered to the ground. He could have flown on the breath of her astonishment. In time she would learn the lesson of letting go and trust. When the congregation sang "Amazing Grace," she heard her name but was yet unaware.

WHEN THE STODDARTS MOVED to Cedarville, friends came to carry boxes from the stock trailer. Tami noticed Isabel trailing her room to room. She took Isabel's hands in hers and asked what was troubling her. Isabel, Grace, and Reuben have ridden in open country from birth. For the first three years of life, they, each in turn, rode in a pack on their mother's chest. When Isabel graduated to a horse of her own, Grace was in the pack. Then Grace was lounging her horse before mounting just like Isabel, and it was Reuben in the pack. Now, Elsie Anna is wrapped just over her mother's heart when they ride, and three older children are mounted on their own horses.

There are no fences at Crooked Creek. The Stoddarts spent every summer in a cabin on the top of Steens Mountain, with seemingly the entire world below. In the fancy of children, they made a sailing ship out of the cattle chute. They found a stone worn by ancient hands that crushed seeds into meal to be eaten by children like them, and roamed the same creek and played in the snowmelt waters of the stream, wild as those children. Now, here in this new place, Isabel looked at the many pastures laid out below the house, fences cutting them into parcels and fields. In every direction, another ranch was within view, and she whispered, "Where are we going to ride?"

Isabel is adjusting to the change. She is starting her own colt. She has ridden the filly and felt the security of her dad holding tight on her belt. Now she knows the excitement that will accompany every first ride.

Deeply homesick for the desert, Dave was riding one horse after another in alternating moments of snow and wind and calm. Tami strung a clothesline in the kitchen to dry their heavy jeans. The girls did their lessons. One day Isabel looked up from her book by the fire and watched Tami carrying

Elsie Anna in the front pouch, taking things from the dryer and folding them on the kitchen table. She asked, "Isn't it hard to get things done when you have to carry Elise all the time?"

"Well, yes," Tami smiled and said. "It's a little uncomfortable sometimes, but that's just part of life. You get busy and forget about it. That's why it's helpful when you hold her for me."

"Do you get mad sometimes?"

"Mad? Not mad. I'm her mother. It's my job as a mother."

"Well, I'm going to be a mother someday," Isabel said. "So I guess I'll have to get used to it, too."

NEARLY TWO YEARS PASSED. Dave had long phone calls with his father and meetings with the family corporation. Finally it was decided that they would move back to Crooked Creek.

"We left because of the feeling of negativity," Tami said. "And that's not changed, but we have changed. In the time we've been away I think we've gained some tools to deal with people. We asked ourselves what do we want to do with our lives, and where do we want to raise our children. And without a doubt, we want to be at Crooked Creek. Once you make a decision like that, it becomes a matter of working out the details, of not focusing on the negative things. We can't stop people from saying what's on their mind. But we can refuse to absorb it. We can look for areas of agreement, if we're willing to work that hard. We have to allow people to have their own opinions without packing their load for them. Once you buy into the negative remarks and take them personally, you give them a place within you to grow and that's when the destruction occurs. We did that and it hurt us. But when things are said that are not really truth, it comes down to whether you believe it or you don't believe it. When you let it go past it loses its power over you, and instead of anger or anxiety, peacefulness comes over you.

"Dave and I have grown in strength together, and we have to deal with things as a family. Dave's father and aunt say they want to see the ranch go to the next generation. We're going to believe that. If we wait for the structure of management to change, it will never happen. We have to do what we can to make it happen and muddle through the communication process. We have a friend who said, 'If nothing changes, nothing changes.'

"We talked to the kids, and Grace is easygoing about things but Isabel has sharper opinions. She put it this way, 'Ranch—good. Creek—good. Horses—good. Dogs love it. Friends—bad.' She is going to miss the friends we've made here. We all are."

Eminent Domain and Land Use

CATTLE FREE IN '93

I was born to ranch people. They were among the earlier settlers in eastern Oregon. My father's father ran his sheep and horse band in the rim rock country of Rudio Mountain, above the John Day River. My mother's family had a small ranch on Butter Creek about sixty miles to the north. They met at a rodeo and were married the next spring.

My parents were born to people of the land who invested their effort in what the land could produce for their living. The effects of the Depression came slowly, like a wind you hear high up long before it stirs the trees. There was no cash money in the country. Three-year-old steers sold for four dollars if they could find a buyer. One rancher shipped his wool to New York and got a bill for the storage.

Young and sick to death of watching their parents living on cream and egg money and feeling depression poor, Mom and Dad moved away from the isolated plains of eastern Oregon.

It was a September afternoon when they brought me home, still mewling from birth. The smell of sage came in the open window of their car. Did I know it then? No. But when John Hussa invited me to help gather the Hussa Ranch cattle from their range on the Sheldon Antelope Game Range in Nevada, sage moistened by the dawn stirred a deep memory. Seventy miles from the nearest town, a hundred years from commute traffic and a job, I rode into a country I didn't know existed. There I fell in love with cows I would know through the years of their lives, and their heifer calves after them, ranch horses as tough as the lava tablelands, and a man who would teach me his ways and want to learn mine. When we married, I made my life around the thing my parents ran from, a cattle ranch in an isolated valley on the edge of the high desert.

IN THE MID-1930S, at the height of the Depression, a federal biologist wandered into the same sector of northwestern Nevada where the Hussa Ranch cattle would summer after 1938. When the biologist first laid eyes on it, the high desert was all but empty of people. The broken land teemed with antelope, mule deer, cattle, horses, and bands of sheep in a flowing pattern like the crosscut of tides. Sage grouse sounding like B-52s flew in by the thousands to water on the meadow where he unrolled his bed. While the country was mired in financial ruin, he had stumbled into a place without breadlines or broken men, as if he'd entered paradise.

He found sheepman Tom Dufurrena, a Basque immigrant, who owned the deeded parcels that gave him control over more than a half-million acres. At Tom's campfire the biologist told Tom if he didn't sell to the federal government, "they'll just take it anyway." Tom didn't understand his rights or the concept of eminent domain. He was an immigrant who did not speak the language well and feared that if he turned the sale down he would be deported and sent penniless back to the Pyrenees. Tom was pressured to sign the sales agreement that would turn the lands over to the government. By order of FDR, the U.S. Department of the Interior (with the cooperation of the Boone and Crockett Club and the National Audubon Society) converted the Dufurrena holdings into the Charles Sheldon Antelope Game Range and Refuge: thirty-four thousand acres in 1931 and an additional five hundred thousand acres in 1936.

The following spring the Fish and Wildlife Service (FWS), administrator of the Sheldon, offered a sixteen-hundred-head cattle grazing permit on that same land to offset operational costs. Three ranchers from Surprise Valley, just over the state line in California, filed an application. John's grandfather, W. H. Hussa, was one of those permittees.

In the early years permittees and refuge employees worked together for the betterment of the system, probably because they grew up in the same

area at the same time; so there were overlapping perspectives of cooperation. If a fence needed attention or a cow got into an enclosure, whoever
saw it, fixed it.

The change came in the 1970s with the first wave of FWS employees
trained in the philosophies of environmentalism. The Hussa family had
a history of four generations on the Sheldon; the other permittees had
similar connections. Refuge employees lacked our emotional commitment;
they came and went like summer guests. Their funded projects were generally restricted to the collection of data. They had no tie to the outcome.
We thought their studies were incomplete. The proof of a theory requires
years of scientific record-keeping. Among us were several ranchers with
sixty years of personal observations, some as many as eighty years, but their
historical insight was dismissed as anecdotal. We could have provided a
baseline of at least fifty years of observations for their data. Without benefit
of that, it was our opinion that their conclusions were worthless.

Basically, our differences boiled down to a clash of perspective. Simply
stated, ranchers use cattle to harvest grasses. The animal-machine converts
nutrients and matter—which the human body cannot convert—into muscle
mass it can. The rancher wants utilization of a resource to the advantage of
people: a productive, healthy world.

The concern of environmental science is, by definition, with the physical, chemical, and biological conditions of the environment and their effect
on organisms. The environmentalist wants a system that works in sync: a
perfect world.

A couple of things lend support to the frustration ranchers developed.
From the first, we and our cattle were cast in the villain's role—the FWS
wanted us off of the refuge. To that end, a high-level employee skewed
data in favor of the FWS agenda. A documented example goes back to the
Dufurrena family and the origin of the Sheldon.

Tom Dufurrena's nephew Buster told me that years back the refuge
fenced in an antelope kidding ground on Big Springs Table. It was meant to
exclude cattle, to protect and provide seclusion for kidding does. However,
once the cattle were fenced out, no permittee, Humboldt County road

crew, or any hunter Buster has talked to ever saw an antelope inside the enclosure.

In 1990, Buster was talking to then Sheldon Refuge manager Barry Reiswig about the Big Springs Table enclosure.

"I was telling Reiswig that antelope need cattle to keep them in there. They follow the cattle and feed off of the tender new shoots, and the cows will keep predators away from the kids," Buster said. "Reiswig told me that in finalizing a land trade with H. B. and Joy Wilson of Virgin Valley, he had agreed to let Wilson turn out some cows on Big Springs Table for a few months. Then Reiswig said, 'Funny thing, as soon as they put the cows in there, the antelope moved back in.'

"I told him, good!" Buster said. "That's the information we've been needing to prove that cattle are beneficial to the antelope herds!"

"Reiswig said, 'You'll never see that documented. Another guy wrote a report like that and he got reprimanded.'

"So he wouldn't do anything about it," Buster said.

Shortly after this incident, Reiswig initiated a plan of *systematic ecological restoration*. Faced with Reiswig's heavy-handed management and doublespeak, the ranchers who grazed the Sheldon felt very much like Tom Dufurrena. They didn't need a crystal ball to tell them that livestock grazing was not a part of Reiswig's future initiative. They sold their permits to an intermediary foundation that turned them over to the FWS. They felt they were getting out before the permits were denied and they lost the value of the permits.

Reiswig gave his parting shot to a *High Country News* reporter: "We had to break that old system in which the livestock industry dominated the management of those refuges."

But in the absence of cattle, the antelope census did not bloom. In 1995, kid mortality was at an all-time high of 99.2 percent. In 1997, it was worse, at 99.5 percent. The reason stated was predators.

IN 1998, Buster and Linda Dufurrena asked John and me to meet them in Lakeview, Oregon, for an FWS information presentation on the status of the antelope herd. Over dinner, Buster said that just the night before he was reading the journals of his father, Alex Dufurrena.

The year of the final purchase, the Dufurrena ledgers record the 1936 livestock census on those acres as follows: 16,000 sheep, 500 cows, and 500 horses. In addition, Frenchy Montero had a cow permit for 500 head and a horse permit for 500, and Harry Wilson had a cow permit for 500 head and a horse permit for 500. Upon the signing, predator control was discontinued and all livestock were removed.

We filed into the Lakeview Senior Center along with other people curious about the current condition of the antelope on the Sheldon Antelope Refuge and Sheldon Game Range. The floor of the center was divided by kiosks, with six-foot-tall charts and graphs, reflecting pronghorn populations and assorted pertinent information. Each table was manned by a refuge employee.

Buster and I stood before the kiosk titled "Setting Population Objectives: Looking at History, Biology, and Expectations." The earliest year represented was 1936, the year the FWS completed the purchase from Tom Dufurrena, the year that topped the chart with the highest antelope population ever, exceeding three thousand animals. From that point, the antelope population dropped sharply to five hundred animals.

In 1936, when the livestock census was at its highest, the antelope population was also at an all-time high. That data was supported by several interviews I had conducted with Modoc County residents in the 1970s, including trapper Leo Weilmunster, one of forty-six federal trappers in Nevada. In one year, he trapped 743 coyotes. His job included the examination of their stomach contents—the majority contained remains of lambs or antelope kids.

Buster and I saw a correlation between the predator control provided by shepherds and federal trappers and the period when antelope flourished on the Sheldon. Buster recounted the figures from his father's 1936 journals to the employee, who had no reaction, no curiosity.

Hoping to make his point clear to the young man, Buster said, "The antelope population peaked during the period of the highest concentration of livestock. Sage grouse, by the thousands, were on all the meadows and springs. That's when the Sheldon was famous for its trophy mule deer. There haven't been any cattle on the Sheldon for almost ten years. You've got nearly a million acres set aside for antelope and their population is in the toilet. What the hell's going on?"

The employee shrugged, pushed a plate toward Buster, and smiled, "Would you like a cookie?"

REISWIG'S PLAN to remove all livestock from the Sheldon came to pass. In the semantics of today's FWS, they "released habitat from the pressures of livestock grazing and began utilizing fire to renew habitat."

To date, not one cow has legally stepped a foot on the Sheldon in twenty years. Nearly a million acres—that once produced feed for nearly twenty thousand animals and in turn produced food for many thousands of people—is wasteland.

According to FWS studies, coyotes and ravens have all but decimated the sage grouse. In the winter of 2007, a federal court decision supported adding the sage grouse to the endangered species list.

According to refuge handouts, "Mule deer and antelope populations have been significantly reduced due to several hard winters, and depredation."

Three wildfires have raged across the refuge, consuming years-old feed, browse, groves of mountain mahogany, and bitter brush the mule deer population relies on for winter feed, costing millions of dollars for fire suppression and the deaths of untold numbers of wildlife.

It is my belief, and of others, that harvesting grasses is key to the health of the plant, and that antelope and deer benefit from the presence of livestock. Managed correctly, livestock grazing the Sheldon could improve the entire ecosystem.

CALIFORNIA RANCHER Phil Stadtler, an internationally respected cattle trader, possesses knowledge of livestock extending back to his relative Joseph Walker, who, in 1834, trailed the first cattle into the Great Basin. The forty-seven head accompanied Walker as beef to feed his men on his exploration of the Humboldt River. Like us, Phil experienced seeing productive land wasted by poor management at the hands of government agencies.

In the late 1980s and early 1990s he owned fifteen thousand acres of ranch land in Modoc County that was made up of several beautiful and productive ranches. He ran cattle on it for quite a few years before the FWS made him an offer.

"The government bought the ranch as a refuge for birds and wildlife," Phil said. "When I was running cattle on that ranch it was alive with waterfowl. They fed around and among the cattle. It was a natural refuge. The cattle kept the feed down so the birds didn't have to worry about predators, and they could feed on the bugs in the new growth grass. After the government got their hands on it, all the fences were removed, at taxpayer expense. In the years since, the meadows have turned into a jungle of old dead feed and tules. The birds are gone, moved to other ranches where they get protection from skunks and coyotes and other predators that work on waterfowl and wildlife. Under the management of the FWS, the value of the land has been completely destroyed. All those acres of wonderful grass and the irrigation system that for generations produced food for the people of this country now *produce nothing.*"

There is a trend in these anecdotes.

THIS FALL, the bale wagon backed into the center of our barn and set down a block of alfalfa that I cut and John baled. We restacked the loads as they came from the field to get more hay inside safe from spoilage. All day long we dragged bales up toward the rafters and stacked them wall to wall. Between loads, hands on the hewn beams, I had the owl's view. How much it felt like resting on a limb with the entire world below. Dufurrena's range, then our range, in Nevada was sixty miles distant beyond the mountains across the playa.

Now our cattle, sheep, and horses run inside on deeded ground under a modest rest-rotation program. We cut the meadows for winter feed and adjust our carrying capacity according to factors we can't control, such as drought and hard winters. John has taken advantage of fault features in developing stock ponds that extend utilization. As a boy, he hiked and played along a creek bed that crosses the ranch and ran six to ten feet below the level of the fields adjacent. He fished in holes twenty feet deep. Thirty years ago he began building dams to divert spring floodwaters onto the fields. Fine gravel and rich silt filled behind his dam constructions, raising the creek bed and the water table level with the fields. He has improved the native feed greatly. He encouraged his father to stop plowing up meadows, losing the moisture in the soil, in order to plant oat crops that succeeded only one year in four. The native Great Basin wild rye grass has returned, giving cover to game birds and providing winter feed for the cattle. These are small but important improvements to our operation.

Standing on hay we harvested and stacked, fingering the cuts on the beam, I know what's troubling me.

I want the government to respect private property rights and to work with landowners in honest and fair ways. I want decisions to be made by people who live on the land, close to it—who know it. I want legislation that will support the industry. I want people to recognize that many of the vast lands of this country are best used for grazing to raise food for our people. Without sustainability, we fall victim to an international market we cannot control.

Perhaps most of all, I want ranches to be family owned, not sold out to wealthy landowners or corporations, neither of which care about the community. Ranch families are needed to care for the land in a way that only those who are invested can care. They are invested, not by market shares, but by history in and love of a place. Their commitment comes from their deep understanding and appreciation for livestock and landscape; their payoff is the family unity of purpose, the shared work and responsibility, the ever-present learning, teaching, rewards, and challenges of productivity. A fundamental dedication to the work that serves the goal is the common thread that connects rural and urban upbringing and is the foundation all young people can build on as entrepreneurs, as legislators, as leaders who protect and renew the environment. It's the way to building and enriching family life in the communities of the West and in our nation. It is *mothering*.

The Tyson Family

Cedar and Gail Tyson

G̲ail Tyson was not born into the ranching culture. But tradition can begin at any moment with one person who has something grown of her
own energy and devotion that she wants to pass on. She merely needs to
find someone she can trust with its value.

GAIL'S MARE, Herdugo, is running wide open when she enters the arena.
At the first barrel in the cloverleaf pattern the mare sets her hocks and, following the inside rein, arcs her body to make the turn within a whisker of
the barrel. In three strides she is coming out of the first turn, digging hard
with her haunches, gathering speed on a line toward the second barrel.
Again, three even strides around the barrel, hind legs driving, shoulders and
front legs pulling, she runs hard for the last barrel. In a copy of the other
two turns, the eleven-hundred-pound mare tightens into the arc, galloping
three compact strides, her body at a forty-five-degree angle to the harrowed
surface of the arena. The brown mare's inside ear is back to hear Gail's
voice, the other tips ahead, locked like radar on a point in the distance. If
you could stop time, you would be surprised by the calm in Herdugo's eye
and the stillness of Gail's body poised above the mare's absolute center. Gail
has learned the precise command of her weight, riding as a surfer tracks
the vertical face of a wave. They are two, but perfect in the balance of one
animal in motion.

Gail saw something artful in Herdugo when the filly was only days old.
With complete abandon she zipped through the maze of grazing mares and
foals in the pasture at full speed. She was happiest when she was running.

Even the mare's name is the expression of astonishment for her speed: *Her-do-go!*

Now, she breaks from the third barrel to the straightaway and with the explosive burst of speed the Quarter Horse breed was built on, she goes full out to the finish and the flag.

GAIL WASN'T a child with a first pony and 4-H in her past. As a teenager she watched the plodding gait of show horses where winners were chosen according to a sedate presumption: *the slower, the better.* Bor-ing! Her interest in barrel horses hit like a lightning bolt when she saw her first race and said to a friend, "Now, this is more like it! This looks fun!"

The world of speed was feeling a feminine presence in the early seventies. Shirley Muldowney was earning her chops driving racecars at the same time that Gail was discovering arena dragsters—barrel horses. The combination of absolute control, a surgeon's cut to the only true line between life and death, and all-out abandon sent her blood thumping. Unlike most horse competitions, the barrel race was not decided by the fallible opinion of a judge. It was a race, after all, and *first one to the finish line wins.* In other words: *speed counts!* As soon as Gail could arrange it, she was taking a test-drive aboard one of the fastest animals in the world, the American Quarter Horse, a horse that from a standstill can run a quarter of a mile in under twenty-one seconds, reaching speeds up to fifty-five miles an hour.

Gail's job with a veterinarian who worked on racehorses led her to a second job as a groom on the track. It was an opportunity to learn from the best trainers about feeding and exercise programs: when to rest and how hard to push to prepare a horse for a strenuous athletic performance. She continued working at the track for five years. "The pay was great," she said. "Racehorses are owned by rich people, and they were always tipping me for the extra-good care I gave their horses. Of course, I was young and spunky back then."

Gail was a quick study and a serious student of every procedure her vet employer did. Those were skills that would serve her through her life, and philosophies she would employ on herself when the chips were down. Don't waste your time trying to make a burro outrun a carrot on a stick. Begin with an athletic animal willing to accept the training; keep it physically and mentally fit; lead it from the starting line to the finish by being its partner in the performance; understand what winning means. Before long, the excitement of training horses to manipulate their power by contracting and releasing it on demand took all of her time and concentration. She quit her vet job to compete full-time at a sport lovingly called by speedsters in the business, "chasing the cans."

Barrel racing tests the speed and handiness of a horse on a pattern run at a sprint. To achieve the body command of a gymnast, the horse must be trained to control its natural movements of play in the pasture and call upon an inborn ability to flee from predators to propel its body through space over a course requiring deceleration, compression, navigation of a direction change, and acceleration, all with accuracy and split-second timing. On a standard course, a barrel horse will cover a distance of one hundred fifty yards, plus three turns of 360 degrees thrown in, at a speed of forty-five-plus miles an hour, in a time of seventeen-plus seconds. The penalty for a knocked-down barrel is five seconds added to the course time. When a hundredth of a second separates the winner from the rest, a penalty of five seconds is a virtual elimination. Precision at that speed requires knowing when to control a horse and when to pitch it its head. Gail has an inborn sense of timing. Speed is the thrill she seeks. The start and near-stop at the barrels plus the abrupt change of direction is a trip on the carnival ride the Wild Mouse after drinking a double espresso grande.

IN 1976, Gail earned the Rookie of the Year award of the Women's Professional Rodeo Association's Sierra Circuit. "I just started doing good," she said. "I couldn't help myself!"

Havadouble, a five-year-old gelding, came into her life about then. He was running at Bay Meadows but not winning. Footsore and badly overworked, he would rather fight than run. She bought the used-up quarter-miler for $650 and took him home for a course of rehabilitation. It took four years and a great deal of patience to bring Havadouble back, but when she did he set records on the county tracks in San Bernadino and Victorville. Then she showed him a barrel course.

While Shirley Muldowney was becoming the first woman to break the five-second barrier at the Popular Hot Rodding Championships, Gail and Havadouble set a world record time of seventeen seconds flat during the finals at the 1978 Reno Rodeo. The team of Havadouble and Tyson qualified for the National Finals Rodeo together in '77, '78, and '79. During the go-rounds and the finals, Havadouble ran the course thirty-one times. That's ninety-three barrels turned clean; he did not touch one barrel.

Gail's list of accomplishments in ten short years is notable. She and Havadouble became major names on the national barrel race scene. But living out of a horse trailer going down the road chasing the dollar points that would qualify her for a fourth National Finals Rodeo was losing its charm. She was already following her own ideas, breeding and producing consistent, superior running horses, and she needed to be home minding the mares and training their babies. She wanted to go but needed to stay. Her marriage was suffering from her time away on the road. Gail sold Havadouble to a friend for thirty thousand dollars.

As luck would have it, the sale of Havadouble coincided with the introduction of barrel race futurities. Under futurity rules, a two-year-old is nominated to be raced in its third year at a scheduled barrel race. It's a gamble on the ability of horse and trainer to deliver the goods on a given day. Futurities are a trainers' contest: the best of the best, horses bred to run coming on in the hands of professionals. Offering big-dollar purses for one race made futurities the hot new thing. They promoted the breeding and development of a new generation of horses. Futurities allowed Gail to redesign her involvement in the sport. From home she could train for the futurities that fit her schedule. Futurity wins provided her with serious money to support her horses and buy a place of her own.

In 1981 Gail hauled two horses she trained to the Arizona Futurity and won both champion and reserve. The meet was just the start of her impact on the futurity circuit that continued for ten exciting years. Until, that is,

After hauling cattle

one spring day in May 1991. It was not shaping up to be a good year, beginning with the death of Gail's mother and the divorce that ended Gail's marriage of fifteen years. A betting person would give heavy odds on a third of Fate's trilogy coming along soon.

On the morning of May 10, Gail was driving up highway 395 from southern California to Winnemucca, Nevada, hauling three horses to a futurity. A friend who often traveled with her had had a change in plans. Gail was alone in her pickup. On a deserted stretch near Victorville, forty miles from home, the driver of a tractor-trailer decided to try to beat her approaching rig across an intersection. Gail watched the truck slowing as she held her speed at fifty-five on the main highway. Then, the truck driver floored it, and the broadside of the truck was a brick wall in front of her. Gail hit the brake, but she was the leading force when she slammed head-on into the tractor-trailer, hitting directly in front of the rear drivers. The top of her pickup was sheared off as she went under the truck's belly. The force of the collision ripped the engine loose and drove it into her lap. The dashboard was crushed against the back of the pickup seat. Gail was pinned in between. Upon impact, Herdugo was hurled through the front trailer compartment wall into the tack room. Her hip was fractured. Rona Royal and Chickapin were thrown forward where Herdugo had been. They were cut and banged up but not seriously injured like Herdugo. For Gail, at the point of impact, it was much worse. Wrenched and twisted metal, shattered glass, the hot engine and the steering wheel and the windshield encased her. There was the smell of burned brakes, fuel running, a blown radiator. There was the hiss and groaning as the stressed metal settled into an eerie silence.

The truck driver bent down and looked in at the bloody rag of her hair, face, and arms. Then he ran backward puking and crying and fell into the barrow pit. Finally, her moaning dragged him to his feet. He had to call for help. The highway patrol dispatcher radioed for an ambulance. The truck driver went back and stood by Gail until they got there. But they didn't have the equipment to free her. Even the Jaws of Life were useless the way her pickup was lodged underneath the tractor-trailer. Gail was trapped, bleeding, suffering from shock, but still conscious as the rescue crew worked to get her out. There was only one possibility, and that was to lift the truck off of her. But there was no physical way to do that. It was fully loaded and they were miles from any heavy equipment. Agonizing minutes passed into hours. As the fury of activity around her ebbed, Gail realized the rescuers were giving up. The futility of their efforts settled into quiet. Quiet enough to hear the approach of a crane driving up the highway in the middle of a nowhere Sunday.

A crane operator wanting to get a jump on an early Monday morning road construction job was moving his equipment on Sunday. He and his crane were the one and only possibility to free Gail from the wreck alive.

The emergency crew explained to the driver what they needed, and without hesitation he pulled his crane into position. The men carefully set the cables in place. It had to be done in one lift; they had one chance. The cables tightened. Gail closed her eyes against the deafening sound of ripping metal. The truck slowly lifted off of her. Three and a half hours after impact, she was carried to the medevac helicopter. Those left behind at the scene—highway patrol, EMTs, and the truck driver—had their private opinions on her chances.

The damage to Gail's pelvis and left leg was massive. She sustained a broken shin, smashed knees, and a shattered hip complicated by the dislocation of her thighbone when it was torn from the muscle and driven four inches out of the socket. It took surgeons seven hours to reconstruct her pelvis and secure it with a metal plate. Friends who picked up her mares and got them to a veterinarian hospital were able to bring her the good news that Herdugo would recover from the hip fracture. If Herdugo could, maybe she could, too.

"A thing like this," Gail said, "you find out who your friends are."

A week later she underwent a second surgery. The doc's prognosis was dismal at best; she would never be able to withstand the strain of training or competition again. He didn't know who he was talking to. When she was released from five weeks of intensive care, she faced three months of bed rest and three more in a wheelchair. All the while, Gail was worrying about her horses.

Just before Thanksgiving, six months after the accident, Gail's rehabilita-
tion therapy started. It was excruciating then, and it's still painful today. But
by following the daily routine of exercise, she has recovered nearly 75 percent of normal motion of her hip, although she lost more than 50 percent
of her muscle strength and probably won't recover more.

Physical therapy was the only path to recovery. Once her therapist understood her commitment to ride again and observed her athlete's ability to
block out the pain, he bought her a bicycle and took her out riding. They
went hiking and rock climbing, anything to challenge her quest to improve.
"He was a hunk," she laughed. "I would do whatever he said just to keep
him around." But Gail had a bigger vision. She wanted to do more than be
able to push a grocery cart or sweep the floor; she wanted to return to training. The horses she had developed to be running champions were standing idle. The foals she had bred for the next round of three-year-old futurities would be ineligible soon. She was struggling to walk, but if she could
endure the pain, regain her strength, balance, and concentration, maybe
riding would be less stress. Her therapist told her, "You'll have to become
the best rider you've ever been to make up for the weakness."

Gail raced Rona Royal, one of the mares in the trailer wreck, in 1992. It
was a brave attempt but not up to her expectation. Later in the year she con-
templated selling her horses and getting out of the business for good. The
pain wracked her constantly. Both her physical condition and confidence
declined. Then she discovered transcutaneous electro-neural stimulation
(TENS), a medical device developed to alleviate chronic pain by blocking
the impulses from reaching the brain. Armed with her TENS unit, she rode
Rona Royal to a reserve championship and repeated wins of two major futurities she had won ten years earlier. Less than two years after the accident
that nearly took her life, she added a third, on Me May First. Gail was back
in the saddle again, in a big way. But it would not be for forever. Competing
exacted a physical price. Additional major surgeries were required; currently the count stands at twelve, including three hip replacements and one
knee replacement due to strain and cartilage deterioration. "I scaled back,"
she said, "and hoped my Royal Go-Go bred mares could stand on their per-

formance record, and sales of their foals would support my horse ranch."
That and more hard work.

In 1993, Gail decided she wanted to make a move north to be closer to
her dad. He still ran a family boating business on Lake Shasta north of
Redding, California. After many scouting trips she found some acres with
a big barn and a nice house along a creek in the oak-strewn hills west of
Cottonwood. She moved in and started welding up pipe corrals and paddocks for her horses. A dozen plus years later there's not a strand of barbed
wire on her ranch except for a perimeter fence line. It's horse-friendly. Every
year she foals and breeds in the neighborhood of sixty mares, and stands
several stallions, including her own, Faxin Go-Go, a son of one of those
original Royal Go-Go mares.

DURING THE NONSTOP WORK of spring, Gail always hired a ranch hand
to share the workload, usually a college girl. In 2004, it was Cedar, a quiet
girl, a little shy, but bright with an expanded sense of her own abilities. As a
part of her high school fitness program she began weight lifting and could
bench-press 130 pounds, exceeding her body weight by 11 pounds. Handling
horses was nothing new either, but she had been her own teacher. She
bought her first horse early in her high school years when she was living in
Fortuna on the Pacific coast.

Cedar didn't have an Ozzie and Harriet life growing up. Her parents
split when she and her brother were very young, and when she was five her
mother dropped the kids off at their grandparents' and left with her boy-
friend. They stayed with their father when he wasn't in the woods logging.
In the winter he spent his time tending his marijuana crop in the backyard,
instructing Cedar on pruning techniques, or hauling the kids along on his
drug runs to Lodi or San Luis Obispo. She speaks of him with stoicism—
a child can do nothing about the failings of her parents, not even make
excuses for them.

As soon as Cedar turned eighteen, she moved away from the depress-
ing life at home and the summer fog of the coast. She enrolled at Shasta

Welding fences

College in Redding. A veterinarian clinic hired her part-time, and she found a place to rent about three miles from Tyson Quarter Horses.

With foaling and breeding season coming on, Gail answered a want ad for a girl looking for a job as a house sitter, pet sitter, or a hired hand. Cedar's roommate had placed the ad, but she wasn't home. When Gail called, Cedar answered the phone. They chatted briefly and made an appointment to meet the following day. Within ten minutes of hanging up the phone, Cedar showed up at Gail's door. "Just to look things over," she said. Gail had already called the vet clinic where Cedar said she worked part-time and gotten a glowing report. The two women walked through the horse pens, and Gail explained the work. The place was in meticulous shape: pens cleaned, no manure piles to draw flies, alleys raked, feed tubs stacked, water buckets full of clean water. The horses were in good shape and came across the big pens to hang their heads over the fence for a rub or pat. Working at Tyson Quarter Horses, Cedar was going to learn to do things the right way, Gail's way, which was okay with her.

Gail and Cedar were at ease with each other from the first. "It was a done deal," Gail said. "She moved into the guesthouse right away and started in here; plus she kept her part-time job with the vet and went to school."

The passing of time is marked by the seasons, and for horse people spring doesn't begin until the mares foal. The hours are 5:00 AM to 9:00 PM, but foaling can happen anytime, day or night. When a mare is close to foaling, Gail begins collecting small amounts of milk in a vial to test the calcium level, which increases as parturition approaches. When the level reaches a certain parts per hundred, she sews one of the radio transmitters she invented on the mare's vulva. The two parts are held together by magnets that are pulled apart by the action of birthing, sending a signal to a squawk box outside in the pens area and to one in the house. The sound is enough to wake the neighborhood, but country people don't complain about a few *ooo-ahs* in the middle of the night. Even starting from a dead sleep, Gail and Cedar can be at the foaling stall in moments to be present for the birth and assist if necessary. The dress code is casual; a coat thrown over pajamas is acceptable in the barn.

Gail's radio transmitter has saved more than one foal's life. In one recent case, they rushed to the mare's stall to find the foal's feet protruding from the mare's vulva but facing soles up. When the foal moved into the birth position, it rolled and was presenting upside down. The foal's head was jammed against the bottom of the mare's pelvis with the force of each contraction. It could not be born upside down. The spine could not arch, like a diver, to deliver front feet and head, correctly. Gail called their vet, Dr. Dawn Shore, a certified reproduction specialist and Gail's good friend.

Dawn and her veterinarian husband live just across the creek, only minutes around by the road. Dawn gave the mare an injection to ease the contractions. They needed time to roll the foal upright. But neither she nor

Gail were strong enough. The situation was reaching the critical stage. The drug was beginning to take effect, but the mare's uterus was still rolling with contractions. If they were to get the foal out alive and save the mare, they had to work quickly. Cedar said she would try. Dawn cautioned her that the foal's foot could rip the mare's uterus, or the hind feet could tangle the umbilical cord and sever the oxygen supply. If the head did not emerge so the foal could breathe, it would suffocate.

Gail held the mare's head. It was important the horse stay lying down and quiet. If she heaved herself to her feet, she could break Cedar's arm. Cedar was lying down behind the mare, listening to Dawn as she tentatively reached into the vulva. She was unprepared for the heat and the billow of the sack like scarves around her arm. Her fingers probed carefully until she found the foal's chin and throat. Dawn told her to take hold of the legs and push the foal back to release the pressure on its head. Then they assessed its position. Dawn explained how the foal should be turned. There was no discussion of the mare's exceptional breeding or the value of the foal; the three women were locked in saving a life, maybe two. In her mind Gail was talking to the foal and thinking of being trapped in the truck wreck, the heat and pressure, the thumping in her temple, and hearing the sound of the crane coming toward her. Cedar was the crane; rescue was in her hands. She felt along the foal's cheek to its ear, and, supporting the head on her arm, she reached down the foal's long neck to its withers and gently, firmly, began turning the foal over. At the same time, she guided its head and body to follow as she turned its front legs. It took all of Cedar's strength, but finally she felt the roll. Her heart leapt as the feet and head came up into her hands. She carefully brought the foal's front legs forward, checking that the head was centered between the front legs. The drug that had quieted the mare's contractions put the birthing entirely in Cedar's hands. With one foot in each hand, she braced her feet against the mare's buttocks and pulled. In steady waves the head came sliding out, eyes closed in that dreamy state of connection to the mare, the sheen of birth on the shoulders, the ribs, the hips. Then with a whoosh, the perfect little horse slipped out into her lap.

The mare lifted her head from the straw, and nickering, reached back to lick the foal's face. The two women Cedar admires most in her life were smiling. It was her finest moment.

GAIL'S FATHER'S HEALTH had been growing worse over the past year. Regularly, they drove to Redding to visit him in the extended care hospital. From the first, Cedar called him "Grandpa." He was always glad to see her come through the door with Gail. At some point he started teasing Gail that she ought to adopt Cedar. They all laughed at his joke. Some months later, Gail's younger sister died unexpectedly. Driving home from the funeral, Gail began thinking about her horses, her dogs and cats, her ranch and how she had worked to build it up, her fruit trees, and what would become of it all if anything happened to her. Her dad wouldn't be in a position to deal with it, and she had no family to leave it to. She imagined an estate sale, horses on the auction block, the proceeds going to the state of California. She kept going over it in her mind and discovered a solution right at hand. Gail broached the subject of adoption with Cedar. At an age when most parents push their fledglings out of the nest, Gail was asking Cedar to make herself at home. Rarely does a nineteen-year-old have a chance at adoption.

They told their friends. There was not a hint of dissent among them. At baby showers Gail answered "Mom" without hesitation. Tyson Quarter Horses took on a different feel. But the first step to adoption had to be taken by Cedar alone. She had to ask her parents to give up their custody of her to Gail.

CEDAR'S MOTHER moved around a lot. She worked for a helicopter logging business, going wherever the contracts took her: the Northwest, Australia, Canada, Vermont. When they did talk on the phone, it was less mother and daughter and more like friends catching up on what had been happening. There was no advice asked for and none given. The relationship of parent and child had gone missing years back on the steps of her grandmother's house when Cedar was five.

When Cedar finally reached her mother, she said she was happy for her and agreed to sign the papers. Cedar repeated a general delivery address and reminded her that her signature had to be notarized. The conversation ended. One down. She called her grandmother, her father's mother, and asked her to relay the message. She did. Her father's answer was, "I don't give a —— what she does." Her grandmother arranged for a notary to witness his signature and sent the papers back to Cedar.

THE PROCEDURE for adoption was available in the county courthouse library. Cedar spent her lunch breaks from the vet clinic doing research and brought home a list of requirements. Together she and Gail checked them off one by one. Court date assigned, papers in hand, and nervous with excitement, they went before the judge the first week in August. He couldn't have been ruder. He berated the way they handled the process. This wasn't right. That wasn't right. He wanted the paperwork done over again and gave them another date on the court calendar in six weeks. Gail and Cedar left the courtroom in a state of devastation. The clerk caught up with them in the hall. She said the judge was having a bad day. Her advice was to do exactly as he instructed. "Jump through his hoops," she told them, "and come before him again."

They were afraid one or both of her parents would be put off or change their minds, or ask Gail for money. On September 17, 2004, they set out again. In a flush of benevolence, the judge congratulated them and signed their petition. The clerk gave them a wink. On the courthouse steps, Tyson and Tyson embraced.

HAND BREEDING STALLIONS can be dangerous. Pasture breeding, or turning the stallion into a pasture with a group or band of mares for the season, is the most natural method. The process follows its own timeline. Each mare finds her footing in the group. Pasture breeding is more convenient and less problematic than leading a stallion high on the passions of spring out of his paddock when he knows what is waiting ahead in the breeding barn. But oftentimes, a stallion won't accept mares coming and going from his harem in the pasture. Or there are complications, getting a mare to settle, that require specific attention. In those cases, Gail resorts to hand breeding. It can be accomplished in one month's time, and that includes a check back to determine if the mare is safe in foal.

Gail has always had a knack with stallions. She is firm, but there's no unneeded force, so they don't get frustrated or angry with her. She constantly reminds Cedar that especially at breeding time, stallions are unpredictable.

Cedar admits that they made her nervous at first, but with Gail's coaching, she gained confidence. The daily routine has given Cedar the experience to understand their personalities, to know which stallion warrants close attention and how to keep the upper hand. If several mares cycle at the same time, Gail and Cedar collect and cool the semen and inseminate them all. The same process allows breeders to ship frozen semen from stallions in other states so mares can be bred without the time and expense of sending them long distances. Mares that compete in horse events during the breeding season can be bred and shown the same day. The semen travels instead of the horses. This procedure is accepted by the registry of the American Quarter Horse Association.

ON THAT LONELY STRETCH OF 395, Gail learned not to take life for granted. If she has to haul a horse somewhere, she throws her bike in and calls one of her friends to go along. Having a daughter now gives her a constant companion, and their circle of friends has expanded. After doing the chores, they take off fishing or sightseeing, boating and trail riding. The two of them pack more hours into one day than most healthy people have the energy for.

Cedar is competent to take on many of the ranch jobs alone now. She's riding their young horses, with Gail at her side. But when she comes up against a colt's resistance, she has no quick reaction, no automatic countermove born of Gail's years and miles of riding. By the time she reacts to Gail's instruction, the lesson is lost. Frustration and maybe a little fear is natural. Young horses are strong and they get frustrated, too, requiring consistent, instant correction, not strength. Cedar is beginning to doubt her ability to follow in Gail's footsteps. Tyson Quarter Horses is built on Gail's

Learning to cut cattle

rare talents, timing, knowledge, and winning reputation. Cedar has none of that to offer customers at this point. She works hard to care for the horses and the property, but wonders if she could manage the successful business Gail has built. She has made remarks that she is merely an adopted ranch hand. Although Cedar doesn't realize it, she has absorbed, as all children do, the agitated tones of her parents' anger. Of these times, Gail said, "It's not a perfect world."

It was Cedar who discovered a neighbor who was a qualified family counselor. She talked Gail into making an appointment. After listening to their concerns, the counselor reminded them of the unique nature of their relationship and pointed out that they are living with emotional traps as wide as the Grand Canyon. Once the challenge of adoption was completed and the celebrations were over, everyday life in all its mundane and

featureless routine was like postpartum depression. At that low point in
a relationship, disagreements can be petty and destructive. She said that
Cedar was expressing kid ideas that she didn't express before because there
was no one to listen. She suggested that Cedar may need time away from
Gail to develop her own friendships, as would happen in a normal mother-
daughter relationship. Discovery often requires separation from the familiar, the safety, the rules. It is a formidable survival instinct that if ignored
can mutate into resentment.

As if the situation was not complicated enough, Cedar's mother was
killed in a car accident soon after the adoption was finalized. She and Gail
never met. Cedar came back from the funeral in a tangle of emotions, guilt
among them. With memories of her father's criminal behavior thrown in,
she desperately needs the simplicity of caring for the horses, dogs, her pet
chickens, and the constant example of Gail's high standards and courage.

The counselor told them that Cedar needs time to understand and trust
her own deep values that kept her from being drawn into her parents' lifestyle, to learn who she is, and find the work that fills her with excitement.
Gail has given Cedar a loving home from which to launch her self-discovery.
She may find it necessary to look outside of Tyson Quarter Horses.

Gail and Cedar are where nearly every parent and child find themselves
at some point. They must decide which parts of their relationship they can
afford to let go and which must be preserved.

The ranch work slows in the fall. Most of the mares and foals have gone
home. Gail has sold some horses and is cutting back more. They have a
little bunch of cows ready to calve. Cattle don't require the kind of time
horses do. Cedar has enrolled in a law enforcement course at the local college. But they still find time to take a lunch up to Shasta Lake and swim off
the patio boat with their dogs. They kayak up rivers that feed the lake, discovering quiet glens where deer and wild turkeys move along shaded banks.
Waterfalls spill into pools, and the turning leaves and the swish of the kayak
in the water delight them. Cedar watches Gail rock climbing, jumping from
ledge to ledge, and, thinking about the highway patrolman's pictures of her
truck wreck, twelve major surgeries, and joint replacements, feels a swell

of emotion grip her. On a blistering hot afternoon this summer, the kayak slipped silently under a canopy of emerald green oaks, and Cedar turned to Gail, beaming: "I'm sure glad you like doing things like this, too." As a girl who hadn't heard the words enough, she might have been saying, "Thank you for wanting me," or "I love you, Mom," even as she wonders if she wants to devote her life to Tyson Quarter Horse Ranch.

Recently the two of them bought a load of hay to carry their horses and cattle through the winter. Gail couldn't find a trucker who was available, so the two of them decided they could haul it. They hooked Gail's flatbed trailer behind the pickup and drove to the ranch in the mountains. Cedar was lifting the three-strand bales up to Gail, who built the load on the trailer. The repetition of the work created a rhythm between them. All in all, they moved and stacked five and a half tons of hay. The bales averaged 104 pounds. The load was four tiers high, with a crown. Soaking wet, Gail might weigh 110, and Cedar 120. As they tied down the load with straps and chain binders, Gail walked down the crown, and Cedar, on the top tier, was one layer below. As they passed each other, Cedar put a hand out on Gail's calf. It was the top of a high load and uneasy footing on the bales, but it wasn't clear who was steadying whom. In a brief, natural movement, as when a mare glances through the band for her foal among the others, there was filiation. Reassurance.

Neither Gail nor Cedar was born to the tradition of ranching. They came by it through their own discovery, perhaps destiny. For now, they carry on.

Entrepreneurs

THE EMERGING RURAL MARKETPLACE

While the number of agricultural operations drastically declined during the last generation, off-farm income is necessary for some families, and smaller family farms are on the rise. The distance to the marketplace is no longer a barrier for many producers because the Internet gives producers and consumers worldwide access. Ranch and farm entrepreneurs like the Evans and Taggart families, as well as the Hammond family in the chapter that follows, are creating a nontraditional rural marketplace that significantly impacts the survival and success of rural communities.

David Evans and Julie Evans
MARIN SUN FARMS AND POINT REYES PRESERVES

Dolores and Dan Evans may not be able to explain why their two children, David and Julie, came home to work after they finished school. The H Ranch, established by Dolores's parents, Alfred and Florence Grossi, has been in the family since the 1930s. Like their mother, David and Julie grew up on land dominated by windswept hills slipping into the rugged valleys of Point Reyes toward the tides of the Pacific Ocean. It's in their blood. And, basic economics made it hard to resist. A no-cost irrigation system in the form of spring storms and summer fog moistens the pasture grasses nearly every morning, and when the sun sears through the overcast, the H Ranch cattle stretch out and soak in the warmth like beach bums.

Like most ranch kids, David and Julie were raised to be independent thinkers. David, the eldest by four years, said, "I returned to the family farm to work there with my parents on the piece of land that I love."

The H Ranch was a dairy operation for many years, but dairies are notoriously labor intensive. In the ranch world, when someone takes on a difficult job that ties them to home day and night, people hoot, "You might as well own a dairy." In the 1980s, Alfred found it increasingly difficult to get reliable help to milk several hundred cows twice a day, and he made the transition to beef cattle.

David graduated from Cal Poly at San Luis Obispo in 1998, with a degree in agribusiness—farm and ranch management. Prior to that, he had gotten an associates degree from Santa Rosa Junior College in business management and entrepreneurship. Cal Poly refined his preliminary studies and gave him the tools to start a business. Unlike his fellow graduates with ambitions in the corporate world, David needed a project to test the value of his education. He was looking for that project back home, even though many of his peers hadn't survived that transition back to their home turf because of rising land costs, taxes, and the impossible distance to markets. But David thought his experience in agriculture provided an avenue, and agriculture was gaining support in Marin County.

The challenge was in using his education to contribute to the family without making changes his parents didn't want. "The ranch was already set up the way they wanted it," David said, "and I could only spread my wings so far because it was indeed my parents' operation, not mine. I had to branch out on my own."

JULIE WAS GRADUATING from high school when David returned from college. She had decided against going to college and worked in Point Reyes Station for the Marin Agricultural Land Trust for a few years. Every summer she and her mother put up jams and pickles made from her Grandmother Florence's recipes. It was something they had always done together. Julie liked having time in the kitchen with her mother, and she was determined to keep the traditions of her grandmother alive. The two women filled their pantry for the winter ahead. They gave jars of fruit and pickled vegetables as gifts to friends. The appreciation and praise for things homemade was noted by Julie, and in 2005 she laid out plans to her mother for a start-up retail company she named Point Reyes Preserves. Within a short time she was producing 7,500 jars of product a year.

"We want the support of the county and community to continue the farming and ranching tradition in West Marin," Julie said. "That support increases our motivation. West Marin looks the way it does because of an indescribable dedication to the land. Ag keeps development away and provides a local food source."

AT THE END OF 1998, while David was still searching for an ag project to apply his energy to, he and a friend started a partnership in a fence company to make some money. The two of them began constructing fences for other ranchers in the area, and built a reputation for straight fences and solid set posts. They made enough money to advertise in the paper and applied for a contractor's license, in that order. The license made them legal to bid on bigger jobs.

David's ambition was still in agriculture. Building fences provided the nest egg to realize that ambition. In 1999, he and his partner launched Marin Sun Farms and leased some grazing property in Nicasio that belonged to a man David had worked for when he was in junior college. The marginal piece of land was about fifteen miles from Point Reyes. David knew that land unfit for cultivation can still be productive when grazed by livestock to produce food, and he hoped to improve the production of the pasture by applying his ideas on rotational grazing and intensive grazing management. They put in a water distribution system and cross fencing, and bought their first stocker animals. In one year David's improvements doubled the carrying capacity of the land. But they still lost money because they sold on a commodity market that had fallen since their animals were purchased.

"We realized the difficulties of this business. It's not necessarily the harder you work the more you're going to get out of it," David said. "It was different in the fence company. The longer hours you put in, the more you got rewarded because everything was based on time and rates and hourly wage. The cattle business doesn't afford you that. You work hard and do the best you can, and sometimes you get paid more and sometimes you get paid hardly anything. It was outside of our control."

David started reading about what was going on in alternative agriculture. Having studied pasture management, he had the background to apply advanced techniques to marketing. Other operators were opening avenues with their marketing and creating new markets.

"That's where I stumbled on grass-fed beef," he said, "and I remember thinking, what a concept—that these animals should only eat grass."

In the beginning of 2001, with the fencing company still growing, David and his partner decided to try to sell their beef in the local community by quarters, halves, and wholes. But dealing with the physical side of the business, processing meat and getting it to market, presented them with a steep learning curve. This initial step of marketing their beef collided with an article David read in the *New York Times Magazine* by Michael Pollan titled "Power Steer."

David remembers the impact "Power Steer" had on him and on the *Times* readership as well. "They are an influential and well-educated group of folks across the country," David said. "The article explained what was going on in the mainstream of agricultural husbandry, mainly beef, to the alarm of a bunch of people."

In "Power Steer," Pollan wrote that he bought a calf from a cow-calf rancher in South Dakota and followed that calf all the way through the industrial system. Of course, it wasn't very industrialized on the ranch in South Dakota, but everything changed as soon as the calf left the ranch at eight months of age and was shipped to a feedlot where he was given a daily ration of antibiotics, implanted with growth hormone stimulants, concentrated in dirty pens, and fed feed rations that are not compatible with a beef's digestive tract. Pollan learned what the feedlots were about, what was going on with his animal, and the economic decisions that were being made to guide his animal through.

CALIFORNIA CATTLEMAN Phil Stadtler was already trading cattle when President Franklin Roosevelt introduced the concept of grain-fattened cattle to the American public in the thirties.

"There was a surplus of grain in the Midwest that farmers needed to get rid of," Stadtler told me in an interview. "Roosevelt suggested feeding the grain to beef cattle. It was premeditated murder. Roosevelt killed people when he forced the government to finance feedlots just to get rid of the oversupply of grain. His plan was to put the grain through cattle to 'finish' the cattle. Instead he 'finished' millions of Americans."

Prior to the era of the feedlot, beef consumed by the American public was processed straight off the pasture. Restricting the movement of cattle in feedlots and force-feeding them a diet of grain does something unnatural to them. On pasture, the fat separates from the muscle. When the meat is prepared, the fat can be cut off. But when cattle are fed in feedlots and they don't get enough exercise, the fat permeates the muscle tissue—commonly referred to as *marbling*.

"The American public didn't like the marbled beef," Stadtler said. "They started buying any kind of meat other than beef. The feedlot investors couldn't sell their marbled meat. They called their Congressmen. The government couldn't just admit they were wrong, so another agency was set up and laws were passed making it against the law to sell any beef for human consumption unless it was labeled USDA *Choice*—in other words, *marbled*."

A marketing campaign financed and launched by the government ran for decades to sell marbled beef to the American public. Over time, the public became convinced that marbled beef was best. What other choice did they have?

"Then they noticed that people were dropping dead from the effects of heart disease, high cholesterol, and other health issues," Stadtler said. "It's not that red meat is bad. *Marbled beef*, that's what's bad for you.

"Meat from cattle that had not gone to a feedlot was used for dog food," Phil said. "Our pets were getting healthier meat than we were because the government would not, could not, admit the mistake. So, after spending millions of dollars marketing USDA Choice, they are now spending millions more to warn the public about the health hazards of beef."

Beef is not the hazard; feeding grain to cattle is.

In "Power Steer," Pollan quotes Dr. Metzen, DVM, saying, "cattle rarely live on feedlot diets for more than six months, which might be as much as their digestive systems can tolerate. I don't know how long you could feed this ration before you'd see problems."

Pollan continues: "Another vet said that a sustained feedlot diet would eventually 'blow out their livers' and kill them. . . . What keeps a feedlot animal healthy—or healthy enough—are antibiotics. . . . Most antibiotics sold in America end up in animal feed—a practice that, it is now generally acknowledged, leads directly to the evolution of new antibiotic-resistant 'superbugs.'

"'Hell, if you gave them lots of grass and space,' Dr. Metzen concluded dryly, 'I wouldn't have a job.'"

MEANWHILE, the beef industry is the unwitting victim along with the public. Ranchers have always known that the concept of feedlots and a diet restricted to grain produced an unhealthy animal, but the government tied their hands. If they wanted to stay in the cow business, they had to go along with the system. Yet on the majority of ranches in the West, the meat served at their dining room table was, and is, grass-fed beef.

Ranchers understood that the quick fix for one segment of agriculture—disposing of a grain surplus to save farmers from bankruptcy—disrupted a balance and had far-reaching effects to the detriment of the rest of the American public. And once the feedlot system was established, farmers expanded their production of grain to service the demand; the feedlot market and the cycle continued.

Marbled beef was so deeply ingrained in the public mind that it took about seventy years and Michael Pollan's "Power Steer" article to change consumer thinking. But the impact was dramatic.

"Pollan kept an economic analysis of everything," David said. "That got him wondering if the system we've set up was the best. The article revealed hidden parts of our food system, places that are not open to the public."

Pollan mentioned at the end of his article that there were alternatives out there with grass-fed animals raised on small farms. He referenced a Web site called eatwild.com—a small forum set up by Jill Robinson in Washington State. "A couple of months before," David chuckled, "I had advertised on eatwild.com for five dollars. It was the first advertisement I ever bought for Marin Sun Farms. The phone started ringing off the hook. People all over the country wanted to buy our grass-fed beef because we were one of maybe twenty or thirty individuals advertised on that site at that time. Now there's probably hundreds. So that kicked us into high gear."

David knew there was no better marketplace for grass-fed beef than in San Francisco, just across the Golden Gate Bridge, a few miles south of his pastures. But the partners of Marin Sun Farms were hoping to ease into the business, learning their way along to supply a market that would open up in about five years. They found out the market was about five months away. Immediately they issued press releases to nearly every newspaper in the Bay Area and landed a major story in almost every one.

To be legal, David and his partner needed USDA-certified processing. A plant was located in San Francisco, and they started sending some animals there. "We didn't have that many head, didn't know how to cut a beef, didn't know the cuts of beef," he said. "We threw ourselves into this whirlwind of fast growth, and through that I lost my partner. He decided he was going to go back to school; he'd had enough of all the stressful monkey business."

With the administration and labor staff of Marin Sun Farms cut literally in half, David was feeling the stress himself. For the next few months, he was alone trying to manage two businesses that were barely holding themselves together.

"Looking back, I can remember the days of driving across the Golden Gate Bridge with this pallet of meat on the back of my truck that's not rated to carry that much meat and it's not air-conditioned," he laughed, "and I'm looking outside hoping the fog will stick around cause I've go to make it all the way to Sebastopol and I can't have the temperature of the meat rise too much, and the pallet starts to shift in the back of the truck because the guys at the meat plant didn't wrap it as good as I would have. I'm worried about what will happen if a few of these boxes fall off in the middle of the bridge and there's meat flopped out all over the road and the California Highway Patrol pulls me over. I've got five thousand dollars worth of meat in the back of my truck, and I'm going to lose it all and go out of business. There were many desperate phone calls to friends at Point Reyes saying, 'Gosh! I'm stuck in traffic, I've got this pile of meat in the back of the truck, I'm doing the best I can, there's no refrigeration and I'm frustrated trying to make this thing work!'"

David had secured freezer storage in Sebastopol, a few miles to the north. He hauled the meat up there once a week from the plant in San Francisco, pulled the meat from the week before out, put up the orders people had phoned in, and drove those orders to their house or a street where they could meet in San Francisco or Berkeley, somewhere in the Bay Area.

"It definitely wasn't making me money," David said. "I was just getting the word out there. And it paid off. I got into the farmers' markets and got some restaurant accounts. Mainly I was trying to offer a high-value, consistent product to my customers, knowing that we were the first ones out of the gate."

There is a definite split in the economics of marketing. The producer targets either a broad-based market or a high-end market. The broad-based market requires volume, and the key is lower pricing, but at the same time it's more demanding on resources: freight, fuel, and energy. Because of the exclusive nature of the high-end market, the producer is able to charge more for a high-quality product; volume is reduced; and the workload and resources are conserved. Small operators lack a distribution mechanism, forcing them to develop markets closer to home. These are the very qualities that have led Point Reyes Preserves and Marin Sun Farms to success: *high-end and close-to-home.*

Marin Sun Farms opened a retail meat shop in Point Reyes Station, where David also features Point Reyes Preserves. The shop affords him control of the quality, the market, and the delivery. It gives a place for the customers to pick up their grass-fed meat orders and allows them to shop for other items, such as grass-fed lamb, range-free eggs produced by his seventeen hundred laying hens, or stewing hens (those too slow on the egg-laying line). Rather than giving the lion's share to distributors or agents, David and Julie are able to put the profit back into their own businesses.

Recently, David realized that he had employees sitting in the meat shop waiting for customers to come in, so he started a restaurant and taught them to cook and wait on tables at Marin Sun Farms Butcher Shop and Eatery. After being open only a few months, the building was wiped out by a winter flood. Rebuilt and reopened, he is once again enticing customers to his meat counter, as well as to the table where grass-fed beef sandwiches, lamb, and free-range eggs are prepared by the chef, and where Julie's gift baskets are sold. He hires employees from the community, his business has generated other businesses, and he has developed a healthy climate of prosperity around Marin Sun Farms, the ultimate goal of the entrepreneur.

In 2005, Prince Charles came to Point Reyes for a visit. As an advocate of sustainable organic farming since 1985, the prince included on the itinerary of his American wedding trip with Camilla a visit to the Point Reyes Station Farmers' Market. He does not accept the contention that organic farming can provide only a small percentage of the world's food supply, saying, "Gradually we are realizing farmers have a very important role to play." As the royal couple toured the marketplace, they chatted with the proprietors, assuring them they would take some understanding of the entrepreneurial success enjoyed in Marin County back to England.

DAVID AND JULIE have always had the help and advice of their parents. But they also understand the demographics of Marin County and share the fears of some county residents who have seen the ruination of many jewel-like areas of the West when land values force agriculture out and the land is paved over for the inevitable urban sprawl. In Marin County, 167,000 acres is under agricultural production: field, fruit, and vegetable crops, aquaculture, nursery crops, livestock products (milk, cheese, butter, meat, etc.), livestock, and poultry. But fewer than one-third of the 276 ag operations have an annual gross income exceeding $100,000. The rest are on the tipping point where sacrificing ag land to real estate development may be their single bailout option.

Marin County has heard their concerns, maybe more now since the royal visit, and with new effort is exploring ways to preserve the agricultural landscape, to maintain the serenity of the costal valleys residents value highly. These goals separate Point Reyes from other suburban towns that are notoriously overrun by fast-food franchises, "super box stores," and strip malls. The county has made provisions for local on-site processing plants, exactly what makes Julie's Point Reyes Preserves, the Strauss Family Creamery organic dairy products, Sue Connelly's Cowgirl Creamery, Kevin Lunny's organic beef, oysters, and clams from his seaside ranch, Peter Martinelli's Fresh Run Farms, and many others possible. Innovative operators protect the land while offering unique products to consumers. These entrepreneurs think beyond maintaining the status quo in the county, focusing on the protection of the culture of agriculture.

Recently Julie ran into a roadblock. Although the county signed off on home production for retail sale, selling wholesale to stores became a state issue. And she has had trouble with the state on the retail side, too, with her pickles. Jams are okay, but pickles require another level of inspection. She's not certain if she is going to carry on with Point Reyes Preserves. Regulations have made it impossible. She's inquiring whether there is any other way to satisfy the state officials, or if they are going to put her out of business. In the meantime, she started a new endeavor with the purchase of twenty-five goats. Just in case, she's backing up her plan with meat. And Marin Sun Farms can sell all she can produce. Florence Grossi's recipes will go back in the folder, to be taken out when her daughter and granddaughter cook for the family. But Point Reyes Preserves may be a tradition of the past for consumers.

"This market we've developed is not open to every producer," David said. "And I would argue that markets don't need to be open to every producer.

I'm in favor of every producer creating their own market. I think smaller markets are what we need, not larger markets. I think that the focus on larger markets is what made it so marginal for agriculture to survive and why we have fewer and fewer family farms. Everything is assumed to have to operate at a larger and larger scale. If we're left with outsourcing or relying on larger corporations that don't have a conscience when it comes to environmental stewardship, we lose in two ways: quality of product and the end of agriculture."

Marin Sun Farms can do what the bigger guys can't do. "They can't compete with me on aging meat; it's not financially feasible for them," David said. "They can't create a 100 percent grass-fed product yet. They can't guarantee that their animals are from within fifty miles or a hundred and fifty miles of a location. Those things are increasingly important. And people will pay more for that, and they have to because it costs more for that type of a system. But the inherent food security and the local landscape and the community, I think people see as a worthwhile investment when they tally it all up with their food costs. It's nice to know that you're contributing to something more than what you've got in your hand after you purchase it. It's nice to know that it reflects other feelings and values, and hopefully it's a part of the sustainable food chain, or at least a food chain that's working on becoming sustainable. Just thinking about the future, a lot of large agriculture is known to be operating on limited time because they definitely do not have a sustainable system in place."

If David is right, that opens a door to new thinking. It is an undeniable fact that farm and ranch operations in this country are in sharp decline. That being said, some people, like David and Julie, think agriculture has turned a corner. There is a movement to return to the farm, to keep the traditions and develop new methods of doing business, with the ultimate goal being more complex and inclusive than the almighty dollar. David sees concern turning into action by a new generation wanting to protect sustainable agriculture.

"I think they have to. I don't know how willing they are, but I just think they have to," he said, "and that makes me feel good and gets me up to go to work every day. Because once that's gone, what are we going to do? Are we going to outsource our food system completely? What if we have zero percent farmers anymore and we import all of our food? What does that mean? To me that means we have to have a bigger military to enforce that we get fed. I'm not into that kind of a world. I don't want to live in a world where we have to survive by our military power. I'd like to think that we become self-sufficient in a certain aspect of that. I'm antiglobalization; I don't believe in it. I don't believe in competitive advantage either on a global scale."

All of us who believe in sustainable agriculture admit to being hypocrites. We have to dress ourselves every day, and we don't make our own clothes. We are products of the present system even as we do our best to adjust our lifestyle to do what we think is important for the environment and for the soul of man. First, oil made us dependent on foreign countries, and now it's food.

"You know, last weekend at the farmers' market in San Francisco where my sister sells her preserves, she sold half of what she normally does. And the main reason was that people couldn't travel by airplane with her goods. They couldn't buy a bottle of pickles and take it with them to wherever they were going, because it has been outlawed."

World politics and terrorism reached a woman in Marin County who puts up goods using her grandmother's recipes and sells them for her living. That's where we are headed if we don't find ways to feed the people without depending on the importation of our food. We have gotten used to buying strawberries and grapes in January. We have let ourselves become spoiled. We put our own farmers and ranchers out of business by legislating against them, and meanwhile purchase food grown by sweatshop labor, using pesticides and herbicides unacceptable in this country. If we had to go back to eating only the produce available seasonally, as our mothers did, would we complain and issue demands, or would we make the miracle of local food production a part of our creative cooking? By driving our children into the country to shop at the farmers' markets, they can meet other people who understand the value of agriculture close to home.

"THERE IS a fundamental problem in the way that this nation in particular operates, and I don't think that it operates on a sustainable measure," David said. "And it's not trying to become more sustainable. I say to people all the time, I don't run a sustainable farm by any means, but I'm trying to keep my sights on sustainability and move closer towards it. That's why when I hear that the local slaughter plant is going to close down and my only other step to get my animals to be marketable requires that I have to drive them farther, these are government-imposed actions. If the plant closes down and I don't have an alternative, then I'll change the whole structure of how I sell. And that's what the entrepreneur offers, that flexibility. There's a greater adherence to principle. There's a reason why I do what I do. I love the ranch and I want to preserve where I live. I want to preserve my community. So, if I can't move in that direction, then I need to find something else to do or find a different way to do it."

Wendy and Jon Taggart
BURGUNDY BOUCHERIE

South of Dallas-Fort Worth, the Great Plains comes to an end. It is the southernmost edge of a great inland sea of prairie tallgrass that runs north through the Dakotas and west to the Rockies. The prairie tallgrass of the Great Plains once supported vast herds of buffalo, elk, pronghorn, deer, and, later, herds of cattle and horses. Species of animals have come and gone, but the prairie tallgrass remains. Wildfires have burned it; settlers plowed it under to plant crops, and asphalt, houses, and cities cover much of it nowadays. But let it alone and up it will come through cracks in the pavement, on schoolyards and vacant lots, on twenty-five inches of rain a year, sometimes less. Give it a chance and it will turn sun, soil, and rainfall into a native grass, nutritious, with fat in the seeds and a sweetness that ruminants prefer over all other grasses. Ruminants will then convert prairie tallgrass into a high-protein food source humans need to survive.

WENDY AND JON TAGGART have been raising cattle for twenty-five years. The new millennium marked their transition from traditional beef production to a new and very personal decision about the way they were doing business. Today it's called Burgundy Pasture Beef; then, it was a shot in the dark.

"I started to be more conscientious about what we ate when we had our twin daughters, Charley and Patsy, and then our son, Ben," Wendy said. "It's partly about how disconnected as a culture we've become from our food. Jon and I were a part of that system. We ran stocker cattle, used chemical fertilizers on our pastures, pesticides to kill flies, and herbicides to control the weeds. Jon said there was a chemical solution to everything. Basically, we were raising grass-fed beef, but when we sold our calves they ended up in a feedlot on a ration of grain and antibiotics and were implanted with hormones to stimulate weight gains."

After reading about an article praising grass-fed beef for its purity and health benefits, Wendy told Jon she would like to get some and try it. "The taste was nutty, with a soft tone," Wendy said, "and there was less fat left in the pan. It was simply wholesome, rich-flavored food."

The Taggarts decided to make a test trial with some of their own cattle to be certain of decisions that were fundamental to producing a healthy beef product, pure and simple. There was no guidebook to producing grass-fed beef. Wendy and Jon relied on their years of education and experience, and their developed eye. The Taggarts never fed any animal-source proteins to their cattle, so all they had to do was shift their focus to improving their native-grass pastures and eliminate all chemicals.

Their own herd of Angus cattle was the basis of their 100 percent grass-fed product. Jon used a no-till drill to gradually reclaim a stand of native grasses that includes prairie tallgrass throughout their pastures. The cattle finish year-round by virtue of a growing season that provides the livestock with high-protein roughage eleven months out of the year. At the peak of summer they experience the least productive season because it is often droughty and hot. There are two sets of grasses in their pastures: cool-season grasses and warm-season grasses. Each is adapted to site-specific

climate conditions. "Through trial and error, we have developed a good protocol for producing culinary beef consistently," Wendy said, "giving our customers our assurance that strict guidelines are met, calf to carcass."

Good-quality Angus heifers from their own herd are exclusive to their
program. In a sustainable, organic operation antibiotics are prohibited—
not used at all, ever. If they had an eleven-hundred-pound steer in the
program that got a cut or had an infection and needed antibiotic care, he
would be pulled and shipped to the sale barn at a loss. A heifer in that same
situation is transferred into the cow herd and bred to produce. Her genetic
quality is not lost to future production. The rate of maturity for heifers is
slightly higher—they put on more body fat, which is distributed naturally
throughout the meat.

Up until a few years ago, Burgundy Pasture Beef was cut and wrapped
by a local butcher shop and sold in a convenient fifty-pound mixed-cut box
directly out of the Taggart's ranch house. But it seemed to Wendy that at
the bottom of the box there were always twenty or thirty pounds of cuts that
she wasn't happy with. "It was the old adage, 'Nobody cares more than you
do,'" she said.

That led them to take a major step: Wendy and Jon built a butcher shop,
a stand-alone three-thousand-square-foot building, and they named it
Burgundy Boucherie. It is not a slaughter plant. That part of the process is
handled at a small USDA-certified facility about thirty miles from Grandview.
"We didn't want to get into the slaughter business because then it's all
about quantity," Wendy said. "That's an overhead issue we didn't want to
bring into our program."

Jon picks up the carcasses in a refrigerated unit and delivers them to
Burgundy Boucherie, where they are dry-aged for twenty-one days before
they are custom cut the old-fashioned way. As a USDA facility, superior
levels of food safety are maintained throughout the operation. The meat is
vacuum packed, suitable for freezing, and sold over the counter or via the
Internet. Delivery dates in the Dallas–Fort Worth area are prescheduled on
Burgundy Pasture Beef's Web site, and Burgundy Boucherie is certified to
ship meat all over the country.

"There are so few custom butcher shops anymore where a customer can buy beef cut and wrapped to their specifications," Wendy said. "Having our own butcher shop gave us a tremendous amount of flexibility. It was really a step up in customer service for us. We were the only ones offering those options to people looking for grass-fed beef produced under strict standard operating procedures. The business has totally grown itself."

THE TAGGARTS were already selling their grass-fed beef when Michael Pollan's article "Power Steer" came out in the *New York Times Magazine.* It was a well-placed stone that whacked the Goliath meat industry in the temple and changed the way many consumers thought of the food on their table. Pollan enlightened the public to choices beyond shouldering up to the trough, like the steers, to eat food that was not healthy for them. The grass-fed movement took a giant step forward.

In a recent *Time* magazine article titled "The Grass-fed Revolution" that featured the Taggarts, Denver cardiologist Dr. Steve Atchley was quoted as saying, "I got tired of telling my patients they couldn't eat red meat." He launched Mesquite Organic Foods, available through the national chain Wild Oats Markets. The company contracts with ranches from the Canadian border to Texas. Sales have quadrupled since December of '05. Atchley guarantees consumers that "Mesquite's ground beef is 65 percent lower in saturated fat, and its New York strips are 35 percent lower than conventional beef, as measured by the USDA."

The challenge of feeding a family on a limited food budget may turn some prospective customers away from grass-fed beef, but the product sold by Burgundy Pasture Beef is from the earth; there is no artificial input. Pricing is based on the longer feeding time required to bring the grass-fed animal to term, and grass-fed cattle need greater land resources because they are not confined to feedlots. Cattle finished in a feedlot on government-subsidized grain reach a kill weight earlier because of the application of chemical hormone implants to boost daily gains. "If the tangled web of government subsidies to commercial feedlots could be unraveled and those subsidies stopped, the feedlot product would be priced much higher," Wendy said.

The American consumer must weigh the value of product assurance where the health of their family is concerned. If a consideration is given to the absence of chemical invasions into the meat, the lower fat ratios, the purity, the high standard to ensure a healthy product, and if peace of mind is important, then the price per pound is justified. Supply and demand also plays a part. Prather Ranch grass-fed and organic beef, sold directly from their plant in Dorris, California, is four months behind on their orders. Other grass-fed operations report similar interest in their product.

CATTLE AND SHEEP graze the western ranges, arid government lands, and land that is unsuitable for crop production. They consume forage that would otherwise be wasted and convert it into valuable human food, hides, and pharmaceutical products. These animals do not compete with humans for food, but furnish us with energy, high-quality protein, iron, and certain B-complex vitamins, especially niacin. B-complex vitamins are synthesized in the fermentations that occur naturally in the rumen that is a part of their digestive system when high-protein fibrous plants that humans cannot digest are chewed and rechewed until they have broken down properly. The conversion takes place in a ratio of six hours of eating to eight hours in rumination. Sheep producer Kathy Lewis calls the rumen "a wondrous piece of machinery that turns grass into highly palatable food."

The Taggarts' mind-set to produce organic beef and to work toward a sustainable operation is something that has evolved over time. Their beef is not certified organic, but common sense and sound judgment dictates their procedures, which, it turns out, are compatible with the organic guidelines. The animals are calfhood vaccinated, but no other vaccinations or antibiotics are given to any animal processed by them for food. No pesticides, no herbicides, no synthetic fertilizers are used on the ranch. Beneficial insects control flies. "If the chemical option is taken away from you," Jon said, "you'd be surprised how creative you can be."

WHEN YOU BUY A VOLKSWAGEN, you suddenly begin to notice Volkswagens all over the road. The same is true for grass-fed beef. Once the

Taggarts focused on organic meat production and sustainable farming, they met a number of people from the community who also have sustainable family operations. One operation in particular is owned by a Mennonite family with a thirty-cow pasture-based dairy, which supplies Burgundy Boucherie with raw-milk cheese made right on their farm. The whey is fed as a supplement to their pasture pork. "I buy live pigs from them and we sell Burgundy Pasture Pork," Wendy said. "We also cut and pack their pigs for them. I offer their raw-milk cheeses in the store because people who want grass-fed beef also want some dairy products, pork, and lamb. It has to be raised with the same philosophy that is our guide. I know these people personally; I know their reputations, and I know their products are what they say they are."

Restaurateur Jon Bonnell responded to Wendy's sales promotion and has been buying and featuring their beef on his menu ever since. But he is the only owner among the high-end restaurants in the Dallas–Fort Worth area willing to purchase and prepare cuts besides the prime cuts. Bonnell's restaurant offers a dinner menu that includes premium steaks, which are the bone-in rib eye and the New York strip. But his lunch menu includes gourmet meat loaf and burgers, and he prepares a Milanese sandwich from the whole top round. He is a chef committed to serving grass-fed beef, not one committed to the cut. Others want Burgundy Pasture Beef but will purchase only 10 percent of a carcass, the tenderloin and the prime rib, leaving the Taggarts to absorb and sell the rest without benefit of those cuts. "Jon has been a great supporter," Wendy said. "It isn't that we sell to Jon exclusively, but he will work with me on his orders and his menu. We can't process animals to sell 10 percent of the carcass."

The USDA is in the process of defining grass-fed. To date, the language they've come up with is not satisfactory to the Taggarts. "I don't have confidence that the USDA will not degrade the integrity of what grass-fed is in the labeling law," Wendy said. "There are a lot of forces that want to water that down. A tremendous amount of lobbying money is spent in Washington DC trying to determine what the labeling laws are. Consumers need assurance that the meat is what we said it is."

The American Grassfed Association (AGA), a newly formed group, has an opportunity to establish a verification method that is credible. Grass-fed is a popular item with consumers who are trying to eat healthy and who pay attention to what's going on in the world of food. "If the AGA labeling was a guarantee to consumers," Wendy said, "then it would mean something to be a member."

The Taggarts share a growing concern that less that 2 percent of the population of this country produces all the food for the rest of us. Wendy sees it as a huge disconnect between consumers and the people who produce their food and where it is grown. "That only demonstrates that we have two or three generations who don't know what real food tastes like or where it comes from," Wendy said. "To me, food has a spiritual meaning, but on a practical level food is something you put in your body that nourishes and builds your body or breaks your body down, every day. It's amazing that parents are not teaching their children to think about what they eat. I don't know if our children will want a career in ranching, but they will be thoughtful consumers and true contributors."

Wendy feels they are witnessing, if not a revolution, an awakening. How else could a two-person operation of a family cattle ranch in rural Texas, armed with only a Web site, have tripled its business every year for the last five years? It's not about quantity; it's about quality. They have eliminated operational input and have no employees. They do not farm; they run fewer animals. Jon moves the cattle routinely to keep the pastures fresh and growing, building the organic materials in the soil to increase production. Other family operations in the Grandview community are being positively impacted by Burgundy Boucherie's energetic marketing of close-to-home ranch products. The competition stimulates the local economy, makes everyone work harder, and gives the public a choice.

"There are lots of ranchers who don't want to be marketers. Personally, I like it," Wendy said. "Jon and I work well together; I handle the books and the business, and he takes care of the livestock."

The grass-fed industry is in its infancy as far as availability to consumers, because there's no infrastructure. Ranchers have tremendous knowledge: they know their animals, they know their soils and what their land can produce. They can guarantee the quality of their product. But when it comes to marketing, they limit the value of their own products and sacrifice the maximum return from their efforts because they don't feel equipped to do it. That's where Wendy has an advantage. "I have a degree in business from North Texas University, and I thought, the kids are in school and I can go out and market our grass-fed beef. It ballooned from there."

Outsourcing has placed the people of this country at risk from a security standpoint. While Congress wrangles over tariffs and subsidies, tainted foods and manufactured products from foreign countries put our children, our pets, and ourselves at risk. We currently import 13 percent of our food, up 56 percent from twenty years ago.

According to an article by Alex Pulaski for Newhouse News Service, 2007 was a year of unpleasant revelations for consumers. According to his research, "federal inspectors have found salmonella in Hershey's Kisses imported from Mexico, illegal pesticides and toxic compounds in peanut butter from India, and scores of shipments of Chinese seafood tainted by unsafe animal drugs, unregistered pesticides or salmonella. . . . Mandatory country-of-origin labeling, passed by Congress in 2002, has been delayed under pressure by meat packers and retailers, leaving consumers with limited information about where their food might come from."

Monopolies and oligopolies in the food business have placed us in that position. That's where the meat industry has gone, along with vegetables, dairy, all of it, bringing into question the quality of food available. "It's not smart for our country to compromise our capability to produce," Wendy said. This country ought to be producing the best food in the world. There's no reason for it not to be. From a worldwide standpoint, it's a security issue for us not to be growing our own food. Wendy and Jon have developed a distrust of the government and the policies of the USDA. "When I see 'organic fruits and vegetables' imported from South America, Central America, and Mexico in our supermarkets in January," Wendy said, "I don't have a lot of confidence in the certification process. Some people think that if it wasn't good for us the government wouldn't allow it to be sold. Well, aren't they in for a shock? Chemicals the USDA outlawed twenty years ago in this country are still being used on produce in those countries."

The Taggarts had some very important mentors in the beginning when things got tough. Now, the rewards are coming their way. Five years ago, Wendy called Whole Foods, a high-end nationwide chain and multibillion-dollar company some people refer to as "Whole Paycheck" because you'll spend your whole paycheck shopping there. The district office wouldn't give Wendy the time of day. "Today the regional director for Whole Foods was in here wanting to buy meat," Wendy said. Whole Foods understands the demand or they wouldn't be looking to change their meat counter. So far, they are not interested in importing beef, which makes all American producers happy. "That's a really strong example of what they think the demand is," she said. "If they think the demand's there, it's there."

Recently, Wal-Mart launched organic food products in their stores. The world's largest food chain, the world's largest employer, said to have a store within fifteen miles of 90 percent of all Americans, will force down the prices for organics. Sustainable production of goods will also be stimulated *if* Wal-Mart buys U.S. produce exclusively. But if it outsources, then specialty producers such as Marin Sun Farms and Burgundy Pasture Beef will continue to grow and prosper because they *guarantee* the conditions under which their product is raised—they *guarantee* strict standard operating procedures, they *guarantee* superior levels of food safety. When it comes to outsourced produce, meat, and dairy products, the USDA is not able to give those same assurances.

SOME FARMERS AND RANCHERS scoff at the concept of farmers' markets, describing it as designer ag. To them it lacks the reality of ranching; tradition bends to accommodate new consumerism, and that requires more sales meetings than roundups. Ranchers would rather ride the range than buck the traffic to market their products to people who share no commonality. And even if they did want to sell their products locally, not every community is blessed with Dallas–Fort Worth's or Marin County's high per-capita income or educated palate. In the rural routes of Idaho or Utah or

Nevada, you'd be hard-pressed to sell a Kobe beef sandwich available in big-city exclusive restaurants for the going price of $150 each, or artfully packaged jams no better than local homemakers put up in their own kitchens, or eggs at a cool six dollars a dozen. But if someone has an idea that stops the family ranch from becoming another golf course, and keeps its kids out in the country where they can saddle up a horse rather than play a video game, then they might agree—any way ranching works is the right way.

The Hammond Family

TJ QUARTER CIRCLE RANCH

Carl, Charley, and Visalia Hammond

When viewed at night from a satellite, Nevada is a dark wedge in the glowing heart of North America, Reno and Las Vegas mere mists of light on that sky map. A small town or ranch headquarters has no hope of interrupting the complete blackness. Still, the Hammond family thinks of their centennial ranch as the center of the universe, much the same as the native people explain the coil of their existence.

Four generations of Hammonds from the late 1800s until the late 1990s were held by the impulse of hard-won battles with nature, economic trends, and political administrations. Carl Hammond lived in that outback of Nevada for more than forty years as if without question it was his only choice.

Now, it is a different ranch on the outskirts of Burns, Oregon, that arranges his life's pattern. Carl regards the gathering darkness of evening as lights come on one house, one street at a time, and he pushes down the feeling of their intrusion. He can't get used to living "close in."

A car comes down the road and turns around in the Hammonds' front yard. Carl wonders if the guy knows where he's going. As a single dad, it's a question he's asked himself many times over the last five years. But not as often anymore. Time and routine have cut a path through regret.

Carl has left stew in the oven for Visalia, his twelve-year-old daughter. When she finishes her piano lesson, she'll come out to the studio, bowl in hand, to draw or work with clay. He stops and listens. The music is fast and happy, just the way she likes it. His son, Charley, and he will probably work on their sculptures until midnight even though they hauled hay all day and had a breakdown with the loader that cost them precious time. Charley jumped on the backhoe and used its bucket to lift the bales onto the flatbed trucks. It made Carl proud that Charley was all loaded before he got back with the parts. On the Nevada ranch where they were both born and raised, sitting idle made no sense. Living more than fifty miles from town gave them the ability to focus on solutions, not stumbling blocks, and to come to their own rescue. Haying is a concentrated chunk of work amid summer thunderstorms, lightning fires, and broken-down machinery. But Carl finds that fatigue is forgotten when the clay softens in his hands.

In the Hammonds' art studio, light lies in a pale sheet across the work-tables. It's tidy and invites creativity. Carl finds comfort in having the kids at work in the same room, and yet it's big enough for ideas to occupy each artist's mind in solitude. Sculptures on revolving pedestals are statements of action or energy translated into flowing lines that develop from wads and chunks of clay. Bits cut or pinched loose are scattered on the table like pebbles on a desert playa, waiting to be reunited with the form as a strand of mane or the curved shank of a bit. Paintings and drawings, things of leather, horsehair, rawhide, silver, and clay make it clear that Carl carries on the vision of his ancestors.

Images are the elements of Carl's remembrance, born in his mind as early mornings when the horses are still fresh and full of play or cattle buck and run off the rim ahead. When a horse is about to strike, Carl adds a speck of white around its eye for widened anxiety. He paints rim rocks shot through with sunrise, aspen suffering in drought, cattle gone wild in their solitary haunts as light thunders down through holes in the sky. These are things he has seen and felt, and feels again, now.

Gloria, the oldest of Carl's children, was also born on the Nevada ranch. Now, she is married and lives in San Diego. In the evenings while Carl, Charley, and Visalia are at work in the studio, she designs jewelry at her kitchen table a thousand miles away, knowing they are all in the studio. She places a turquoise stone against one spidered with green. Her memory absorbed the intricate details of the desert until it was as much a part of her as the matrix is to the stone. When darkness falls and her concentration overrides the noise of traffic outside, art unites them.

Trappings of the buckaroo life are all around the studio. Some would say as props or models. That might be part of it. But more to the point, things of horses and horsemen belong where the Hammonds are. Mecates, ropes of twisted horse hair, made to be tied onto a bosal or hackamore and used in a horse's training, have a place here as art. Carl's father learned the craft from buckaroo and bunkhouse inventor Glenn Walcott. Carl's dad would take his boys over to visit "Walcott" at the Little Humboldt Ranch, and they would help him twist the strands of his mecates together. Carl continues Walcott's work with Charley and Visalia, who have each designed and made their own mecates. The process becomes a family project initiated by one of them. But the one who envisions the pattern, states the size, and twists the first strands is the maker of the finished rope; theirs is the name on the tag.

The tapaderos, thirty inches top to tip, hanging on the studio wall, were on the saddle Carl ordered from Visalia Saddle Company when he was ten years old. The saddle was paid for with his first wages for helping put up hay, and it was the saddle on his horse when he went out with his dad following the cs Ranch wagon. During the day, the buckaroos rode up to where he sat his big gelding, and one by one they asked, "Who rides the longest tapaderos, Carl, you or your cousin?" Carl stuck out his chest and answered, "I do!"

The Nevada cattle ranches that surrounded Hammond Ranches were made up of millions of acres, from Winnemucca, north and east into the Owyhee Desert on the Oregon and Idaho borders. The Circle A ran twenty to twenty-five thousand head of cattle. The cs ran seven thousand. Ellison Ranch and Company ran eight to ten thousand head of cows and an equal number of sheep. The 25 was the largest, with thirty to thirty-five thousand head.

The cs, Hammond's nearest neighbor, ran a big wagon, spring and fall, and had a crew of a dozen to fifteen buckaroos hired permanent. Jay Fowler was the cow boss. He was also Carl's uncle, so there was no argument when Carl's father, representative for the Hammond Ranches, asked to take Carl along on the spring gathering to brand the unmarked calves. As the rep,

Carl's dad took part in every rodear for their neighbors on the range. It was his job to make sure any TJ Quarter Circle cattle, those belonging to Hammond Ranches, were branded with the proper iron.

Gloria, Charley, and Visalia, the children of Carl and his former wife, Helen, come by their place as fifth-generation Nevada ranchers because their great-great grandfather Frank Hammond was brave enough at age thirteen to stow away on a freighter leaving France in the 1860s. Frank was accidentally pistol shot onboard the ship that carried him around the Cape of Good Hope, but he recovered before the ship entered the port of San Francisco. He caught a scow across the bay and began walking inland into the foothills of the Sierra. Gold mining did not lure him. On the ship he heard about cattle and land barons, Miller and Lux. In working for their company, he learned that hard work could build an empire. All he needed to find was the right country and hearty cattle. He kept a northeast reading on his compass for the next four or five years, working, walking, working, walking. Near the end of Frank's search for a place to settle, he took a job at the flourmill in the northeast corner of Paradise Valley. One morning Frank saw a Paiute raiding party approaching the mill. With no time to get away, he ran to the mill, pushed open the door, and hid behind it. The Paiutes rushed in after him, but they didn't think to look behind the door. He waited until men arrived from town before he came out from his hiding place.

Not long after that incident, Frank left the mill to locate a homestead of his own. A small meadow on Kelly Creek looked promising. Any water in a dry land is valuable, and he was told that Kelly Creek flows nearly all year long. He built a little dugout and put in a garden. About the time he got the garden planted, the creek quit running. He followed it to its source and found someone had dammed up and diverted the water. Out of respect for a prior claim, or fear, or wanting solitude, he migrated on to Jake Creek. But before he laid a shovel to the sandy ground, he walked up to the headwaters to determine if there was a claim upstream. Finding none, he built himself a dugout.

It was on Jake Creek that Frank had his second encounter with the

Paiute people. A small family group moved in and built a stick shelter on the hill above his place. He kept a sharp eye out for any sign of trouble, but none came. After a few days they were gone. They left the shelter standing. Fearing an ambush, Frank waited and watched through the afternoon. Finally he investigated their camp. A Paiute girl lay sick on a grass mat inside the shelter. She had been bitten by a rattlesnake. He carried her downhill to his camp and there applied a poultice to draw the poison out of the wound. Slowly, the girl recovered. When her people passed through the country again the following spring, they took her along. By then Frank had grown so fond of her, he was sorry to see her return to their nomad ways. He was alone once again.

In time Frank married, built a house, and fathered nine children. The Jake Creek Ranch was, according to his great-grandson Carl, "nine hundred and fifty acres of some of the prettiest country in Nevada."

Seven of Frank Hammond's children moved on to various parts of the country. Frank and two of his sons bought more land and incorporated all the properties into one operation. One of those sons was Carl's grandfather, Carl. Sr. Frank Hammond had gone from teenage stowaway, dayworker, and homesteader to the founder of one of the larger family ranches in Nevada. His holdings encompassed forty-three thousand acres of deeded land in both Humboldt and Elko counties and four thousand cows.

IN 1939, Carl's father, Francis Hammond, was propped up in a hospital bed in Winnemucca with a broken leg when his sister-in-law came to visit. Her friend Dorothy McNinch, a young woman of uncommon good cheer, accompanied her. Francis, or "France" as some called him, fell in love with Dorothy. They were married and moved out to Hammond Ranch within six months. "I had him at a disadvantage," she said smiling, "but it worked out fine. We raised a family and worked together on the ranch for fifty-five years."

Their first child, Carl, was born in 1953. It was a flood year and every road in Nevada was washing out. Francis drove Dorothy in a four-wheel-drive Dodge Power Wagon on planks laid over the washouts to get to Winnemucca.

It was a close race with the stork, but Dorothy won. "I was glad I came in on a good year," Carl said. "It was a wet fall, and that means a lot of grass for the next spring and extra feed that fall."

Carl was the first of three boys born to Francis and Dorothy on the land that became known as Hammond Ranches, Inc. In those early days there were no outside fences at all and the cattle mixed. Being a small outfit in the middle of all the larger ones presented Francis with a good opportunity to ride with their buckaroos. Francis was the rep for his outfit. When any of the larger ranches gathered and worked cattle, Francis worked with them and protected his interest. Later, he was able to take Carl along with the cs wagon.

"I'd start getting butterflies about the middle of May," Carl said. "As soon as school got out, we left for Walcott Creek to get all of our saddle horses together. My dad had about twenty head of his own, and he loaned me five of the older bridle horses in his string, and we tied our bedrolls on his old brown horse. It was six miles over to Kelly Creek. We drove our saddle horses and caught the cs wagon there. We set up our tipis and had supper at the wagon. Our horses ran out with the cs cavy. That bunch of horses was something to see. The cs had over a hundred head of horses, plus ours. My dad always kept a bell-mare with our horses, and they would stay with her. That's how my buckaroo days started."

The next morning at four thirty or five o'clock Carl could hear the bell-mares leading the horses into the big round corral at Kelly Creek, and the boss would rope the men's horses out before sunup. Having kids along changed the dynamic of the work slightly, but in Carl the men saw their own youth again. No one seemed to mind. On the third day with the cs, Carl and his dad rode into Kelly Creek Basin up above Snow Storm. It was a good grazing area. The cows fed into the basin and stayed there. Carl was helping the riders push the cattle out of the basin to the branding spot when he saw a mountain bluebird wing by.

"I just couldn't help but go after it," he said. "It was a small one and just the brightest blue as blue could be."

Cattle, buckaroos, work were all forgotten. A boy went in search of a bluebird. The men pushed the cattle toward the rim before anyone noticed that Carl wasn't with them. Jay, the cow boss, rode back for a look-see.

"I caught the bluebird or had him cornered," Carl said, "and all of the sudden this big shadow comes over me, and Jay says, 'Carl, what in the heck are you a'doin'?'

"'Well, I'm just trying to get a look at this bluebird,' I said. He had to laugh. He was thinking that maybe my horse fell and he came clear back there.

"He said, 'Well, better get mounted up, it's time to go. Everybody's goin' on and we're gonna' be out of sight pretty soon.' He waited for me to get on, and we caught up. I don't know how it would have been someplace else, but then, he liked kids, otherwise I wouldn't have been out there interrupting the day."

Jay respected Francis's position. Once the cattle were settled in the rodear, Jay let Francis and Carl go first so his men didn't put the cs iron on Hammond calves by mistake. The ranches could trade calves later, but that meant extra work. Jay chose to handle the situation with neighborliness.

Buckaroos of that era were wizards with a rope. Generally they used a reata of braided rawhide ranging in length from sixty to ninety feet. Any of them could throw a loop thirty feet or more. The etiquette of the rodear was observed; each roper took his turn while the other riders kept the cattle quiet. The cow boss would designate the ground crew, and normally he worked on the ground. It was his responsibility to make sure that the vaccine was given and the marks and brands were right. The big rodears would have upward of three hundred to four hundred cows and hundreds of calves to mark. Each man would start out at the backside, away from the fire, and rotate around. As soon as the roper had a calf caught and started to the fire, another guy at the backside would do his rotation and come through the rodear, always roping toward the front end, never away from the fire. They would put a coil with the loop to give them an extra six to eight feet of distance when they threw; their loops would cartwheel to head or heel the calf and bring it to the fire.

"The men had respect for the cow boss," Carl said. "He always rode in the lead and he didn't put up with any baloney. You were told what time to be up for breakfast, and you better be there, regardless. Those guys worked hard for not a lot of pay, but they all liked being out there. All they had were good horses, good grub, the scenery to look at, and the spiritual nature of the desert."

Each morning the riders would trot out from camp. At a certain point, Jay scattered them out and gave each person a circle to ride. It was an area of responsibility, and the rider was expected to make a clean sweep whether he was seven or seventy. If a buckaroo didn't have his directions straight, he could jeopardize the day's work. Carl developed pride in knowing where he was at all times, and to do that he picked out a landmark and kept it in sight.

"Getting your directions and watching for landmarks is a skill that can come in handy even in a city. A landmark can direct you to your hotel," he said. "I have a sense of direction even when I'm indoors. But I don't think my kids use it as much. Although they grew up on a ranch and went with us, the scope of the country they covered was smaller than an adult's."

There is an unwritten etiquette of gathering, based on the idea of safety. It is also about courtesy and teamwork, but that's not obvious to children. They have to be taught, as they are taught to respect their elders or carry their dishes to the sink.

"One day my cousin and I were on the inside of a circle," Carl said. "We gathered our little bunch of cows and headed to the branding area. If you're on the outside, you have twice as far to go as someone on the short circle, so we were moving too fast. Everybody was to meet and shove in to the road. We were supposed to wait for the other riders, to help them and all go in together. One of us had the idea of getting there first. In about an hour I could see a guy coming at a trot. It was my dad and I thought, 'This can't be good.' When he got there we got a chewing out—'Don't you guys ever go off and leave anybody farther out on another circle. You wait until they're there.' So I learned that it's not a big game. You have to be patient and wait because that's how you communicated with the next guy and the next guy and then you all got to the rodear ground about the same time."

There was another reason to slow down and arrive with all the other cattle. It had to do with efficiency. When the cattle reach the rodear ground and stop, the calves are more apt to mother-up and nurse. When ranges are shared and the cattle get mixed with those from different outfits, the calf has to be identified with certainty before it is branded, and that is proved only when it sucks from its mother. The brand she carries is the brand that goes on the calf. If they come in and suck, they will be satisfied and likely get separated from the mother and may not reconnect for hours. It is most efficient if the rodear forms as the branding fire is lit. Then the branding can begin as soon as the irons are hot.

Carl was just a second-grader that first year, but he absorbed valuable lessons from the adults. When the time came, he taught his children. Carl also learned he could live for three weeks without his mom, although she and her sister, Jay's wife, went along some years. It was unheard of for women in those days to ride and rope. To a boy who had no experience with the privileges of marriage, Carl thought the women got special treatment, such as tents with the good floors and getting to rope first when they reached the rodear grounds.

"I went with Francis before I had children," said Dorothy, who was also ranch raised. "When I could, I went along with the men afterward, too. Those buckaroos were so special to me. They never swore in front of me; they treated me like a queen. The cooks let me sit behind the stove when it was cold. I would help them do dishes and pack wood. When you work with a bunch of men, you're in their world. You need to keep your mouth shut and observe."

Jay Fowler led them around the desert for three weeks. Every day there was a roundup and a branding of all the slick-eared (unbranded) calves. It was twenty miles from where they started at Kelly Creek to the center of the range between Hammond Ranches and the cs and their last camp. The cs stayed out to haul salt and fix up the corral fences. Carl and his dad trailed their horses to Walcott Creek, and that was the end of the wagon for the year. Carl had mixed feelings as he looked down the back trail and waved good-bye to the cs crew. He was lonesome for his mother, but he had found something in the company of those men that would stay with him always.

Summer at the home ranch meant haying. "I always looked forward to joining the cs wagon," Carl said, "but no one looks forward to haying."

In 1969–70 the Bureau of Land Management (BLM) started fencing all that public land into individual allotments. The tradition of working the range became localized within boundary fences, and the community of the big rodears ended. The cattle didn't migrate outside of their allotment. The wagons stopped running and the ranches cut back on full-time buckaroos. Carl was right on the edge of that change. "Fences didn't benefit the ranchers; they separated the ranchers from the working community they had developed out of necessity," he said. "Before the BLM took over administration of the Taylor Grazing lands, ranchers were respected and had input on the way it all worked. Fences made the job of the BLM easier, and from that point on the rancher took a subservient role to the BLM. They didn't know the country like we did, they truly did not understand the water or the wildlife, but they were in control."

"We had a resentment toward the changes forced on us," Dorothy said, "but there was nothing we could do. Long before Visalia was born, Francis and I had a saddle stallion that we bought and turned out with our mare band. They stayed on our mountain. But when the BLM fenced the country, our stallion got fenced off from his home territory. We wanted to go get him and bring him home. They told us, 'You can't run horses, you can't go get him. It's against the 1971 Wild Horse and Burro Act.' So he died over in the BLM country, and every time we rode, if Francis came on a pile of bones, he would say, 'I wonder if that's Rojo.' Visalia remembered her grandfather telling that story, and she made a sculpture of a lone horse. She named it *Rojo*."

The cs didn't pull that big wagon out after the fences went in. Carl never got any pictures of it, so he paints those days of gathering in that vast country.

FRANCIS AND DOROTHY had a habit of discussing the ranch history and the buckaroos they had known at the supper table, and Francis always had a story to illustrate a point. "Carl would sketch little pictures while he listened to his dad," Dorothy said. "I thought that we should do something to help him with his art. So I took some art classes in town to learn what kind of paints to get for him so he could get the sagebrush just right. He started out working in watercolor, and I got him a coloring book: *World Champion All Around Cowboy, Jim Shoulders*. It had horses and cattle in it. That was Carl's world, too."

The principal of the grammar school advised Dorothy to encourage Carl's interest in art. When it came time to choose a college, Carl decided on Casper, Wyoming, because it had a great rodeo team and a great art department. What more could he ask for? Directly after graduation from high school Carl packed up for his first formal training in art.

Carl's sculpture

Despite the changes that time has wrought in the high desert country of Nevada, Carl succeeds in capturing the moments of peace, or drama, on the range. His palette, like the men Carl looked up to for guidance and justice, is somber. Subtle and chaste.

"I admired Jay Fowler because he was a fair man," Carl said, "and my dad, of course, even as their abilities and skills were being diminished by time. Dad found it harder to get on his horse and began using a mounting block. But he told stories that were so real to him because he had experienced them. I thought it was a shame these men would not be remembered after the stories were forgotten. I vowed that the ordinary buckaroos, ones who would never be inducted into the Cowboy Hall of Fame in Oklahoma City, would be recognized for time earned."

Carl started the Great Basin Western Art Roundup in 1982 to encourage western artists who depicted the buckaroo life authentically. In 1988 he added the Great Basin Buckaroo Hall of Fame to honor the common workingman who laid his life on the line every morning when he stepped into the stirrup. For the first eight years an art show carried the event. In 1990 the first buckaroos were inducted, and a place was set aside for photographs and memorabilia of each one in the Winnemucca Convention Center. Among the first four inductees, men who gave their best every day of their working life, was Glenn Walcott.

TRADITION is a pillar of the Hammond family, or in the buckaroo vernacular, tradition is their snubbing post—the place from which the action and the learning begins.

Gloria, Charley, and Visalia were all born in Winnemucca and raised on the TJ Quarter Circle. When they were ready for school, Carl and Helen took turns driving the kids out fifteen miles to catch the bus, just as Dorothy and Francis had done. When they were ten or eleven, they drove themselves out just like Carl and his brothers had done in their little VW Bug. It was an hour to get to school and an hour home, worse in the winter when the roads were bad.

"It was a hardship for my parents to get us to school from there, and then for Helen and me, but the alternative was boarding the kids out," Carl said. "Mom and Dad tried boarding me out with a relative in Winnemucca when I was in first grade. But it didn't work out. We never tried it with our kids."

It was a long trip to town for Gloria and Charley to be involved in school sports programs. Charley made good use of the time to study. "I had two hours every day to do homework," he said, "and stare out the window."

High school rodeo offered them a means to compete at sports designed around their ranch background. Most of their practice could take place at home, although competition required driving the length and breadth of the state every weekend of the fall and spring. Gloria put her ability separating and sorting cattle to work in the girls' cutting event. Charley rode bucking horses and was the Nevada State bareback riding champion in 1997 and was reserve in 1998. The wins qualified him for the National High School Rodeo Finals in both 1997 and 1998. "We had big banners on the side of the trailer that said, GO NEVADA!" said Carl. "It was a great experience for all of us."

When the kids were little, they all started out riding with Carl on the front of his saddle, or on a pillow behind Dorothy, before graduating to their own horse. After the fences went in, Francis would make a crew out of all the kids and go up to the camp in the Snow Storm Mountains and stay for up to two weeks gathering and branding calves and packing salt. Francis built the same relationship with his grandchildren as he did with his sons. He took time out to teach them about the beauty of nature as they hunted for pretty rocks, and taught them to fish from their horses, especially in rattlesnake country.

A cow and her calf may graze the country alone for months and forget about humans altogether. The sight of a rider can spook them into flight. Gloria remembers that when she was about four years old she was riding with her father and grandfather in the Snow Storms. A little bunch of cows out on a rim spotted them, threw their tails over their backs, and spilled off the mountain toward the Owyhee Desert. Francis galloped hard to the outside to bend the lead cows. Carl brought Gloria along at a trot. When Francis got the leaders turned, Carl left Gloria on the ridge and told her to wait there until someone came to get her, as he bailed off after the wild cattle. Finally, with the cattle in control, he looked back to see his father and his daughter coming along about three miles behind.

Francis had seen Carl bust after the cattle and figured what he'd done, so he backtracked to find Gloria and her old mare waiting just where she'd been told to stay.

Children learn the importance of following directions and trust. Explanations will come later.

IN THE FALL, Charley would take a week off from school, with his teacher's approval, to help gather. He made up his schoolwork and was asked to give reports to the class on the experiences of going to cow camp with the men to help bring the cattle home for the winter. His classmates listened enrapt. His experiences seemed to be coming out of a lost time; his heroes were not their heroes.

All of the children loved to ride in the desert. Adults placed important responsibilities in their hands, yet someone was always within sight if there was trouble.

"Visalia would go horseback in her little diaper the whole day and not want to get off," Carl said. "It was not very comfortable with two in a saddle for one, but as long as Visalia wanted to go, she went along."

At age four Visalia got her first horse, Mooch. "Then she really didn't want to get off," her dad said. "It would be sundown and Mom would bring the trailer to haul her home, but she wouldn't get off Mooch, and I couldn't make her get off. She's independent that way."

All three of the children learned a great deal from doing work that can be experienced only on horseback. They know that the desert grasses can be harvested by cattle and converted to benefit people. The also learned that a day wasn't over until the work was done and that work could be fun, too. Those lessons learned working with their parents and grandparents matured their thinking. Gloria graduated with a 3.5 grade point average, Charley with a 3.0. Visalia works to keep her 3.90 average and, as a seventh grader, is in the National Junior Honor Society. She studies piano with enthusiasm and hopes to be a professional musician. At a recital in the spring of 2007, Visalia earned a scholarship to an Oregon state summer music camp. Meanwhile, ranching provides her with a peaceful life and many opportunities to refine her own ability with horses and cattle.

THE NEW MILLENNIUM brought predictions of cataclysmic events on the planet Earth. For the Hammond family, the predictions were personal in nature and true. Hammond Ranches came under a forced sale by a majority of the stockholders. In an attempt to save the operation from being put on the auction block, Carl acquired a silent partner who agreed to buy out the shares for the family. Unfortunately, Dorothy and Carl were unable to purchase the ranch under the agreement of the trust. They sold their interest. Hammond Ranches still exists, but not for them. In Dorothy's and Carl's mind, the only blessing was that Francis didn't live to see it happen.

The Francis Hammond Trust bought a ranch near Burns, Oregon. Carl and Helen moved there with Visalia, the only one of the three children still at home. Gloria was working in Reno, and Charley took jobs away from home, but when the jobs were finished he always came back home.

Dorothy bought a small ranch five miles from Carl and Helen's. They all tried to adjust to the changes, but time only seemed to rip them farther apart. When Visalia was eight, Helen left. Visalia stayed with her father. Since that day, he has served both sides of parenting. For Carl and Visalia, living together has made each stronger and better prepared to deal with whatever comes their way.

"When you're a mom and a dad," Carl said, "you have to handle both sides of that. Visalia is edging toward the teenage years. I'm paying more attention this time around. It seems like it just happened with Gloria, but I'm watching the steps and stages. Mostly I'm really proud that, with a dad for a mom, she has learned to play the piano and the clarinet, as well as staying a'horseback. Visalia takes pride in getting all A's in school. We live close enough to town where the bus can pick her up and she doesn't get home as late as we used to on the Nevada desert. I'm grateful for that. When you have children, you have to think about more than just being a rancher or a buckaroo. I'd like to see them stay in the ag world, though there are other opportunities that they should have access to that I didn't have. It wouldn't have changed my goal or the road that I traveled, I don't think. Ranching got in my blood early, starting out with Dad and Uncle Jay and the wagon at age seven."

As Visalia tried to make the adjustment to being a ranch kid in a town school, Charley kept an eye on her. "She was starting to change, to be like the town kids," he said. "She started questioning the way we did things at home and the clothes she had. They weren't what the popular girls wore. I told her to be true to herself and not try to be like somebody else. Just be herself. Now she's finding friends who are like her, girls from ranches around here, and she's happier. I try to help her because I went through it, too."

The lack of respect for people who make their life in agriculture disturbs Charley. He sees it on a local level, in the middle of cattle country. "I was in the local feed and equipment store, and in a sarcastic way this girl asked her mother, 'What are all these *farmers* doing in here?' So I listened to see what her mother would tell her, and she said, 'They're just farmers.' Well, she missed the opportunity to teach her kid that farmers and ranchers put the food on her table. Without them, where would she get her food? That's the problem in this country. People have forgotten us. They think food comes from the store, not the ground."

Charley and his grandmother Dorothy enrolled in a real estate course a year ago, and, as investment partners, they bought a townhouse in Bend. He laid new tile and wood floors, and she gave it a fresh coat of paint. "We got a new Jenn-Air stove that cost us a lot, new countertop on the sink," Dorothy said. "We stayed right at our remodeling budget, so now we're going to resell it and I think we'll make a profit. It's been fun working with my grandson. The time we spent together means the world to me. He laughed a lot and he got to know me as a person, not just a grandma."

Charley took a job in Reno for a well-drilling company, and when it was finished he came home. He misses the ranch, his animals and horses when he works away. Sculpting brings him back. Lately, the periods back home

Dorothy working the chute

have gotten longer. "The ranch is his anchor," Dorothy said. "Now he wants to get a place of his own. He went to the ASCS office to apply for a loan for a purebred operation. The real estate course taught him how to write a business plan. It was a good, solid plan." Dorothy smiled, marveling that Charley wants to make his way back to ranching, and she said, "I'll help him any way I can."

After 1970 when the BLM fences went in, the Nevada ranch turned into a family operation. There were no more big crews riding to gather and brand. Each operation tended to its own work, so it took all of the Hammonds to help with the cattle, the haying, and the feeding. Their children gained a lot from that responsibility.

"They're good hard workers," Dorothy said. "Gloria's boss in San Diego told us she's the best help he's ever had. She's efficient and knows how to get things done. I think she learned that from the ranch because she was on her own and she had to think for herself. A lot of kids today don't have to figure things out. Both she and Charley had to do that. Observation is a part of that."

Gloria is an administrative assistant for Solar Turbines, a subsidiary of Caterpillar Tractors. True to her upbringing, she is a jane-of-all-trades, from fixing paper jams in the copy machine to coordinating executive meetings. But a career with the company is of no interest to her.

"It disturbs me that we're losing machinists at the plant. We have a training program we can't fill," Gloria said. "No one wants to learn a trade. They aren't proud to be working. I grew up loving to work, but everyone there is waiting for the weekend so they can sleep in or party. As for the future, I'll find something to do that will unite the things I do well. I've learned to be resourceful."

Divorce is hard on a family no matter how old the children are. Gloria suffered being away from the storm when Helen left Carl, but it gave her a perspective that she values. She listens and stays neutral. Preserving her relationship with both parents is most important to her.

"I have them over for dinner almost every Sunday," Dorothy said. "It's a grandma's job to set up in the dining room, lace tablecloth, the silver and napkins, and we all sit together like ladies and gentlemen. At home they can just grab a sandwich and go, but I think it's good for all of us to remember that there's more to meals than that. Visalia joins in the conversations, and she fits right in. I tell her to get some cooking ideas because it's going to be her job. So she comes over and I've taught her to cook and to sew. She makes potholders and pillowcases and does a pretty good job. I tell her I'm not going to be here forever. I love just sitting back and observing them. I love being the grandma."

THE 25TH BUCKAROO HERITAGE WESTERN ART ROUNDUP was held on Labor Day in 2007. At the main floor entrance in a complex of display areas Carl's sculptures and paintings were at the center, Visalia's whimsical bronze study of Chief Crooked Horn and the statue of Rojo were to one side, Charley's sculpture of a buckaroo and bronc was on the other. Mecates made by the Hammond team were scattered throughout, and beside Charley, Gloria displayed silver and gold handmade jewelry of her own designs.

"WE'VE ALL LOST SOMETHING," Carl said. "It's nice here at the ranch in Burns, but we don't have those long desert rides. Visalia experienced that, and when we left the desert it must have bothered her some because she always wanted to take our house back from the new people and live there. That's been six years, so she's over it now, I guess. It bothered us all to have to move away from Nevada. It was our family's ranch for over a hundred years. The change is hard when you've all worked together as a family to get the cattle fed, branded, moved out in the spring, and gathered up in the fall. It's the great open spaces and the camaraderie that we loved. I can only give that world to them through my art. I teach them by depicting scenes from that time and from before my time that will always be in front of them.

"Everybody used to ask how can you stand it out there, it's so lonely and despairing. But you're not alone. You've got God for one thing. And once you've met Him you can't forget Him. You've got your horse, the cattle, and your dog. I never feel alone."

Advantages of Being Ranch Raised

GINGER GRAHAM AND JESSICA HEMPHILL

W hat stirs in the steady eyes of a champion? Clarity of purpose? Determination? Concentration? Ginger Graham and Jessica Hemphill each bear the calm poise born of digging down to do their best. Both have ridden into the arena of the National High School Rodeo Finals behind cowboys and cowgirls gathered from across the country, with their state flags snapping in the wind of galloping horses. They first experienced the value of hard work on the family ranch. Despite the separation of years, they are two of a kind, sharing common ground in a personal need to excel at academics, the advantage of considered preparation on the harrowed surface of the high school rodeo arena, and in the world of business.

THE UNPLEASANT PRICK of a needle begins each day for Ginger L. Graham, president and chief executive officer of Amylin Pharmaceuticals. The regimen is done to test her blood sugar. People with diabetes must do this daily to keep a close eye on their diet to avoid dangerous fluctuations of glucose. The thing is, Ginger is not diabetic. But her clients are, and she doesn't want to lose sight of the people she serves.

"I just think we don't appreciate how hard their lives are," Ginger said. That's why she is particularly proud that in 2005 her company launched two new drugs that have revolutionized health care for people with diabetes. Her gesture of solidarity with those who suffer from diabetes and her dedication to producing a superior product for the public health sector is how Ginger Graham has made Amylin Pharmaceuticals, a company that is expected to surpass $1 billion in annual sales in the next few years, a leader in the biotech business world. The media flocks to interview Ginger because of the dollar figure, but it's the patient in the waiting room who has her undivided attention.

GINGER'S PATH to success began on a meandering dirt road through northwestern Arkansas. She was born and raised on her parents' chicken farm. That's where she learned to lean her shoulder into the hard times and keep working for the good. Her plainspoken business demeanor falls away when she speaks of home. Some might hear the cadence as "southern," but it's more any-place-in-America warmth from living close to the soil. Her parents were the entire labor force on the farm. She and her brother started helping as soon as they could walk, carrying feed, working cattle, filling water tanks. Besides chickens and the occasional batch of turkeys, her folks raised five acres of grapes, a herd of pigs, sheep, cattle, and horses to handle them. Agribusiness was built on commonsense diversity. The law of averages teaches that when one crop is dropping in price, another will be on the rise. Farmers and ranchers have always understood supply and demand as the underpinnings of all markets. They try to maintain some measure of liquidity to take advantage of the fluctuations. Downswings in pork bellies are offset with fat lambs, or pasture steers, or sorghum, or corn. The meat the family operation produces has nearly always been organic in the true sense. Their animals have long been raised on natural feed without medication because the animals have never left home and were not exposed to diseases that are by-products of mixing, shipping, and stress. Markets were developed in local communities. Reputations for consistent, high-quality products were established over the long term. They were entrepreneurs before the world knew what the word meant.

Ginger was a horse addict from the beginning, like many young girls raised on farms and ranches. To celebrate her fiftieth birthday, her husband Jack flew to Arkansas and dug through old family albums with her dad and brother to surprise her with a video. "He found pictures where I'm maybe four years old, barefoot, in a dress, and have real wild curly hair, riding on my Shetland pony with a switch in my hand," Ginger said. "I think it just happened genetically."

While Ginger was riding her horse or grooming her pet sheep, Tinkerbell, she was absorbing important early lessons in business administration as she helped her mom and dad on the farm. It came to her as an understanding of the value of effort for the animals that supported the family. "There's so much you learn from animals, but you have enormous responsibility," she said. "You have to take care of them and pay attention to them, and do it on their schedule of needs, not your own. When you're tired or it's really lousy weather and you have to do chores anyway—you have to clean the rabbit cage or muck the stalls—you learn responsibility for something that is dependent on you."

Ginger applies that thinking on the human level to her employees. "If you don't trust the people you work with, that what they say is true, that they care about you as a person, and that they are committed to doing the right thing in business, then it's almost impossible to build a team-based relationship." She was very young when she realized that an investment is not necessarily made in terms of money. In a rural environment, whether it's the horse you ride to move the cattle or the cows themselves, "You have to invest time, you have to be consistent, you have to be available," Ginger said. "All those things take time, something this world is forgetting."

In the present business environment of high-speed and remote access, the benefit of time is often sacrificed. It's not personal. But work on the farm or ranch is defined by the season, the age of the animals you have built a relationship with, death and birth. It is a reality that the animals contribute to your life, not simply as pets, but as partners in the way a living is made. "Tragedy is a common occurrence on a farm or ranch, as is the realization that life is beyond our control. Certain things must simply be accepted. That's one thing about farming that I admire the most," Ginger said. "Like my dad when a hailstorm ruined everything, or we couldn't get enough help to harvest the grapes, or a cow died having a calf. You dig a hole and you bury them and you move on to the next cow because you've got to keep going. I think that sense of marking seasons, knowing the inevitability of life, and perseverance in the face of difficulty are hallmarks of people that are raised on farms."

But she is quick to remind us that urban people work hard, too, building a business. Ones who succeed face setbacks and tragedy and are not diminished by the adversity. Early in her business career she worked for a man whose parents were bakers, and they had to get up at three o'clock in the morning and work hard hours. The whole family pitched in. Everybody had a role to play, in good times or bad. "That same set of attributes can be learned, and I know it's learned by work," she said. "There's no doubt in my mind that hard labor teaches you how to be a better person, and on family farms and ranches there's a lot of hard labor and a sense of grounding less able to be expressed specifically in other environments. Work is the greatest gift parents can give to their children because it teaches them self-esteem and accomplishment. Any twenty-year-old kid I can find who, through hard work, has understood the value of that perseverance and personal accomplishment and gotten that self-esteem benefit from it, I'd like to get to know them."

THE BAREFOOT GIRL with wild curly hair grew up to compete in 4-H, junior rodeo, and high school rodeo in every event open to girls: breakaway calf roping, goat tying, barrel racing, and pole bending. She competed in rodeo events at the college level and, as an undergraduate at the University of Arkansas, won the 1976 Miss Rodeo Arkansas title, qualifying her for the Miss Rodeo America Pageant. At that pageant, Ginger won the public-speaking portion of the contest for her speech about her home state of Arkansas. After graduating from the University of Arkansas with a BS in agricultural economics, she got a "good job." But she was hungry for something more. She decided to enroll in the master's program at Harvard Business School. "My parents had never gone to college. My brother and I were the first generation on both sides of the family that got to go to college," she said. "Then it seemed we were never out of college." Their dad drove a mail route and their mom did part-time catering, on top of working on the farm, to help with expenses.

"I didn't even know where Harvard was," Ginger said. "Going to Harvard was this huge deal." She sold everything she owned to finance her tuition, including her car. Her brother had a car that he'd bought from an uncle when he went to pharmacy school. "It was literally the typical rural Arkansas vision," she laughed. "Up on blocks, under a tree, hadn't been driven for I don't know how many years. It was a 1972 Oldsmobile Ninety-Eight, as big as a small building. The vinyl top was all rotted, and rust ruined the wheel wells, and it had about 160,000 miles on it."

A friend of Ginger's from high school was a mechanic. He agreed to get it running as cheaply as possible, and her dad found some used tires. She piled everything she owned in the back, and, with her mom as co-pilot and navigator, she took off for Boston.

"I pulled up at the Harvard Business School with a rusted-out, rotten-topped '72 Oldsmobile Ninety-Eight, and there were Ferraris, Mercedes, Bentleys, and Porsches in the parking lot," Ginger said. "It was a perfect image for my trip to Harvard, because I was very afraid I couldn't compete."

The Business School published a book of everyone's resumes in the class that first semester. It was Ginger's worst experience. "I sat down and read it and thought, 'Why am I here? How did I get here? I don't belong with these people.'"

But she found a way to compete and earned a master's in business administration to boot. Sometime during college she developed a plan for her work life. Years before, she abandoned her initial career goal to be a veterinarian because that work would have restricted her area of impact to the animals and their owners she served. Ginger cut out a bigger territory for herself in theory, not knowing that her future in business would achieve worldwide impact. After graduation she went to work for Elanco, an agricultural chemical company, then owned by pharmaceutical giant Eli Lilly and Company. As one of the few female Elanco sales representatives, she drove a truck down the backcountry dirt roads selling herbicides to soybean, cotton, and rice farmers in the Mississippi Delta. Ginger called on her customers in blue jeans and cowboy boots, looking like a neighbor. Her clients were men very much like her father: in the farmer's office, underneath a tractor or setting irrigation headgates, or driving a harvester down endless rows of crops. The men weren't put off by a woman who knew the tolerances of certain plants to the application of fertilizers, the when and how. Family farm operations are gender blind. The work, except for strength requirements, is interchangeable, man to woman. Beyond farm skills, Ginger expanded her turf of expertise considerably when she mastered the male-dominated world of rodeo. If that didn't work, her Miss Rodeo Arkansas beauty and charm certainly did. Some company farmers who managed corporate accounts were reluctant to deal with a woman. But Ginger's ideas on maximization of dollar invested in a weed prevention program with the Elanco product line changed their minds.

Management at Eli Lilly recognized Ginger's potential and moved her through the cosmetics, investment banking, and medical technology branches of the company. During that period she developed strategic planning for its cosmetic division, Elizabeth Arden. "It was a great experience. I learned how to take a business apart," she said. Apart, indeed, and put it back together again and make it irresistible to cosmetics industry competitor Fabergé. In 1987 she managed the sale of Elizabeth Arden to Fabergé for $735 million—then, the largest cosmetics deal ever. As a result of the sale, Ginger was offered a market research job in Eli Lilly's pharmaceutical division, where her interest turned to medicines and disease risks like diabetes and heart disease. According to the Centers for Disease Control and Prevention, chronic diseases, including diabetes and obesity, account for more than 75 percent of the nation's $1.9 trillion health-care spending. Diabetes is listed as the fifth leading cause of death by disease in the United States. "We needed major advancements in science, and we had a health-care system that needed to rethink how medicine is delivered," she said. "I got addicted; I have never been able to leave health care."

Advanced Cardiovascular Systems offered Ginger the position of president and CEO. In 1994, she helped create Guidant, where she served as group chairman, office of the president, developing advanced therapies in cardiovascular disease and building a global medical device company that became the world's leading provider of coronary stents and angioplasty systems. Leading a workforce of more than ten thousand employees, Ginger focused on the strategic development of business collaborations, talent recruitment and development, and the company's women's health initiatives, promoting awareness of heart disease as the number one killer of women. During her administration, Guidant was included among *Fortune* magazine's "100 Best Companies to Work For" for two years in a row, and for four years out of five.

Ginger was serving on the board of directors for Amylin Pharmaceuticals in 1998 when the company suffered a severe blow. Johnson and Johnson backed out of a critical research partnership, causing Amylin's stock to drop to thirty-one cents and threatening the company's NASDAQ listing. Amylin executives did what any doctor would do to keep a patient alive: they cut to the bone—250 employees to 37—and invested their own money, hoping they could hold out for U.S. Food and Drug Administration (FDA) approval of Symlim and Byetta, two diabetes drugs that could dramatically improve the lives of people with the disease. In time, those two drugs would prove to have distinct benefits: help control blood sugar, and the sidebar advantage of lowering the weight of many people with diabetes. When the news broke of the FDA approvals in the spring of 2005, Amylin was instantly transformed from pure research to a player in the pharmaceutical business. President and CEO Ginger Graham celebrated by jumping into the fountain outside company headquarters.

"Our parents raised us saying, 'You can do anything,'" Ginger laughed, "so I truly believed I could do anything." Ginger moved into the work world during a period in history when the thinking was that women were not supposed to do certain kinds of jobs. "I knew better," Ginger said. "I had been taught that I could do many, many things to be self-sufficient, to be self-reliant, to contribute. Hard work can teach you almost anything. If you don't know how, you just start and you learn. That has helped me tremendously. The only thing my parents asked of us was, 'Please just choose to be a good person in whatever you do.' That was their only requirement, and it was always based on the fact that *the sky is the limit*. My mom always said I was going to be the first woman secretary of agriculture. That kind of faith—that we could go do anything—has served me and my brother very well."

Health care was her passion and her work, but agriculture was her home turf. While she was away working to develop health-care products for the benefit of Americans, the fertile valleys of Arkansas were being raided. The relentless crawl of strip malls and subdivisions is taking the best out of Arkansas soil. Farmers are pushed out because their tractors are too noisy, roosters crow too early, pigs stink, and cows bust through fences. Now she sees motor homes parked in driveways that cost more than most farms, and horses in paddocks with no work to do, and she wonders where home has gone.

Her first transition to thinking about corporate farming and the economic deterioration of family farms happened in the early eighties, when President Carter embargoed Russia and the U.S. agricultural economy went belly-up. "I watched farm after farm after farm go down," she said. "They lost their homes, they lost their livelihood, and the kids lost the sense of what they were going to do because, for many people, their kids would run the farm someday."

Ginger was working for Elanco when the company produced an annual television special for National Agriculture Day called "Who Will Farm the Land?" She was sent across the country with the production crew to connect with farm families whose children were affiliated with Future Farmers of America and ask them, Who is going to farm? "The family farm was on the decline. This story is real and it's progressing very dramatically," she said. "If you go today to the Central Valley of California, which most people understand to be the breadbasket for the world, it's turning into suburbia. It does cause one to think very aggressively about what is our national policy for food, what is our national view of self-sufficiency as a nation, much less as individual communities or families. How do we have smart growth as a country and still allow for those national and regional farming and food resources, because we're fast approaching a place where it's hard to see where food production can occur. A decade ago the government issued a buy-out program of dairy cows. Small dairy farms sent their cows to slaughter so that milk production, which was in "overcapacity" and being subsidized by the U.S. government, could drop in capacity. That impacted the beef industry. It's a very interesting social dilemma.

"Interest in this issue does exist in certain places," Ginger said. "It's not on the national agenda and the opportunity for discussion at that level. For me, education, health care, energy, and agriculture ought to all be on the national agenda, because all of those are fundamental to a functioning society. If you look at the debate about the cost of gasoline, what we're looking at as a nation in terms of the risk to the economy; the lack of adequate education, science and math disappearing as curricula, the lack of competitiveness of U.S. students; healthcare, the cost of health care, the demand for health care, the innovations in health care but the poor delivery system due to all kinds of perverted incentives in the health-care system; and agriculture as a natural resource both for sustenance and also for economy— those four topics should be on the national agenda. Our leaders and legislators should see their role as framing how each of these affect the economy. Regretfully, I'm afraid that's not what we spend most of our political energy on today."

Ginger Graham announced she would retire from Amylin in 2007. Getting Symlin and Byetta, what she affectionately called her Sleeping Beauties, through the FDA approval process and keeping her company and loyal employees intact, was a big job. To realize their full potential in the marketplace is her successor's job. There is global production and distribution to oversee. Certainly, she knows how important timing is. She may move to Colorado permanently and ride her horses over the parks of the Rocky Mountains with Jack, and learn to play the harp he gave her when she considered retirement once before. Certainly, she deserves time to enjoy life and reflect on her contributions to the health-care industry of the world and to American business in general. Her leadership will be missed. Those with the most to offer their fellow man, who are deeply committed to the health and welfare of humankind and, therefore, the country, who work without personal ambition or hidden agenda, are those who deserve to have a potting shed out back and enjoy the embrace of silence. But then again, there's that national agenda Ginger's mapped out in her mind, and her mother's unfailing faith in the country girl she raised to take on the office of secretary of agriculture.

JESSICA HEMPHILL is at the opposite end of her life's work from Ginger and yet their influences are similar. Both have had the benefit of strong and supportive parents, both are secure and loved, both were encouraged to "shoot for the stars" and, in doing so, have a wide horizon of promise.

In the spring of 2006, Jessica graduated from high school as salutatorian of her class. "Which is no big deal," she said bluntly. "There were only twenty-nine kids in my class at Tulelake High." The valedictorian and she knocked academic heads through the years. Still, her 3.86 GPA, to her classmate's 4.0, is based on grades not census, and she has a right to be proud. Especially when you consider that as soon as haying starts every year, she bales hay all night and heads for school when the sun comes up. "I've enjoyed it," she said, "because you're always outside, not stuck in the house."

Jessica was born at the Center of the Earth. The Modoc People of the Tulelake Basin in northern California think of their homeland in this way. It is volcanic country, both in terms of geography and history.

The violent Modoc Indian War came to a climax on the western side of the lava-strewn valley in 1872–73, during a post–Civil War campaign to rid the country of Indians. Captain Jack, leader of the Modoc people, and a handful of warriors played a deadly version of hide and seek with the U.S. Army in the lava tubes. During the standoff that lasted for the better part of a year, at a cost to the taxpayers of more than a half-million dollars, only seventeen Modocs were killed compared with the loss of eighty-three whites.

At the start of World War II, another population of Americans came under the control of the military. The Tulelake War Relocation Center, built on the eastern side of the valley during World War II, housed many Japanese-American families and those Japanese-American citizens termed "troublemakers" or "no-no boys"—those who would not pledge loyalty to the USA alone. The buildings have been scattered to the far corners of Modoc County, ending up as bunkhouses, saddle sheds, field shops, and storage buildings. After more than fifty years, all that remains is the collective memory of shame and sadness for a time of distrust and fear of our countrymen and women.

During the severe drought of 2001, the Klamath Basin was the scene of another kind of war—a water war ignited between environmentalists and the area farmers and ranchers. Unrest escalated when a federal court ordered agricultural irrigation canals to be locked shut in favor of preserving the Klamath River endangered salmon, sucker fish, and waterfowl. The air vibrated with the conflict around the sacred uplift of rock in the southern end of the valley where the Modocs inscribed images of antelope, deer, waterfowl, sheep, and fish—their homage to the creatures who gave them life. Or maybe it was just the shimmer of two hundred fifty species of migratory waterfowl gathered in the millions at the Klamath National Wildlife Refuge, a feeding rest stop on the Pacific Flyway. Judicial regulation of adjudicated rights to water in favor of environmental concerns is being considered across this nation. It has affected the way Jessica thinks about her future in agriculture.

AT THE END OF WORLD WAR II, veterans were given the opportunity to settle in the Tulelake Basin. The Ackleys, Jessica's grandparents, were among those who established a ranch and farmed acres that were cleared of the ubiquitous lava rock. Her mother grew up farming and working cattle only a few miles from where Jessica, a fourth-generation rancher, was born. Jessica feels uncertain about coming back home after college to continue the family business. Hard work is not enough any more. Recently the balance of the family ranch has been thrown off by the unexpected consequence of the condemnation of legal water rights.

"Ranching is a hard life," she said. "And the government doesn't make it any easier." Water delivery has become a major concern. "In the summer of 2001, we had to give up our right to irrigation water from the river. We drilled wells that cost us over a hundred grand apiece, and watched neighbors who couldn't afford to drill wells go out of business." Some farmers cut wilted alfalfa that was barely as high as the sickle bar to get something in a bale or because they had to do something to try to stay sane. "If they had gotten their water rights," she said, "the crop would have been four times that high.

Besides the water war, the price of fuel is about to run them out of business. "You count up the number of times you run across these fields to get up a hay crop," Jessica said. "You plow, disc, harrow, drill, fertilize, irrigate, cut, rake, bale, and haul; plus there's oil in the fertilizer and oil in the baling twine. So you charge all that fuel to every crop of hay and the price of hay hasn't gone up enough to compensate for the rising fuel prices or the cost of equipment. How do you figure to make a profit?"

Their power bill has doubled, and there is always uncertainty about grazing permits. "We don't know if the Forest Service will cut us off, or what," she said. "We have to play by their rules. We put up a fight when they try to reduce our aums (animal unit months) on the permit, and then we worry that because we do, they'll reduce our numbers out of spite."

The difficulty with grazing permits for government lands comes as rules change with transitions in administration. Jessica has experienced employees fresh from college with little or no practical experience holding positions of authority. "They don't even ask us any questions about how things are going," Jessica said, "or what we need for our cattle. It's like they don't want to know us."

Jessica's GPA and skill as a rodeo contestant has earned her a scholarship to National American University (NAU) in South Dakota. She's leaving home in a few weeks, excited like all kids going away to college. South Dakota is a long way from California, but Jessica already has a friend there she met at the National High School Rodeo Finals last year. Her friend will be a senior at NAU and has already taken Jessica under her wing. "She knows everything about the college," Jessica said. "I'm going to the business college to study marketing. I want to get into the pharmaceutical department so I can be a sales representative. I want to specialize in drugs for beef cattle. That's what I know best."

The rewards of rodeo, a sport she's been involved with since her days in 4-H, are evident in trophies and photographs proudly displayed in the Hemphill home. Rodeo and the rodeo team will be her home and family for the next four years. Jessica earned a place on the California High School

Rodeo Team, qualifying her for the National High School Rodeo Finals in her sophomore and junior years in pole bending and goat tying. She and her kid sister, Kendra, both qualified for the finals in 2007. Jessica will compete in goat tying and Kendra in breakaway roping. Rhonda and Joe, the girls' parents, in the middle of haying, can't be away from the ranch for two weeks. They don't want their two young daughters making that long drive across country alone, so the girls will be flying back to Springfield, Illinois, the end of July and will compete on borrowed horses. "They're good horses," Jessica said. "It's not the best way to compete, but this year it's the only way."

Rhonda and Joe bought their ranch when they married twenty-two years ago, and every year they aren't sure they'll make it work. They both devote their lives to the ranch. They have different interests that work for the whole of the operation. Joe heads up the farming and takes care of the equipment. Rhonda handles the livestock. Either is always available when the other needs help. Still, it's become increasingly hard to reach a balance, and every year the profit margin narrows but the work never does. As an example of their difficult times, Rhonda remembers that early in their marriage winter came in the form of freak storms that dumped two or three feet of snow at a time, three years in a row. They breed their cows to calve in early spring so the calves are old enough to utilize the feed as it comes, and so they are ready to wean for the fall market when the price peaks. In the Tulelake Basin, winter lasts until April. That means you bump heads with storms that take a toll on baby calves. In those early years, they were losing calves at an alarming rate because of the conditions. Joe took the day shift watching the calving cows, and Rhonda took over at night. Every two hours, she strapped three-year-old Jessica in the car seat and drove across the pastures looking through the calving cows. She checked for cows having trouble calving and for calves too cold to get up and nurse, and made sure that the blowing snow didn't smother the babies. When she came across a newborn calf, she would get out of the truck to see if it was okay, or get it up to suck the cow's colostrum, warm milk rich in immune factors that are essential for protection against the stress and cold. When Rhonda got back in the truck, her sweet little baby girl would chime out with a child's frankness, "Dead or alive, Mom? Dead or alive?"

The Hemphills take their losses and go on. In the early spring they drive the cows and calves onto their Forest Service grazing ground in Clear Lake Hills, about twelve miles straight east from their house across highway 139. If they are moving cattle to the far allotment, they split the drive into two days. "The calves are young when we make that move," Jessica said, "and if it's hot, we have to go slower. If we get a cool windy day, we can do it in one."

The calves born in the snow of January and February are sold on the video livestock market where more than 250,000 head of cattle sell over three days in July. The entire world of cattle buyers comes to the marketplace via the Internet and cable TV to purchase truckloads of cattle that never leave home until shipping day. They can watch the Hemphill cattle pass in front of the camera and judge their size, age, conformation, and condition. They can see the cows they come from and know the quality of the feed they've been eating before the bidding starts. The buyer sets the conditions of delivery. Essentially, for a deposit, they sign a contract to purchase calves to be weaned and delivered on a date that is mutually agreeable. Come fall, the Hemphills gather their allotments and drive the cattle home to settle them in for winter on the home meadows. The calves are weaned from their mothers, put into conditioning lots, and started on hay. They ship in December, according to the terms of the contract. "Our calves average seven hundred pounds when we ship," Jessica said. "The steer calves average twenty-five to fifty pounds more than the heifers. The video is the best way for us to sell our calves. It's quite a bit better than taking them to the sale ring in Klamath Falls. There is no stress on the animals, and they are never exposed to disease. Anyone in the world with a satellite dish and a telephone is a potential buyer."

Jessica grew up in a family that focuses their time and money on cattle and hay production. A horse-breeding program would diffuse their energy and money, so they buy the horses they need. "I own three horses right now, separate from the ranch horses," Jessica said. "I'm going to take two of my rodeo horses to college. My working horses, they're like wild horses, and if they get hurt in that lava country, you're not out much."

AT THE BEGINNING of life's road Jessica can't know what the obstacles will be, nor can she appreciate the value of her experience and the skills that hold her up like her long legs. When she was a junior in high school, her college options were outlined thoroughly.

"You can never be too prepared. You just never know," Jessica said. "Like on the ranch, some years the rains don't come, so you have to be ready with your plan to take care of your herd. Other times, there's flooding and you manage your hay fields for that. Or the public lands rules change and you've got to find other means of grazing your cattle. You've always got to think ahead and have options ready to reach your goal." It's a skill learned on horseback, one that makes her a threat in the rodeo arena and will lead her forward in her business career.

Ranching promotes practical thinking. Eighteen years with parents who taught her as best they could about the pitfalls of being a rancher in the twenty-first century has toughened Jessica to any eventuality. She's honest in her opinions of herself as well as of others. She hasn't packed for college yet, but she's ready to leave. It might be a relief to be away from the pressure, but she won't abandon thoughts of what her folks and Kendra are doing back home. She will know their day and how it's gone with her eyes closed. It is the touching back that will drive her to succeed.

Rhonda's parents host an annual ranch barbeque, a block party of western dimensions. This year it was held in Jessica's honor after graduation to celebrate her scholastic achievements, her success in high school rodeo, and her going away. Four hundred neighboring ranchers from the basin came to wish her well. If she wants it or needs it, this Center of the Earth will be waiting. That's what gives Jessica the confidence to leave. If she didn't know that before, she does now. For a few hours the music of the country band drowned out the raucous cries of waterfowl passing overhead on their northern migration.

The McKay Family

WALKING BOX RANCH

Luke, Joan, Joe, Martin, Anna Rose, Gabe, Joyce, and Clare McKay

Joe McKay went to work for Mary Arrien in 1978. She desperately needed help to keep the ranch going. Her husband, Julian, was in a nursing home nearing the end of a long battle with Alzheimer's, and her daughter Joyce, the only one of her children with an interest in the ranch, was in her final year at Portland Nursing College.

Right away, Mary was on the phone to Joyce singing Joe's praises. The calls continued, more enthusiastic. Joyce was relieved to hear Joe was working out, but she was not surprised. She had known him all her life, at school and 4-H meetings, and every Sunday the McKay family filled several rows of the tiny chapel in Juntura.

Joe had been raised on a cattle ranch in Harper, the next town downriver from Juntura, in a house that levitated with the glorious noise of the McKay's eight children plus an undisclosed number of foster children. The "foster" kids were not bound by formal procedures. Any abandoned kids who needed food and a family found both in the McKay household. To this day, boundaries between children of blood and those of good fortune do not exist.

"They're good people, Mom," Joyce remembers saying. But when she finished her degree and came home, she also remembers fighting with Joe over every deviation from the way her father managed the ranch. Her head buzzed with Julian's favorite saying, "Breathe in fresh air that has not yet been touched by the sun and you'll get more work done."

Julian Arrien was a sheepman at heart. Later, when he changed his operation over to cattle, he worked them as he did sheep, as he learned from his father in the Pyrenees Mountains. He drove the cattle to the corral, tied his horse to the fence, and worked them on foot. Joyce loved being shoulder to shoulder with her father as he proudly watched his cattle string by. But Joe McKay was a horseman, and he worked cattle by staying in the saddle, teaching his horse to help do the work.

Disagreements between Joyce and Joe led to loud discussions and long periods of silence that carried over to her mother's supper table. Mary didn't like to ride or work cattle; she gladly left all the decisions to Joe. But Joyce wanted Joe to have respect for Julian. Fighting for her father's ways kept him alive.

Relief from their running battle came when the first snow flew. The dry cows bred to calve in spring wintered on the Shumway Ranch, high on the mountaintop twenty miles southeast of Juntura. When Joe told Joyce that he would look for someone to stay up at the Shumway to feed the cows through the winter, she volunteered. She needed to study for her state nursing board exams, and she wanted to be away from him for a while.

Most years, fall lingered even in the high country and the cattle grazed until the first snow came sometime around Christmas. But that year, a polar express packed the fury of winter on the wind and dumped a foot of snow on the level. Then the temperature dropped to zero. Joyce tarped boxes of supplies and her books in the back of the truck. With her border collie, Moss, beside her in the cab, she left for the Shumway at first light. The truck crawled up the road that snaked up the ridges and into canyons, the snow axle deep all the way from the valley to the ranch at the top of the mountain.

As she packed her bedroll into the old Shumway house, she stopped and tapped the thermometer by the back door. At 10:00 AM the mercury seemed frozen at minus thirty-five degrees. She built a fire in the cookstove and went out to load the hay on her truck. The cows smelled the hay when she rolled bales down from the stack, and they waited by the gate. At that elevation the world was white except for the long string of cows on the wavy line of the feed trail. After she finished feeding, she loaded for the next day, drove the truck into the cinder-block garage, popped the hood, started the generator, and hung a drop light over the engine to keep it from freezing.

As she chopped ice to clear the trough, the cows were already coming to water.

Joyce was warm from the work and packing wood into the house, and the popping of the fire gave her comfort. Moss curled on her blanket beside the cookstove, and while the soup heated, Joyce opened the carton of books. The first one she drew out flooded her with the memory of leaving the ranch for college as if those days were written on the first page.

After high school she had stayed on the ranch working with her dad where she was always the happiest. In that close contact she started seeing confusion in Julian's eyes when he was faced with a decision. She did what she knew he would want and said nothing. Always his good right hand, she tried to give him her mind also. Eventually she had to admit to herself that it was more than an occasional lapse in memory. Alzheimer's was destroying his mind.

Just when Joyce's dad needed her most, her mother informed her that it was Julian's wish that she leave home and go to college. She refused to discuss it, so her mother sent away for enrollment forms to Portland Nursing College, filled them out, and signed Joyce's name. When the letter of acceptance came, she packed Joyce's best clothes in a bag, put it in the car, put her hysterical daughter in, and closed the car door. "Your father wants you to go!" she said. Then she turned back toward the house and went inside.

Joyce could not disobey her father's command. It would be a long time before she would understand that her mother's pushing her away was the most painful kind of mothering.

FROM THE KITCHEN WINDOW at the Shumway, there was no break of light between earth and sky. The world of white silence enveloped her troubled mind. She let it go and focused her attention on *policies and procedures.*

Joyce didn't dwell on the dangers of being there alone until one day she put the truck in low and, as usual, climbed up three tiers of bales on the back. She was flaking the hay to the cows when the truck jolted over a big rock and sent her cartwheeling off the load. The snow broke her fall, and she climbed back on as the truck inched forward. Had she been hurt or broken a leg, she could have frozen solid while waiting for help that wouldn't be coming until March. After that, she was more careful.

In time, she found a balance between the physical work and the familiar territory of her medical training. Words and definitions she thought were forgotten returned. Yet, nursing bleached pale and antiseptic when weighed against loping her horse to turn a cow and hearing Joe yell, "Good job, Joyce!"

Weeks passed. One afternoon when she took Moss for their walk out to the road and back, she found herself standing looking at her truck's tracks that disappeared under the drifted snow. Any sign of her was obliterated. She felt truly alone in the world.

As days passed, her mind began to stray from hospital procedures to spring calving, plans for the young horses coming on, trimming the budget, things she wanted to talk over with Joe.

Halfway through February, headlights glowed through a whiteout. A truck stopped in the yard. Moss got up and went to the door. Her tail was wagging when Joyce opened the door. Joe came out of the dark with a Valentine box in his hand. Inside was an engagement ring.

EVERY FALL, cattle buyer Dick Mooney made a swing through eastern Oregon to look at calves coming off the short, hard feed of the high desert. Mooney knew the cattle and could have bought them on the phone. But he looked forward to his annual visit with the ranch families, Joe and Joyce McKay in particular. Mooney had a fondness for the couple. The condition of their ranch was improving. Sagging fences were mended. Fat cattle. Good horses. A good ranch.

Rusty basalt cliffs reflected the afternoon sunlight as Mooney entered Juntura Valley. Swaths of green meadows surrounded ranch houses built back from the highway. They could be one ranch. Every stackyard full of winter feed, every field full of cattle. Ranchers of the high desert are in step through the seasons. When prices are up, everybody meets the mortgage payments. Without favor, drought takes its toll on land and business.

Neighbors helping neighbors is a matter of survival. Potlucks bring them together. The little chapel on the edge of town holds them to a larger truth.

Two forks of the Malheur River encircle the valley and flow together below town. Joyce's maternal grandfather was an early settler in the valley. He planted the cottonwood trees that shade the town and named it Juntura, Spanish for joining: water, purpose, *people's lives,* perhaps.

Joe and Joyce drove Mooney through the fields to see their calves. He smiled to himself, listening to the two of them talk about the feed year, market trends, fuel and freight costs, things ranchers discuss when they are with people of a like mind—a man and a woman formed by a commitment to their land and livestock. The silence that passed between them deepened with unsaid details gained by living and working together.

They walked to the house to settle the conditions of the contract. The kitchen smelled of fresh baked bread and roasted beef. Three places were set at the dining room table. He was expected to stay for supper. With gentle curiosity Mooney looked around the big room and asked, "Well, no kids?"

Joyce understood: Dick loves kids, his kids, all kids. He meant no harm.

Fifteen years went by. Mooney was still visiting the McKays every fall, hoping to find a baby bottle in the dish drainer, or a crib near the window. And every fall, seeing none, he repeated his question, "Well, no kids?"

His affection for Joyce and Joe increased his concern that they were becoming resigned to being childless. It was obvious that every bit of their energy was going into the ranch, and he worried about Joyce—that she would have nothing left for children.

Joyce, nearing forty, and Joe, forty-two, sat at the dining room table. Mooney's relentless question was the uninvited guest. Joe is a steady man and straight speaking. He said, "We've lived in this house for fifteen years, and there are still empty bedrooms upstairs."

As the evening passed, Joyce and Joe united in a decision that deflected their lives from its course. They agreed to try adoption to fill those rooms.

Adoption for Joe and Joyce should have been without obstacles. For starters, a child would have a large home in the country, fresh air, horses to ride, home-cooked meals, a life secured by an established business, and

parents of impeccable moral character. They are respected by the community, both individually and as a married couple, and active in their church.
They offered all of that to a homeless child. The adoption agency would not
be swayed. Their caseworker's reasoning was "the lack of cultural opportunities on a ranch." Sadly, Joyce and Joe discovered that it was easier to get
a half-million-dollar operating loan than it was to adopt a homeless child.
They lost heart.

Mooney told them not to be discouraged, there were other agencies. He
steered them toward CASA, a children's advocacy group in Boise, Idaho.

Preliminary introductions with CASA took place over the telephone. They
followed up with a trip to Boise, one of many. At the CASA office they were
given a clipboard and a pen. More paperwork. More questionnaires. More
interviews that pried into their financial and personal lives.

One afternoon there was a call from CASA. Three black children were
available for adoption. A woman dying of AIDS was giving up her two children. The mother of the third child had been found guilty of a serious crime
and given a long prison sentence. Adoption by the McKays would rescue
three children.

There was no question about adopting black children into the McKay's
Anglo family. Both the Arriens and the Harpers raised their children without prejudices. Joe and Joyce believed the most important part of parenting
is love, not raising someone in their image.

But the caseworker stopped the process. It was her opinion that the
McKays didn't fit the profile of adoptive parents for black children and that
ranch life in eastern Oregon would be culturally wrong for them. To fulfill
the mission of CASA, children must be given the opportunity for interaction with others of their race. Later Joyce learned that CASA gave the three
children to a black woman on welfare with four children of her own. In
essence, the message to Joyce and Joe was, "It's okay to die in a city, but it's
not okay to live on a ranch."

Once again Mooney bluntly moved them off-center by leaving a business
card with Joyce for Robert Luce, a lawyer in Boise, Idaho. Luce and his wife
were adoptive parents of a Haitian child. He had mastered working through

Hat's off!

red-tape tangles that can undermine international adoptions. Armed with the statistic that one in five Haitian children die before reaching adulthood, he dedicated his efforts to improving the odds. He put the McKays in contact with New Life Link, a not-for-profit adoption agency located in Port-au-Prince, Haiti. New Life Link's mission, more directly than that of CASA, is to help couples willing to open their homes and their lives to orphaned or abandoned Haitian children. The agency offers hope to the children of Haiti.

2005—Juntura, Oregon, Population 50

Joe McKay and his son Gabe, next up in the open team roping at the Juntura Ranch Rodeo, enter the arena side by side. Joe backs his horse into the roping box, and Gabe waits on the right. Their horses compress, eyes intent on the chute where the steer waits, and when the gate opens, steer and horses break as one. Joe's horse is one stride back as the head loop drops over the steer's horns. Gabe's loop sings high overhead and downward to set a perfect trap. Steer steps in, ropes come tight, flag drops. Joyce and the other five McKay children are at the arena fence cheering.

Passing tourists, drawn from the highway by the unexpected sight of cowboys on horseback, capture souvenirs on film of wide-brimmed hats, straining muscles, the expressive eye—images that will have lifelong currency back home.

Their cameras find another layer of the cow country rodeo to focus on. Kids on horseback are contestants, too. Teamed with adults, they sort numbered cattle through a gate between two pens. If the number sequence is broken, the team is disqualified. Like the roping events, sorting teaches them to think and act quickly. Maintaining control of a cow can be like staying one jump ahead of a lightning bolt. It's a skill many adults find hard to master. These ranch-raised kids handle a rope with confidence and ability beyond their years. When they aren't competing, they mess with a water snake in an irrigation ditch, gallop races on the shady grass, and run up a bill at the hot dog stand.

Joe has been patiently working cattle with his six kids since early in the day. He cinches up his horse and slips into the saddle as if he is weightless. Gabe does the same. They ride to a fourth place in the team roping.

Nothing separates this ranch family from the others. Only strangers see that Joyce and Joe are white and the children are black.

THE SUN is just beginning to set when the rodeo is over. People load their horses and head for home. Joe drives his pickup and trailer into their ranch yard, just across the valley from Juntura. Quail flush from the garden when Joyce opens the front gate. She and the girls go to the house to start supper. Joe and the boys unload the horses and lead them to the barn.

Evening light floods the barn as the horses are tied to the long manger and unsaddled. They pull mouthfuls of hay from the overhead rack, and the old barn is filled with the sounds and smells of other days reaching back to the turn of the century. Horses and humans. Hands on hide. A partnership.

More than a dozen saddles line the south wall, and saddle blankets are draped over a pole sweat-side up to dry. Six saddles are small but well used.

When the horses are turned loose in the corral, they drop and roll dried sweat from their backs into the soft dirt. At the irrigation ditch they lean deep into the sliding surface of the water and relieve their thirst.

The youngest of the McKay children, eight-year-old Joan, sits under a maple tree in the yard, a baby cottontail rabbit cuddled in her arms. Martin, also eight, found the dead mother and then the babies. "The cats got a couple. There's only two left." She whispers, hugging the rabbit protectively to ward off further tragedy. Joan has learned the hard reality of life's cycle, ever present on a ranch, ever present in her native home—Haiti. Deeper implications are waylaid by the tenderness of her fingers in the rabbit's mottled fur.

Luke and Martin are relaxing in the TV room. Ten-year-old Luke, an excellent roper at home and at the neighbors' brandings, rarely participates in public. He seeks the edge of the room, does not raise his hand in school, but knows the answer. He supports the others with his presence.

Martin has a special ability with horses. He gets more out of them with less effort, knowing when to ask and when to wait. Cinnamon, the four-year-old he rode today in the barrel racing, had never seen a barrel unless it was full of gas or oil or contained a branding fire. He held the anxious colt together through the cloverleaf pattern and won third place.

Clare and Anna Rose are setting the table, talking as they put forks and spoons beside the plates in no particular order. Clare is eleven, but she has the poise of an older girl, laughs easily and makes others laugh. Today she won the barrel racing on her Paint gelding, riding hard to the first barrel, checking him lightly, and sending him into the turn. At each barrel she was in control of his speed, and pushed fast to the finish. Winning is in the tilt of her chin.

All animals fascinate Anna Rose, as if she and they share a private language. First to notice a calf with droopy ears, or a doddering trot, the nine-year-old points them out to her dad and follows the treatment until they are well again. Nothing about Anna Rose reveals that her twelve-year-old mother gave her up for adoption, unless it's her ambition to keep the animals of her world healthy.

Gabe plays with a tiger-striped kitten on the floor. At twelve and a half he balances on the outer edge of childhood. A competent roper, he is deliberate, never one to be rushed unless it's in a footrace. Then he is a force to fear. Heading back to camp after a day of driving cattle, it's not unusual for Gabe to ask his dad's permission to get off his horse and run. If it's okay, he ties up his reins, hops down, and leaves the horses far behind.

Handling a rope came naturally to him. He mastered building a loop and roping a bucket on the ground as a six-year-old. When he was ready to try it on horseback, Joe gave careful instructions. Adding a horse and calf to the mix increases the chance for accidents. Joe tried to keep Gabe from getting in trouble, just as he has done with all of the children. Carelessness in a branding pen can get people hurt.

Joe washes up and comes into the kitchen. He sits down in a chair and leans back, hands behind his head. Joyce takes a beer from the fridge and gives it to him. "Clare got a check," he says. "And this guy here," gripping Gabe's shoulder, "double-hocked that steer and won us fourth place."

He doesn't mention that beyond his wins, the entry fees for working every event with each of the kids amounted to three hundred dollars. And their bill at the hot dog stand exceeded seventy dollars. The McKay kids know what it's like to be hungry, so when they eat, every kid eats.

Gabe puts the kitten on Joe's pant leg, and the kitten digs in its claws. Joe is trying to talk with Joyce. He tells Gabe to quit. The routine is repeated several times, and Gabe is grinning, enjoying the effects of his game. The kitten is moved to Joe's shoulder, arm, back. In a firm tone Joe finally says, "Now, Gabe, stop that." Gabe gently unhooks the kitten from Joe's shirt and puts it on the floor. Then he drapes his own arms over Joe's long leg, cheek on his knee, and Joe rubs Gabe's back. This solemn moment moves from the boy's face inward to where the man he will be has begun.

HAITI, where the average annual income is slightly over four hundred dollars per year, is the poorest country in the Western Hemisphere. Abject poverty is responsible for the sale of more than four thousand Haitian children into the slave trade every year, according to a joint report by UNICEF and the International Organization for Migration. Smuggling is a lucrative trade. Parents needing income pay smugglers in the Dominican Republic up to eighty dollars per child to take them across the border into Haiti. Many children end up as forced laborers on farms, doing construction, or as domestic help, beggars, or prostitutes.

Even within Haitian borders poor children are grist for the mill. Serving as house servants to the elite, they are not given living quarters but turned out of the house at night to sleep in the street without bed or blanket. Young

Rodeo conference, Joe and Gabe

girls like Anna Rose's mother, especially vulnerable to the conditions they are forced to accept, are let go if they come up pregnant.

According to the joint report, Haiti has other demons that impact the children's lives: it's a major Caribbean transshipment point for cocaine en route to the United States and Europe and experiences substantial money-laundering activity, Colombian narcotics traffic, and pervasive corruption.

Luce introduced the McKays to Dr. Jacob Bernard, a Haitian theologian and director of New Life Link, a Baptist orphanage. Dr. Bernard, educated in the United States, works tirelessly to get children out of the corrupt and war-torn hellhole his country has become. Word on Haitian streets is that Dr. Bernard can be trusted. Desperate mothers appear at the door of the orphanage.

"The mothers bring their children in so they will live," Joyce says with reverence. "We told the little kids that it's not that your mothers don't love you. They do!"

The Haitian women give their babies life twice, first with their bodies, and then by giving them up to the orphanage.

A packet of photographs came in the mail from Dr. Bernard. Sweet children's faces—dark to mocha brown, smiling, scared, shy—were laid out on the McKays' kitchen table like playing cards. Joyce and Joe found themselves with the awful power to choose. They decided to begin with two, a boy and a girl. For a fleeting moment they wanted to take them all, to empty the orphanage and the streets of poverty, to still the cries of the hungry and homeless. But there would always be more than they can afford to care for, more than they can get their arms around. They drew back to a point of reason and shuffled through the photos again, finally settling on two-and-a-half-year-old Gabriel and thirteen-month-old Clare.

But before the arrangements with the orphanage were finalized, Clare's mother came from the village and took her away. Joyce understood the woman's grief-stricken walk to retrieve her little girl, hoping to be in time to take her baby home.

Dr. Bernard gave her some time to realize what keeping her baby would cost in the end. He went to her village and found little Clare lying on the mat flooring, stomach distended, crying as she ebbed toward starvation. He stayed and talked with Clare's mother until she lifted the baby into his arms.

Haitian babies are at high risk for AIDS, and those testing positive are not allowed to leave the country. During the process it was discovered that Gabriel tested positive for sickle-cell anemia. Dr. Bernard called and spoke with Joyce. He said that they would be given another baby. She hung up the phone, and when Joe came in, she told him.

Joe said, "No. We chose him. He's ours."

Joyce got out their medical manual and read aloud words anyone could understand. Gabe would be doomed to continual hospitalization and inevitable death. Financially, it would be staggering. Emotionally, it would be worse. She closed the book and pushed it away.

As Joe dialed the orphanage he told Joyce, "We're keeping Gabe." He spoke with the orphanage, hung up, and turned to Joyce with a stunned look. "They said, well, okay. They'll throw in another baby for the same price."

Although it would be discovered later that Gabe did not have sickle-cell anemia, only the trait, on the morning of June 1, 1994, when Joe took the freeway exit to the Boise airport, they both thought Gabe would be a terminally ill child. In the long-term parking lot Joe turned to Joyce and asked, "Ready?"

Often Joyce saw a doe cross their horse pasture. Recently, twin fawns trotted out of the willows behind her. When the doe stopped, the fawns stretched their necks to suckle at her flank. At first glance they might have been a different species, the doe with her sleek golden hide, the fawns spotted and mahogany brown. The doe and fawns were in her mind that morning. She was ready.

The flight to Miami was a strange combination of excitement and boredom, going at breakneck speed yet strapped in a seat for long hours. The cloud bed moved beneath the plane like white silk, as exotic as the thought of arriving in Florida. None of it had any relationship to Juntura. Again and again Joe fished in his shirt pocket for the pictures of the children, as if taking out a map to assure himself of the way ahead. The plane made its descent into what seemed like a foreign country to the McKays. Islands strung out into the infinity of the blue ocean, palms, sand, city, and incredible heat as they disembarked. Inside the terminal, public announcements were made in Spanish first, then English.

"Dr. Bernard and his wife met us at the airport," Joyce says, "and handed over Gabriel, Clare, and seven-month-old Luke, some Haitian art, which is real cumbersome, a satchel of the babies' belongings, and said, 'Well, okay. Bye bye.'"

People on the hotel shuttle gave up their seats to the couple with three babies and their belongings. There was more confusion at the hotel. Getting everything to their room was like packing supplies to their cow camp up on the Shumway Ranch during the fall gather. When they got to their room, they put the babies on one bed and they sat on the other, thinking that the children needed their space. Little Clare was the first one to slip down. She tottered over to the full-length mirror and looked at herself like, That's me, all right.

The real impact came when the tiny girl turned and looked at them with no recognition, no idea who they were or where they would be taking her.

The next morning Joyce woke to two little faces peeking over the bedside. She tossed her clothes on and started changing diapers. While she fed the little ones baby food she brought from home, Joe took Gabriel downstairs to breakfast in the dining room. In a jungle of exotic flowers and ice-sculptured flamingos, platters were heaped with sausages, bacon, ham, eggs, bowls of fruit, drinks with straws, everything a little boy might dream of, especially a boy from a Haitian orphanage.

"I fixed Gabe a plate, and he started eating," Joe said. "That little child had never seen food like that. He'd never been full. I finally realized he wasn't going to stop. He was like a horse with a sack of oats; he was gonna keep eating until his belly busted. I had to just pick him up and take him out of there."

The children were plagued by health issues common to those born into the poverty of a tropical country. Little Clare's naval was herniated from lack of food, and Luke was very sick with strep of the skin.

After they boarded the plane for home, Gabe went wild when they tried to fasten his seatbelt. Joe recognized a colt's panic at being hobbled the first time. The little boy tore at Joe's face trying to get free. Joe convinced the stewardess to leave the seatbelt off and Gabe calmed down, but he clung to Joe, crying. Joyce held Luke, leaving Clare to sit alone in the window seat beside her.

"I wished someone would have held her," Joyce said, "but they didn't. She sat there the entire flight to Portland and never made a peep."

THE MCKAY RANCH spreads like fingers reaching into the corners of the Juntura Valley. Their cattle, branded with the Walking Box, range over deeded and permitted land that stretches west toward the community of Drewsey. It is a cow/calf operation, and the cows are the foundation of the herd, culled for quality, maintained in good condition the year round, and bred to calve every spring. The calves are carried through the summer on the cows, weaned, and sold in the fall. Hay put up in the summer is fed out in the winter. Life on a ranch is mapped by the cycle of the seasons and altered only momentarily by catastrophes if it is to survive.

In the early fifties when Julian Arrien still had his sheep, a freak spring snowstorm hit as the bands were moving from the desert toward the Steens. The sheep were marooned in two feet of snow, unable to move and with no feed or shelter for miles. A neighboring cattle rancher by the name of Stoddart knew Julian had been caught by the storm. Stoddart saddled up and took his men to find the sheep. Once found, his men rode ahead of the sheep, breaking a wide trail for them to follow to safety. Cattle ranchers are often characterized in history as ruthless enemies of sheepmen. Some were, but many more were not. Without the action of the cowman, the sheep would have perished and the Arrien family would have been wiped out of business.

AFTER JOE graduated from high school, his father sold the homeplace and moved to a desert ranch near Ely, Nevada. When the time came for Joe to strike out on his own, he headed toward Juntura. On the way he bumped into a friend who told him that Julian Arrien was ill, Joyce was at school, and Mary was running the ranch alone. Joe went to see her, and she hired him on the spot.

The ranch was sorely in need of a man's strength, energy, and ideas, and Joe was not one to spend someone else's money foolishly. He kept the purse strings tight, gave the land its full allotment of water, and saw to the livestock's needs before he thought of himself.

Joyce graduated in 1978 and moved home where she always wanted to be. After Joyce and Joe married, they built her mother's herd of cows to seven hundred head and increased the deeded land. BLM and U.S. Forest Service permits expanded their grazing over fifty miles.

THE ADOPTION OF CHILDREN changed the McKays' working partnership. In an instant Joyce was a housebound mom with sick children to tend. Joyce's mother helped with the children. Relatives and friends were a godsend. Joe was left working alone, and for Joyce, confinement in a house she had seen only before sunup and after sundown for sixteen years was difficult. Tending three sick infants in a household of revolving caregivers increased her longing to be outside with Joe doing their ever-changing ranch work. The only thing ever-changing for her was diapers.

Luke's medical condition was her primary concern. Acutely aware that the mortality rate of strep of the skin is high if left unchecked, she took Luke to the clinic every week, and every week the doctor put the baby on a different drug. When she overheard him telling the nurse they were going to lose the baby if they didn't get the strep under control, she was really frightened. Experimentation with drugs was leaving the baby vulnerable to acceleration of the infection.

They took Luke to a man in Caldwell, Idaho, who practiced natural medicine. He examined the baby and made an infusion of tea tree oil, echinacea, and goldenseal. Immediately Luke began responding to the herb tea. Soon, he was completely well.

All of the children were infected with a relentless diarrhea that defied every medicine. Finally Joyce learned about a clinic where the doctor in charge had been a military doctor in the tropics. He immediately recognized Giardia, which the infants had contracted from drinking unclean water in Haiti.

"The doctor put them on a seven-day regimen of medication and cleared them of the parasite," Joyce said. "When we went to Miami for the other children, the medicine was in our suitcase."

Clare, the mimic of the family, entertains the other children with stories dramatized by the rolling r's of a Scottish brogue or the clipped patter of a Liverpool accent. But it wasn't always so. Clare was tongue-tied. A simple surgery fixed the problem, and now she has a beautiful voice. Had she stayed in Haiti, it is a certainty the surgery would not have been available to her.

Being a mother of three babies under the age of two and a half proved to be more difficult than Joyce imagined. "Joe and I were exhausted," she laughed. "Someone asked me if the kids sleep through the night, and I said, I don't know, but we do."

THE MCKAYS CHOSE RANCHING. It is their heritage, compatible with their best qualities. They have common sense in the face of problems, the ability to laugh when they want to cry, and to cry when they need to. Joe is a seat-of-the-pants mechanic, patient and inventive. Joyce is a master organizer, cooks in quadruple quantities, and somehow maintains her sense of humor. Both are devoted to the ranch no matter the weather, the hour, or the effort required—the very virtues needed for mothering. And there were still three empty bedrooms upstairs.

In March of 1996 Dr. Bernard delivered eleven-month-old Anna Rose to Joyce and Joe. She had the condition present in all of the other children, a herniated naval caused by hunger.

The arrival of the first three children was novel. Help was unscheduled but faithful. The children are a constant reminder that there are so many more children in Haiti who need a home. When Joe and Joyce went back for

Trail drive

Anna Rose, the attitude of family and friends was a little like Dr. Bernard's: "You're on your own now. Bye bye."

Two years after getting Anna Rose, they picked up Martin, who was born in October of 1996, and Joan, born in November of that same year. Four years earlier Joyce and Joe had sat alone at the kitchen table. Six children later Joe was wondering what they had got themselves into. The simple word "bedtime" made the tough cowman weak in the knees.

"Just getting them bathed and diapered and into bed at night took two hours," he sighed. "We tried teaming up in the bathtub to cut the time down, but it was always two hours—*every single night.*"

The good news is that the last two children were physically healthy. Neither has been to the doctor for more than simple immunization. But they had other problems that needed solving. Joan was malnourished and extremely weak. She wasn't doing age-appropriate things. At two she couldn't hold her own bottle, and she would fall all of the time.

"I think her motor skills were delayed because she was struggling so hard physically to survive," Joyce said. "But one day, I was trying to find the shoes of one of the boys, and I said, 'Luke! Where are your shoes?' Suddenly little Joan was standing there with Luke's shoes, and I'm thinking, she's okay."

Martin was at the far end of the behavioral scale—high-strung, disruptive, and very aggressive. In order to survive in the Haitian orphanage, he learned to be a scraper. When Joyce's brother-in-law, a teacher in Portland, saw Martin, he told her, "If Martin was in our school system, they'd put him on Ritalin."

"Joe put him on a horse," Joyce says, smiling.

Realizing that Martin needed a physical outlet, Joe took the little boy with him on horseback every day. If he couldn't, Martin would throw terrible fits, pacing the yard fence, yelling for his dad to come back. He wouldn't settle down until Joe came in sight. He needs his dad. They are inseparable.

"Joe is such a fierce parent," Joyce says. "He's committed to these little kids, and he's turned out to be so nurturing. It was interesting to see that in our relationship, because his gifts really came out having children. It would have been so sad for that never to be a part of his life, because they're his strengths. He's really a wonderful father. He was taking the little children horseback so young. That was his time with them."

The McKays' office is lined with six school desks. Bookshelves, posters, maps, a globe, and a computer draw the world into their schoolroom. Joyce follows the homeschooling lesson plans, but also realizes the value of the ranch as a rich source of education. The children help her plan and plant the garden. They sit beside Joe at the kitchen table as he figures the tons of hay required to winter a cow. They sharpen their eyes to the condition of the weaned calves and observe Joe teaching a young horse to accept his weight in the stirrup. And they play.

Joan smiles brightly. "Sometimes our recesses get carried away."

MOTHER'S DAY is a major holiday in the McKay household. All of the children's mothers are alive in Haiti. The fathers are rarely listed on their papers. Joe and Joyce keep the kids in contact with their mothers by helping them prepare packets of letters and pictures and photographs to be sent back to Haiti.

"We want to let them know their babies are alive and doing well," Joyce says. "Dr. Bernard told us, 'You must bring the children to Haiti to visit, but . . . they will not want to stay.' It is so poor in Haiti. It's almost like they will understand what they left and what they have. I think there will have to be a certain level of maturity for a child to handle that."

Robert Luce organized a Haitian reunion to honor a visit from Dr. Bernard and his wife. The McKays drove the longest distance, and when they came walking across the park with the six children all together Dr. Bernard ran to meet them.

Home schoolroom

"The love that Dr. Bernard has for these little children is extraordinary," Joyce said. "He greeted them by their Haitian names. It was wonderful, all those families."

As the afternoon waned, some of the city families started leaving. But the McKays are country people. They took a day out of their lives. One couple that lived nearby asked them over to their house.

"Dr. Bernard had concerns," Joyce said. "He showed us how to keep the boys' hair clipped short. He said the kids on the street wear their hair long. It was really important to him that we groom the children properly. As a people they have a lot of pride. Every little Haitian boy got his hair cut that evening."

The children love playing make-believe games like, "I'm going on a trip and I'm taking . . ." Each child's story builds, with their birth mothers superimposed onto their own lives in Juntura.

"I think it was really healthy for them to do that as little ones," Joyce said, "to keep connected. They'd say, 'Oh, my mother has long hair and she lives on a ranch. Oh, my mother has chickens.' But the reality is that animals don't live in Haiti because they've all been eaten long ago. There isn't even grass. At the border, it's barren on the Haitian side and on the Dominican Republic it's lush and tropical. Haiti should be green and forested, but they cut every tree for firewood and destroyed the ecosystem."

PARENTS RANCHING in America's outback have to face difficult decisions when it comes to educating their kids. Many communities can't support upper levels of school, making it necessary for parents to homeschool or to send their children to boarding school. Some of the mothers move with the children. They buy or rent a house in town in order to maintain a home environment, and dad is left home alone. Either way, from the time the oldest child goes away to boarding school until the youngest graduates high school, family life is condensed into weekends and school vacations. In the case of the McKay family, the third scenario would mean that Joe could look forward to an empty house for ten years. It's a sacrifice no one should have to make, and yet every September ranch families across the West do exactly that.

Crane, one of the last public boarding schools in America, is an hour's drive west of Juntura and offers a summer school program. Joyce and her friend at the neighboring ranch, Linda Bentz, decided their kids needed a little socialization. They scheduled a carpool.

The nuns running the summer school were enthusiastic about enrolling the McKay children and found a film about Haiti to introduce the children's homeland to the student body. With the McKays at the center of the semicircle in the darkened gymnasium, the screen throbbed with stark scenes of a wasted landscape and the dire poverty of Haiti. When the film ended, all the McKay kids' fantasies of their mothers' beautiful lives in that imaginary land dissolved. The teacher spoke into the deadened silence, "Well. Who would like to be from Haiti?"

"Our little kids raised their hands," Joyce said, "and the other kids didn't raise their hands. But the little Bentz kids raised their hands with our kids, in solidarity. The other little kids were saying, 'Who'd want to be from there?' I don't think we understand poverty in our culture. The women bear the burden. Our kids need to realize there's nothing to go back to. The mothers don't want them to ever come back. In Haiti the mothers realize that it's their gift to let them go."

IN JUNTURA the McKay kids are already admired as polite, smart, honest, as well as good ranch hands, like their white counterparts. Ability with a horse or a rope indicates a deeper level of experience but has nothing to do with their worth. They're accepted because they are just plain decent kids. But prejudices are met outside the valley. Joyce had business in Burns, Oregon, and she took Joan along to swim in the community pool. Joyce sat at the edge of the pool reading while her very social daughter played in the pool and made friends. After a while Joan got out of the pool and told her mother that she was ready to go. They had to wait another hour for a part for Joe's baler, so she asked why Joan didn't want to swim any longer.

House chores

Joan glanced over at an Indian boy gathering his things beside his mother's chair and said, "Those kids are being mean to him, saying mean things. He's going home. I want to go home, too."

Sometimes that unexplained prejudice is closer to home and affects the lives of the children in real ways, hurtful ways. Joyce and Joe try to shelter them and talk honestly to them in those cases, knowing that painful situations are ahead for all children, and especially the McKays. Joyce and Joe work hard to give them confidence and pride, knowing these are tools against prejudice, and the kids are strengthened by a good home and loving parents.

"In a sense it's breaking new ground to have black families on the land in ranching," Joyce says. "They're not going to stay children all their lives. Their future, if they want to choose, is in ranching. We have plans to build a gas station where the kids can work and learn. A gas station would help the community, too. We are fifty-six miles in either direction from a gallon of gas. We plan to let local artists hang their work in the station, so they'll have a chance to sell some things and keep their art going. We also want to build a slaughter plant so the local ranchers can have their own meat processed. It's so far to those kinds of services, and the children here need more employment options. They will be raising their families here. I pray that goes well."

LIVE TELEVISED COVERAGE of the National Finals Rodeo Championship extends for ten evenings in early December. The kids' bedtimes are postponed so they can watch professional cowboys working some of the same events that translate to their ranch life. For the past dozen years one of the top contenders for the calf-roping title has been Fred Whitfield, six times World Champion Calf Roper, and the third cowboy in history to surpass the $2 million mark in earnings. Fred Whitfield is a cowboy from Texas. Fred Whitfield is black.

Gabe watches Whitfield through each of the ten go-rounds of the 2002 World Championship: watches him back his horse into the box just as Gabe does, rope fast just as Gabe does, and with hands like lightning, tie the calf just as Gabe imagines he could do. When Whitfield completes his final run to cinch another world title, Gabe raises his hands in victory. Gabe says, "I want my name to be Fred Whitfield!"

Joe McKay is a fine roper who has won many contests, including the prestigious Big Loop in 1989, in Jordan Valley, Oregon. In addition, he is an exceptional roper in a practical ranch setting. Gabe loves his dad. Joe has raised Gabe since he was two and a half, loved him although he expected the child would not live, lifted him on his first horse and placed the bridle reins of freedom in his hands. Yet, the man in whom Gabe recognizes an identity to strive for is a black cowboy because they share color.

CHARLES GORDONE, a black playwright who won the 1970 Pulitzer Prize for his play *No Place to Be Somebody,* said, "the aspirations and happiness of black Americans will remain trampled and shattered as long as they continue to be caught up in urban chaos with its utter degradation of soul and psyche. A people whose history is with nature and whose instincts are essentially bucolic cannot endure as a viable American tribe if they remain packed away in city ghettoes. Now, as a Westerner, I believe the thwarted instinct of African Americans for a dignified involvement with nature is the biggest cause of their troubles. Making them realize their heart's true habitation is not urban is a simple idea, radical in the true sense of the word."[1]

JOYCE AND JOE believe in the family of mankind, both are optimistic, and they teach the doctrine of the Catholic Church to their children by living example. Weekends all through summer they seek relaxation from the work at home in rodeos and roping events. But when it's time for mass, no matter where they are, even if Joe or the kids are up in an event, Joe tells the secretary, "Just move us down in the draw. We'll be back in a little while." They tie their horses to the trailer and enter the church as a family.

"In both the Irish and Basque culture, the males or the firstborn inherit the land. I did not inherit; Joe and I have bought and worked for everything we have. But I'm the first woman of our family to continue on the land. That's another example of breaking new ground," she says, taking the idea further, "and now we have our little kids who are black, and that's breaking new ground, too. I don't know how they will feel about it, but I think it's very exciting."

The life cycle turns within the earth's cycle. The McKay children lead one to believe that a life on the land and the husbandry of animals can build a stronger child. Civilized people have the unswerving duty to provide every child with shelter, good care, education, and the opportunity to seek their potential. By virtue of a parent's promise, every child is owed someone to believe in, someone who believes in them with unconditional love.

Ranching communities are often bound by tradition, and not every child can fit that rigid mold. Yet, new blood can advance traditional thinking, open eyes to new ways, and both generations can benefit. Cultures can be bridged and the best of each guarded and allowed to flourish.

AFTER DINNER ONE NIGHT, guests pushed back their chairs from the table, and the McKay kids began performing Jonathan Winters skits. It took a little while for the guests to catch on. These children were born in Haiti, decades after the retirement of the rubber-faced comedian who gave us the antics of a wise-beyond-its-years baby, a saucy, albeit elderly Maude Fricket, and other characters. How would they even know about Winters's characters? The answer was evident in Joyce coaching from the sidelines, her delighted smile encouraging them on.

Gabe had asked for permission to be excused right after dinner. He was on the last chapter of a book he wanted to finish. But when the peels of laughter from the dining room reached him, Gabe flew down the stairs to join in as everyone sang "America the Beautiful" and "The Star Spangled Banner." The finale was "Big Bad John," a fifties song about a courageous coal miner who held a broken timber from falling until the other miners escaped a cave-in. Gabe, Clare, Luke, and Martin were loud on the chorus. Anna Rose and Joan kept up with them until they broke out in giggles.

After the hugs and "good nights" at the back door, the guests crossed the yard to the bunkhouse under a sky streaked by the last of the day. Bats swooped above the meadow, filling up on mosquitoes. Kittens chased each other up and down the tree, in and out of the porch light as night settled. The Malheur River that splits at the top of the valley and joins downstream holds this family in its embrace.

NOTE

1. Charles Gordone quotation from Buck Ramsey's address to the National Endowment for the Arts.

The Public Trust

In memory of Dr. James and Nancy Jane Slosson

For weeks in the early 1990s, Vivendi, the world's largest water procurement company at that time, ran a full-page ad in the *Reno Gazette-Journal*. Under a picture of a sweet-faced little girl drinking bubbling water from a hose, the copy read, "Water Is Life."

Question is, "Whose water?" And, how do a people divvy up natural resources?

In many western states, under the guise of providing for the "public good," companies and politicians try to justify, in the name of the majority, efforts to mine water from rural places and pipe it hundreds of miles to cities. This is done even though the removal of the water from the area of origin results in environmental disaster, denying life and livelihood to those within the scope of pump and pipeline. With every stroke, these decisions remove food production from our country's table.

Bonnie Slosson takes a GI shower every day of her life. She's not in the army, never has been. But her father, geologist Dr. James Slosson, taught her early on that there is a bottom to every glass, every well, every aquifer, and if not refilled, replenished, or recharged, *it will run out of water,* and that's a fact.

The GI shower got its name from soldiers in combat who bathe in the amount of water they can scoop up in their helmets. The shower version goes like this: get in, wet down, turn the water off, soap up, shampoo, and turn the water on to rinse.

In 1958, the Slossons took a summer cabin in Modoc County with no indoor plumbing. That's where Bonnie learned something about packing water in a bucket. It caused her to give deep consideration to the well she drew from for her purposes. From then on she made a private ceremony of balancing her existence within conservation's principle: "You may use, but you may not squander."

More and more of the rural West is being sacrificed to the unreasonable doctrine of disregard. Rivers no longer run to the sea. Landowners, farmers, ranchers, and entire irrigation districts in Arizona, Colorado, New Mexico, Utah, Nevada, and California have made deals to stop producing food and sell their water rights to support urban sprawl. We, as a nation, choose to ignore truth: If we continue to neglect our responsibility to the environment and humankind, we will, in the words of Bonnie's father, "create the Sahara of the West." In return for our betrayal, we will be given thirty pieces of silver.

This cautionary tale pits a handful of ranchers and landowners against the might of greed. If no other lesson can be gleaned from the experience, there is this one: Without the ranchers on the land to care for and protect the environment, water-grab schemes such as this one, and the one that currently threatens White Pine County, Nevada, will succeed and the environment will suffer the consequences. Those people who protect their property rights and property value also protect water for the benefit of land and wildlife—the entire environment in a balanced system. The danger is the illusion of insignificant modification. The broken web of interdependence is revealed only in retrospect. The system must be protected against intentions that oppose nature's balance. Resistance to that lesson of truth is a mortal human flaw that needs to be put right, or we, as a species, will fail. For that reason, all land must have a champion if it is to remain intact, functioning, and prospering to the best of its natural ability. The honor and duty fall to those who love it most. That was the purpose of our home-based offensive. Champions would be coming to help. But we were to begin the journey alone.

This is the story of one of many environmental conflicts taking place across this country.

THE BATTLE to keep our water from being pumped by the state of Nevada and exported across state lines can be traced to a single point in time. In the spring of 1987, the *Reno Gazette-Journal* ran an article that described the project Washoe County, Nevada, had proposed for importing water to metropolitan Reno. In its entirety the article was no longer than a recipe for a two-egg cake. Yet, if implemented, it would be responsible for the death of many thousands of square miles of land.

A rancher read the article and alerted his niece Bettie Parman in Surprise Valley. She called three other women to her kitchen. We were Sara Gooch, a schoolteacher, Sophie Sheppard, a painter, and Bettie and myself, who were ranchers. In the cozy spot where we normally discussed valley history or got Bettie's advice on the benefits of Jonathan Hale peach trees, a battle would be launched by this small band of insurgents.

As Bettie read the article aloud we were locked on trying to understand the scope of the proposal. It was a good thing we could not know that trying to stop this water importation project would last twelve years. Foresight would have killed the deal.

Nevada's Silver State Water and Power Project (SSWPP) would change names as investors came and went like players on a slot machine. The proposal, already a year old, stood as evidence of the concept of water as a commodity that could be sold, bought, and transferred without regard for the area of origin's natural landscape, wildlife species, historic use, prehistoric use, or local need.

Back in October of 1986, unbeknownst to anyone outside of the Washoe County commissioners' boardroom and Peter Morros, then Nevada state engineer, the commissioners had already filed applications with Morros to "appropriate all the unappropriated water in Washoe County."

It was a lavishly simple phrase, but the gathering realization of its true meaning chilled us to the bone. Eight words would grant physical and legal control over *all* the water not already claimed in Washoe County. *All* the water would become the property of Washoe County from Reno to the Oregon border in every interstate aquifer and every shared basin flowing beneath the land's surface to the unplumbed depths.

The Washoe County commissioners validated their claim with the prediction that at the turn of the next century the Truckee Meadows, like Los Angeles at the turn of the last one, would be on the verge of a water deficit, with demand and supply nearing an extremely critical situation in a county with a projected population of a half million by 2030.

A small map accompanying the article was sprinkled with fifty-two well filings, four within the Surprise Valley Basin in California. The map gave no indication that the area to be pumped dry was classified as semiarid to arid. By filing the sswpp applications with the state engineer, Washoe County was saying that in order to support the demands of growth in the Truckee Meadows, it was acceptable to reduce northern Washoe County and the California counties on shared hydrologic basins to wasteland.

We could not shake the idea that pumping all the unappropriated water from a desert was a joke. Until the early 1980s, residents and businesses in metropolitan Reno still paid a flat fee for water service, regardless of how much they used. Until this time, in the driest state in the Union, people in one of the state's major cities still demanded unlimited cheap water, no constraints on growth, and no water conservation. More elaborate and taller and bigger hotel/casinos were being built, and historic ranches were paved over for sprawling housing tracts and shopping malls, with more in the planning stages.

I would like to say that the four of us were bold, but on this issue we were foot-draggers and scared. None of us wanted to get involved; our lives were already overloaded. But what we lacked in commitment we made up for in indignation and outrage. We fumed about the number of golf courses in Reno, the greening-up of each one requiring *one to four million gallons of fresh water every day*. Still, the evil of the project eluded us, and it would until we looked the proponents in the eye and saw their total disregard for the cost. Soon we would learn that the proposal was written around a very serious backstory of greed, lies, bribes, threats, and ultimately the unquenchable desire for power.

Bettie made more coffee as we formulated a strategy. In time we were to learn that with the right chemistry, four inert elements could be combined to make a bomb.

THE SHARP STICK that goaded us into immediate action was the last line of the article. Protests opposing the project were required to follow the formal process of filing within two weeks on an official form available from the Nevada Department of Water Resources office or by telephone request.

If we requested a stack of forms to be sent by mail, we wouldn't have them for three days. Subtracting another day to hand deliver the protest forms back to Reno cut our two weeks to ten days. A community meeting had to be set up to inform the landowners and connect them to water law attorneys who could help them fill out and file the protests. We couldn't forget to tell them about the upfront cost to the attorney and the filing fee of twenty-five dollars per protest.

There seemed to be a dozen first steps. Modoc County Planner Pam Townsend could provide us with a list of water law attorneys. We had to reserve the all-purpose room at the Cedarville Community Church and bake cookies, just as we did for all get-togethers. And get the word out. Our newspaper was a weekly—no help. So we resorted to our usual means of communication: we painted a sign and taped it to a barrel in the middle of Main Street in Cedarville, put posters in the post offices in Fort Bidwell, Lake City, Cedarville, and Eagleville, and got on the telephone.

IT WAS IMPORTANT to understand that the protests could be filed to protect three separate things. First: landowners could file to protect their water from being pumped and exported. Second: landowners could file to protect their grazing allotments in Nevada. Surprise Valley ranchers historically relied on Nevada's high desert—stretching east for nearly one hundred miles, north to the Oregon border, and south to the Black Rock Desert—to graze cattle and sheep. Third: any concerned citizen could file in protection of the environment, wildlife, and habitat that would come within the scope of Washoe County's water-importation plan. But we, as Californians sharing a hydrologic basin, had no legal basis for complaint simply because we were worried. Scientific data predicting the effects of groundwater mining were needed to support our protests.

That night at supper, I told John I was worried about our firing the first shot over the bow of the sswpp. He listened as I explained that the thrust of the project was not about advancing the community; it was about mining a resource without regard for consequence to ecology. We would be attempting to keep the bad guys out, and to do so, we would have to attend meetings with government agencies and powerful corporations. Mostly we would be losing time. No one, nothing, can give back time.

"Who will do it if you don't?" he asked.

THE HUSSAS have owned a field up against the mountains since 1913. South Deep Creek roars through our field in spring and slows to a trickle by June. Rocky, gravelly, alluvial soils are evidence of meandering creeks cutting the banks when limbs blocked the flow, the work of nature's scouring. Trash dams or those engineered by beavers slowed the water, allowing it to soak in to recharge the aquifer.

In California, adjudicated surface water rights, decreed by local courts like property rights, are tied to the land, as elemental as the soil. Most neighbors paid sharp attention to their water rights and, in the spirit of cooperation, developed and maintained irrigation projects, headgates, and diversions to ensure maximum benefit to all from the free water. But on nearly every stream of water up and down the valley, there was a bully or a *night irrigator* who took advantage by turning water his way while the other users were working elsewhere or home in bed. The California Department of Water Resources (cdwr) governs its code within the language of a plainly defined responsibility—to put water to beneficial use. In California it is against the law to waste water. But, as in the case of the sswpp, there was no one who would enforce the law in any meaningful way. Warnings are useless when there is no follow-up penalty.

The South Deep Creek system worked well until the late 1960s. P. B. Harris, a neighbor and co-user on South Deep Creek, had a plan to increase his hay production. He approached my father-in-law, Walter Hussa, with a request to bury an underground pipeline the length of our field to transport his water right directly to his land. The pipeline would eliminate his ditch loss and evaporation. In exchange for that easement, Harris would *give* the portion of his water that wouldn't fit in the pipe to Hussa Ranch via the free-flowing ditch. At the end of the irrigation season, Harris said he would turn the entire flow out of the pipe and back into the ditch for stock water and to recharge through the winter. Walter agreed to the proposal, and we live with the folly of that handshake.

Construction began immediately. It didn't take long to realize the mistake. As soon as the irrigation season began on May 1, Harris took his share down the pipe. By the end of June, the creek dwindled to the point that there was no surface water, no livestock water, no recharge. Shallow-rooted shrubs were the first to show the effects. The cottonwoods along the dry creek bed began dropping dead limbs, and the niche was filled by noxious weeds, thistles, and junipers. Only the most drought-resistant plants were able to exist on the scant moisture that fell in winter. The native rainbow trout was the first to be eliminated from the stream. Birds and squirrels disappeared, and the Brush Field became as quiet as a cemetery.

Even on a small scale the effects of exporting water from a parcel of land were clear, unemotional science. The environment of the Brush Field balanced on the dominant feature: the water system that supported the community of wildlife and plants that lived within its parameters. The seasonal reduction of available water compromised the habitat, leading me to the conclusion that if water is pumped out of the ground and transported elsewhere, the landscape will be damaged and guzzlers or wildlife stations cannot mitigate the harm. In a climate classified as semiarid, any amount of water removed will alter the environment, and the effects are irreversible. When an organism dies, restoration is decades away, perhaps centuries, and then some species may be lost forever.

STARTING that spring afternoon in 1987, the four of us were on our own. All negative thoughts of overreacting or being labeled busybodies were brushed aside. We had to trust our impulse to stop the sswpp. We would begin without professional knowledge or expertise, without lead support from any California agency mandated with the protection of the water resource. Later, the Modoc County Resource Conservation District would give us unlimited advice and help in the development of an independent water district in Surprise Valley, but neither Bettie, Sara, Sophie, nor I had the benefit of financial or legal aid. The work of twelve years was out of pocket for us.

Had it not been for the community effort of Surprise Valley, and of those communities in valleys to the north and south of us and the Washoe County residents who joined as allies, northern Washoe County, Nevada, and the adjacent borderlands of California would today mirror the irreparable destruction that befell Owens Valley, California, at the turn of the last century when its water was exported via aqueducts to grow Los Angeles.

STEWARDSHIP, a modern buzzword, is a centuries-old concept of symbiosis: take care of the earth and the earth will take care of you. Cooperation and respect are embodied in that concept, even love. Yet, around the world with every tick of the clock, things essential to our survival and to Earth's survival, are polluted, damaged, or destroyed.

The families on these pages are the quintessential stewards. Their livelihood depends on a holistic framework of balancing production within the needs of the environment. Overgrazing can be laid at the doorstep of the fly-by-night operators, people like the proponents of the sswpp, who suck the sustenance out and leave wreckage behind. Ranching families who make a home on the land cannot damage the land they rely on. Their effort is to improve the conditions by developing water tanks, springs, and troughs, and by using rest rotation to condition the plant community for seed production. These people are in a constant state of preparation for the worst so as to ensure themselves a future. Fields are set aside as insurance against drought or fire. If by some act of providence it turns out there is abundant feed, or rain, or the cattle prices take a swing up, they don't boast or take credit, for they know the right and the wrong of things swing from the same point.

These ranchers would also say that the people of urban communities must share in the responsibility for the care and condition of the rangelands of the West, just as they must share the blame when conditions, species, and the habitat they depend on fail. If city dwellers continue to demand that water be pumped from the rural valleys and piped curbside without regard for the cost to the environment, they must understand that the drying up and desolation of the arid West in great measure bears their personal signature.

Even with that knowledge, the human drive toward progress continues to sacrifice nonrenewable resources. Our decisions to burn, to kill, to plow, to pave, to dig, to cut, to take are eased by worldwide trends. ("If you've ever gone to China, you would understand why it's a waste of time to conserve and recycle," one man said.) In the seventies we took conservation seriously for a short time. ("Our family all came to the kitchen in the evening to read or study to conserve, and I learned newly developed energy-efficient cooking methods. Then we experienced the rolling brownouts of the nineties and realized we had been spitting into the wind with our good-citizen practices," a woman told me.) In Reno, one of the local radio DJs took it upon himself to read the *Water Waster Report*, which amounted to something like: "In the block of Plumb Lane and North Center a sprinkler's been running all night. Folks, there's a drought going on. Let's get that timer fixed." ("After a while our listeners told us to drop it. So we did," the DJ said.)

When an ordinance comes up for discussion, or when, as with the SSWPP, a project that requires scrutiny is proposed, invitations are sent out to the impacted groups, political systems, and individuals for comment. But we discovered that it is common practice that before the "call for comments" is announced, the decision to act has already been made. A comment period is just a part of the process. Words of dissent to such plans are heard, read, and ignored. Data or models are tweaked to support a desired response. Bureaucracies give ground to big companies with big plans. *Mitigation* of environmental concern has been honed to sound sensitive, inspired, and reasonable. The public has grown used to being ignored. They may grumble and write their representative, but that, too, will only get them lip service. The green light for a proposed expansion or major development is predicated on a promise of economic growth, jobs, houses, that is, money to be spread around. The taxpayers who are fooled into bankrolling these projects are left out of the decision-making process entirely. Ultimately, approvals for such projects are based on the payoff. No one rocks the boat. That's why when over 250 protests to the SSWPP were delivered to Peter Morros's desk short of the deadline, it caused quite a stir in the Truckee Meadows. According to an engineer in Morros's office, they usually got one or two protests, the most was six. Until then.

THE PACE OF LIFE has always been fairly calm in Surprise Valley. The economy is based on ranching: livestock and hay. That's it. Our good years and bad years, gains and losses, are often decided by the weather, our greatest friend and most wicked adversary. One summer midway through a seven-year drought we had only two rainstorms, one on our first cutting of alfalfa and one on our second cutting. For those who don't understand the standards of a hay buyer, rain would have been a benefit—a blessing—one week before or one week after we laid the hay down. But at that stage, the nutrients in the hay and the bright green color are leeched out by the rain, devaluing the crop by as much as a third. I believe that ranchers—people of the land who build lives around the fickle and unpredictable forces of nature—become reconciled to taking a beating and getting to their feet again. Those were the people who responded to our calls, the folks with the most to lose. We greeted them at the door of the church.

"Water is topic A in Reno," said Pam Townsend. She knew that what she was about to tell them was the worst kind of bad news. "Washoe County has a plan: the Silver State Water and Power Project. The estimated cost is $262 million. With typical cost over-overruns, the figure will double. They're committed."

But this wasn't a California-Nevada fight. Forty-three of the eighty-seven

The Public Trust | 147

ranchers in Surprise Valley own property in Nevada, and they don't think of the borderlands as separate states but rather as one region straddled by their lives. The scope of the project was overwhelming on such a scale. After Pam outlined the process and identified the protest to the project as their only means of protection, the ranchers felt the blow but did not waver. They scanned the map to locate their deeded land and looked on their property as if it were the face of a loved one lost to them. Orderly lines formed at the attorneys' table as each person received instructions in filling out the forms.

It was dark when we walked the last of them to their cars. Of the twelve years ahead of us, that is one of the days I remember clearly.

WE HAVE ALWAYS MARCHED to our chosen drum in this valley, and ranchers are called *independent*. The term can be an endearing observation, or hurled as an insult, but the dichotomy of our lives and livelihood requires we maintain some distance. Ranchers depend on a community of neighbors who are also their toughest competitors for the same beef and hay markets. We may gossip in the coffee shop, but we play our cards close to the vest because cattle buyers pit us against each other on the price and the shrink and the slide when we sell our yearlings. Equipment salesmen exploit the envy principle to boost sales. We compete with our nearest neighbors on the same ditch for our share of water, and the system designed to be judicious in the handbook rarely operates at that level in practical application. Enforcement is the key to honesty, and we could not count on the California Department of Water Resources (CDWR) for enforcement, not locally, and not against Nevada. The CDWR showed us to the door with a dose of platitudes. *Don't worry, it will probably never happen.*

Imagine the receptions when four women introduced the wide-sweeping plan of the SSWPP at the Rotary and Farm Bureau meetings, and to the cattlemen's associations and the volunteer fire departments. Vastly different from the Lake City Women's Club or the Fort Bidwell Civic Club. But they surprised us; they had done their homework, and soon we had a thick stack of letters to carry to our California representative as proof of support.

Imagine also how we felt years later when we learned that behind closed

doors in California, powers agreed to allow the sswpp to pump the interstate aquifers that Washoe County shared with California's Sierra, Lassen,
and Modoc counties if Nevada would divert a larger share of the Colorado
River into the Los Angeles water system.

Eventually, those powers would have to back away from that agreement.

RANCHERS also take a lot of heat for the relics of old haying equipment,
trucks up on blocks, tractors settled into the dirt, broken-down equipment.
It's true. Out behind the corrals John's first car is rolled on its back like a
stinkbug, but it shades the lambs in the heat of the day and harbors a bou-
quet of scarlet nettles into fall. We don't take offense and admit to being
savers and rat-holers. Our parents' memories of the Depression still linger
at the outer seams of our financial ledgers, and you can lose a bet if you
think these people won't have exactly the bolt you need, like a hex-head, fine
thread, ⅛ by inch and a half.

One summer afternoon, I was broke down in the desert with John's
cousin. I'd been touring her around when the truck abruptly stopped. Outta
gas? Nope. Broken belt? Nope. It didn't take a mechanic to identify the
cause of the breakdown. I leaned down to have a look-see, and there was the
drive shaft dragging on the ground. A bolt had dropped out of the universal
joint.

When we didn't show up at suppertime, John and his dad came looking.
About dark I heard Walter's CB radio buzz. I grabbed it off the hook and
said, "Walter, I'm in Shoestring Gulch just southwest of Dave's Cabin."

John's cousin, who was a part-time school bus driver, snatched the radio
from my hand and scolded, "That's not how you talk on a CB!" She depressed
the button, "Breaker, breaker, any takers? This is Honey Bee . . ."

There was a long silence before Walter said, "Linda?"

The cousin dropped the radio in my hand and went back to tend our
campfire.

I was glad to see headlights inching nearer through the dark. I explained
the problem. Walter was the on-call guy on our ranch when anything me-
chanical went amiss, and his truck was a shop-on-wheels. That's why he

had a CB. Somewhere in that crazy old blue Dodge he had every kind of part for the bailer, swather, all the tractors, irrigation bikes, bale wagon, pumps, wheel lines, you name it. We looked through his glove box, on the dash, under the seat, and then he began to unload his iron toolbox into the bed of the truck, oily thing after oily thing, and in the very bottom, stuck in a corner, there was the one and only bolt we needed: a hex-head, fine thread, ⅛ by inch and a half.

I've never apologized for the ungodly pile of treasures that track up our shop, shed, and beyond. Work and life are all rolled into one around here. The house and garden are not the things that occupy our weekends—the entire ranch is, and all the animals, just like every other day. I pray that I never have to organize it, yard sale it, and move, because we are stuck here like rust on iron. The patina becomes our own, the glow of our aged skin, the scars and grooves. That is why we are moved to protect the place where our life unfolds. Simply, it is us, we are it. We know every low point where water can be turned. We cuss and caress. And if the water of Surprise Valley ever runs in the gutters of Reno, it will be over our dead bodies.

MONTHS DRONED ON in the tedium of letter writing, phone calls, and meetings. We were horn flies buzzing around the head of a beast that was developers and politicians. They were fairly certain we would get bored or discouraged and go home.

Enter: The Knight on the White Horse and his Lady Nancy Jane.

John and I were invited to a barbeque to meet some folks from Sacramento. Bonnie Slosson was standing by the gate when we arrived. She shifted her scotch to shake my hand. "What's news in the Valley?" she asked. Her eyes never left mine as I gave her my scaled-down version of the SSWPP saga. She bid me to follow her into the house, went directly to the phone, and dialed a number.

"Hi, Daddy," she said. "I've got someone here you should talk to," and handed the phone to me.

A wizard or a hero must have a certain way of speaking. We've been trained by literature and adventure stories to expect a flash of flame or thunder clap on a historic moment. There should have been some drama to clue me to the genius of the man behind the quiet voice on the phone who said, "Hi. I'm Jim Slosson. What's news in the Valley?"

It was a phrase I would hear a million times over the years, one that would make me smile every time. On the other end of the phone was Dr. James Slosson, chief engineering geologist of a consulting firm; former state geologist under the administrations of both Governors Edmund G. Brown and Ronald Reagan; chief, California Division of Mines and Geology; member, Seismic Safety Commission; author of numerous articles and abstracts on the geology of Surprise Valley on the borderlands of Nevada and California. Nor did I know the conversation Jim and I began that summer evening would go on into the next century.

A week later Bettie, Sara, Sophie, and I waited on the boardwalk at the Modoc County Fair for Dr. James and Nancy Jane Slosson. We teased about wearing carnations in our lapels so the Slossons would know us. But there was no doubt who the handsome couple approaching us was. The man flapping a file the size of our county phone book against his pant leg. It turned out to be Jim's resume, as if he had to interview for the job. We had no money to pay him. He didn't want our money. From that day to the end of their lives, Jim and Nancy were a team who would see us through to the end no matter where that might take us.

The best advice we ever got was given to us by Dr. Slosson that day: protect the area of origin, demand good science, don't let them segment the project, because once a pipe is in place it won't be allowed to run dry. And don't forget, not everybody is honest.

BY 1989 the CDWR was still treating us like we were a foxtail in their sock. They made it painfully clear to us that they did not want to be drawn into another water battle with Nevada like the ongoing Colorado River disputes. Nancy Slosson gave us her address book and told us to write to everyone that might stir the CDWR into action, saying, "You never know who they'll meet at the next cocktail party." The cc at the bottom of our letters was an added attention-getter. Our persistent letters to the CDWR state director gained us the attendance of his field chief at our weekly meetings, albeit in an advisory capacity only. Better than nothing.

Dr. Slosson advised the four counties in the path of the SSWPP to petition the USGS for a four-year moratorium while it studied the proposal. The study would give us time to complete what Jim said was our most important means of defense: a legislative act to create a water management district, an entity with which agencies could communicate. The Surprise Valley Groundwater Management District (SVGMD) would be controlled by the users, residents, and landowners, and required the support of our state representatives through passage. The district established a board of directors to manage and negotiate on behalf of the residents. As a closed basin— all water that comes under the control of the district originates and ends within the basin—no opposition from outside could stop its formation.

The board had examples from other districts as templates to cut and paste paragraphs together to satisfy the specific demands of our situation. Start to finish, the development of the district required the board's attendance every Wednesday night for five years. It was a duty a few citizens performed for no pay, and no real credit, as it turned out.

AS TIME WORE on the project wore us down. The SSWPP was refined by the elimination of the power segment of the plan. Every step ahead was followed by a new twist in the newly named Silver State Project (SSP). The proponents and county commissioners continued to push the project forward by putting out hype and bogus data. When we presented our case, Jim reminded us not to get emotional, " . . . just stick to the facts."

Jim and I represented the valley before the Nevada Legislative Public Lands Committee in Carson City. We were last on a full agenda, and it was late in the afternoon of the hearing when they got to us. A proponent for the SSP spoke first, assuring those present that Director Morros would not allow the project to over-pump the water available. I was very nervous at the idea of speaking before the state senators and made a garbled appeal to the committee to deny the application for the ssp. They looked at their watches. One member left to catch a plane.

Jim sat before Dean Rhodes, chair of the committee, who said, "According to what we just heard, I guess we can say that there is no danger of the project exceeding the safe yield."

Yes," Jim replied in an offhand way, "you could say that. But you'd be wrong." That woke up the proceedings. The senators leaned forward to hear Jim explain the ssp. "The projected cost is grossly underestimated and the water available grossly overestimated, and if the project fails, the Nevada taxpayers will carry the burden of the accumulated debt up to that time."

In other words, the taxpayers wouldn't be happy about being forced to bankroll an ill-advised project, and when the next election rolled around, they might rethink their choices.

When we left, the Nevada Legislative Public Land Committee had some information they had not gotten from Director Morros.

JIM AND NANCY were the ultimate teammates. Their relationship was never in conflict, although they worked together at their geologic consulting firm every day of their lives. Nancy was a devoted and absolute supporter of Jim's honesty and integrity. She had witnessed the bribes and threats over the years from developers and construction companies in attempts to get him to sign off on their projects. Sometimes she was frightened, but she always backed his judgment. And when we were worried, she would say, "Jim will know what to do."

They worked for us for more than ten years for no remuneration, traveling to meetings and hearings, often driving straight through to attend to their paying clients' business back in LA. Both were lifelong residents of the Los Angeles basin. The water of Owens Valley ran from their faucets, and they knew a wrong when they saw it.

I SAT in the crowded Susanville auditorium with Jim and Nancy when the usgs was to present their findings on their four-year examination of the ssp's proposed water-importation project. The usgs shocked everyone in the room when the lead geologist upheld the ssp's proposal to extract and export in excess of seventeen thousand acre-feet of water. Jim had an explanation, but he chose to keep it to himself. We would never know how they reached that conclusion. The ssp was being given the green light by a federal agency. It was a long, quiet drive home that night.

EACH AND EVERY TIME WE LOST HEART, Jim and Nancy shined hope our way in the form of new information, a new lead, or a suggestion to look through our files for a supporter we'd forgotten. It was during the lows following the usgs decision that I fingered a *Peanuts* cartoon pinned above my desk. Charlie Brown faced his defeated baseball team, looking thoughtfully sad, and asked, "How can we keep losing when we're so sincere?"

ONCE THE DISTRICT FORMATION WAS COMPLETED, we needed irrefutable scientific evidence to stop the ssp. The ssp chameleon shed another skin to become the Truckee Meadows Project (TMP). The proponents of the TMP bought the Fish Springs Ranch in Honey Lake Valley, a failing alfalfa hay ranch. The plan was to let the hay land dry up and kick-start the TMP by pumping water directly to the Truckee Meadows.

In Jim's opinion, good science will provide the answer to every question. If evidence is collected without bias and tests are properly executed, you will possess truth, and if you are patient, nature will prove your theory.

He contacted his colleague Dr. Alan Mayo, Department of Geology, Brigham Young University, a specialist in the aging of water. Together they conducted isotope tests at various well sites in northern Washoe County. The tests were time-consuming and very expensive. Dr. Mayo dropped his fees, and the Resource Conservation District picked up the balance of the costs. The results of the isotope testing established that if the project was allowed to go forward, pumping would be mining fossil water, illegal according to the Nevada water law. The TMP was beginning to feel the pressure. It would get worse.

BACK IN 1991, Captain Culver, the attorney representing the U.S. Army at the Sierra Army Depot, had requested Jim's help. The ammunition depot at Hurlong was the site of contamination from hundreds, perhaps thousands, of World War II ammunition bunkers. Culver's concern was based on the proposed pumping at the nearby Fish Springs Ranch. If aggressive pumping occurred, it was reasonable to assume that a plume of contamination could be drawn into the zone of the well.

Culver joined with Lassen County in requesting a hearing with Michael Turnipseed, then director of the Nevada Department of Conservation and Natural Resources, to object to the TMP's application for permits to pipe water to Reno-Sparks. Water quality was the issue, and he wanted it on the record.

Turnipseed, acting as the administrative law judge at the hearing, disallowed the testimony of Drs. Slosson and Mayo based on a technicality. The tests they referred to were not yet completed by the federal and California EPAS. Further, Turnipseed ruled that the TMP could safely export thirteen thousand acre-feet from Fish Springs Ranch.

IN JANUARY OF 1992, a friend of Sophie's was out hiking in the Never Sweat Hills, a little southeast of Fish Springs Ranch, the TMP's home base, when he came on long areas of recent subsidence that ran under hummocks and out the other side. Jim told Sophie to get pictures and contact the *Reno Gazette-Journal*. This was the evidence needed to uphold his prediction of subsidence due to drawdown by the irrigation wells at the Fish Springs Ranch at a rate of only five thousand acre-feet per year, and it was strong evidence that pumping at thirteen thousand acre-feet would not be a sustainable yield from that basin.

The photographs and story ran in the *RG-J,* right in the TMP's home court.

THEN IN 1993, the *RG-J* broke another story that we had not dared dream of, calling into question the integrity of Nevada state officials. An engineer from the Nevada DWR's office blew the whistle on highly seated state officials who he said had pressured him to support the amount of water the director of Nevada Water Resources determined could safely be exported from Washoe County. After being upbraided when he would not pass on the state office's estimate that exceeded twice the safe yield, he called a reporter with his story of dirty backroom politics.

BY 1994, the TMP had sunk millions of dollars into the development stages of the project. The proponents and opponents were still at odds on the amount of water that could safely be pumped. The numbers varied: the TMP said twenty-seven thousand acre-feet, the USGS estimated it at more than seventeen thousand acre-feet, while our expert consultants said the number was closer to seventy-five hundred. The TMP needed a scapegoat to recover their losses. The U.S. Army seemed a reasonable choice, and a suit was filed blaming failure of the project on contamination of the aquifer by the Sierra Army Depot.

Captain Culver needed proof that information was made available to the owners of the Fish Springs Ranch regarding the possible contamination from aggressive pumping. He called Dr. James Slosson.

Despite constant haranguing by his secretary to throw old files into the dumpster, Jim saved everything. He, too, was a child of the Depression; he learned to save things. The evidence list from the 1991 hearing with Judge Turnipseed was safe in his storage unit. Jim took his flashlight and went prospecting through the box labeled TMP-1991. Drs. Slosson's and Mayo's testimony warning about water-quality problems owing to the proximity of Fish Springs Ranch to the Sierra Army Depot was on the court's evidence list. Slam, dunk.

A NUMBER OF FACTORS led to new water policies in Reno in the early 1980s. The drought, raised public awareness of environmental issues, and the impact of rising demand for a limited resource led Sierra Pacific, which at that time oversaw the main distribution of water in the Truckee Meadows, to require the installation of water meters on all Reno businesses in 1983, followed by voluntary conversion to meters in residences in 1985 and mandatory installation of meters in all residences constructed after 1988.

Nonetheless, some of the remaining flat-rate users each consume over 2 million gallons of water a year (the average metered residence uses 137,000 gallons per year). In 2007, the Board of Directors of the Truckee Meadows Water Authority, which was formed in 2001 to succeed Sierra Pacific and oversee water distribution in the Reno metropolitan area, voted to convert all remaining unmetered customers to meters by 2010. After 2010, all customers in the Reno area will pay the same rates for the water they use.

However, there is still some resistance to residential water metering in older sections of Reno built before runaway development began. Metering opponents reason that conserving water will encourage even more development, although in fact unused water remains stored in TMWA reservoirs in the nearby Sierra Nevada, to be made available during times of drought. Moreover, developers are now required to obtain water rights from other sources in order to support their projects, since the Truckee River's water is fully allocated. In a further effort to promote conservation, the TMWA has developed programs to educate the public about water use, as well as a program that allows people to report water waste.

All these efforts, however, have done little to discourage development, and currently in the planning stages are a number of ambitious projects that purport to have access to adequate water to supply the houses and businesses that will perhaps one day sprawl further into the desert. The developers of one such project promise that the new city they propose to create in the desert north of Reno would use no water from the Truckee River and no water imported from outside Washoe County. Since there is little year-round surface water in the county other than the Truckee River, this water would have to be pumped from aquifers that lie beneath the desert and sustain the plant and animal life that has evolved over millennia to survive the high desert's challenging environment—and that sustain the ranches and communities scattered over the county's rural terrain.

And this brings us back to the question that began this essay: is it right, from the perspective of environmental responsibility and from the perspective of social and economic justice, to desertify one region of this arid state in order to support urban development elsewhere? Is it right to destroy the habitat of countless life forms, the livelihood of hard-working ranch families, and the very existence of small rural communities so that city dwellers can enjoy green lawns and long showers? Water is the arid West's most precious resource. It is our responsibility to future generations to use it prudently, even frugally, rather than expend it to sustain a lavish lifestyle unsuited for the region.

ON FEBRUARY 5, 1998, Jim and Nancy called. Nevada State Engineer Mike Turnipseed had pulled the plug on the TMP. Jim explained that the TMP proponents had missed all the filing deadlines for renewals, and said they had no plans to proceed. I didn't know if the echo was Jim and Nancy's speaker phone or a voice in my head trying to get through. It was over—over—over . . .

LOOKING BACK, it's crazy how it all unfolded. Jim and Nancy were the encouragement, the experience, the knowledge, the wisdom in our twelve years war. Stirred by their involvement and faith, others came forward with additional information and support. The grunt work was done by the community of Surprise Valley and other people in neighboring valleys. It was the unified effort that was needed. If not for that, the pumps would be running around the clock, pouring the lifeblood of this land into reservoirs for country club fairways and swimming pools, car washes, and hotel showers—and sand mountains would march before the wind.

The thoughts that occupied my mind that evening traveled the path we had walked for twelve years. From the perspective at the end, it was an allegory. I asked myself, what was at work here? Each time evidence was needed, it appeared. Each time the walls were breeched, a soldier rose. Had our resolve swayed, would the outcome have changed? Dr. James Slosson lived his life upholding the principle of the public trust: that "certain lands and resources belong to the whole people and that the government, which serves as a guardian, has an inescapable duty to manage these properties well, including wildlife habitat, nature study, and simple beauty of scene."

I would add something. The "whole people" are an active part of the equation as guardians. That's what makes it work. We cannot sit back and leave the decisions to government; this small story proves government can make appalling errors. We, the "whole people," must make certain our existence does not hurt others.

We owe our very existence here in Surprise Valley to our friends and advisors. Together they taught us: written law provides no guarantee. It is our responsibility, if we call a place home, if we find safety and sustenance, friendship and community to defend this place at all costs. We will always be the final barrier the enemy must scale.

The phone was silent for a few moments before Dr. Slosson added, "But let me add a word of caution. Don't think it's over. It's never over."

EARLY IN 1999, the Bureau of Land Management completed plans to designate certain lands on their inventory as disposable, to be offered for sale. The list included the entire Smoke Creek Desert, leg two of the original importation project. When questioned, the BLM—protectors of the public lands—gave assurances that their planned sales were currently under reconsideration. Meanwhile numerous transactions were finalized. The ghost of the proposed pipeline for the SSWPP, all the ranches and small acreages necessary to see the project safely to conclusion in a direct route to Reno, were purchased by a man who came among us as an absentee rancher, just as the proponent of the water exportation project in Owens Valley had. The properties are his ace in the hole. He built a grand house, forty feet high, with a widow's walk atop a copper roof. Up until the building of that house, we were all ordinary ranching families in this valley, living in a rhythm of good and not-so-good years. In a stroke we all became paupers to his ostentatious display of wealth, his helicopter that disturbs the quiet, the mountain his men patrol to keep people out. Selling the water from his lands to Reno will make him as wealthy as a king. If not him, someone like him. And his neighbors will suffer when the pumping begins, first those just across the fence. But the pumping will go on until all water in this part of the world knows him as *master*. And then the desert beyond.

Surprise Valley is ahead of the curve. The legislative act created by landowners of the valley and signed into law in 1994 was put on a shelf until implementation became necessary. Responsibility, though not unanimous—for there were those who hoped to avoid regulation at all costs—was accepted by the majority because, if left to the federal government, developers, or investors, restrictions and costs would be greater than we could stand to witness.

The moment will come when the district is taken off the shelf and implemented, employing guidelines necessary for the benefit of industry, community, and environment. Discussion and compromise will be part of the process. What the district does here will not limit, control, or damage anyone outside of this valley. But, the district is our guarantee that no one outside of this valley will limit, control, or damage us.

As a society we must decide which is more important: the urban dwellers' right to a luxurious lifestyle without restrictions on use or cost of water; or rural land where food is grown and water serves communities of wildlife and plants and rural people? Farmers have always lost out to cities. Perhaps it's time to remember the testimony of Harvard anthropologist Timothy Weiskel to a U.S. Senate committee two decades ago: "There is no such thing as a post-agricultural society." To deny the necessity of self-sufficiency as a nation is to guarantee its collapse.

In our heart of hearts, we know the right thing to do. But it requires us to act and to encourage others to act—for decades, for centuries into our future. We stand at the edge of our survival. Ultimately, we stand at the edge of the survival of Earth.

How will each of us spend our life? Will it be spent protecting this place we call home?

NANCY AND JIM SLOSSON met and married at the University of Southern California. True to their lifetime partnership, they passed away in 2007 just one day apart. Our personal loss of their friendship, counsel, and sound judgment goes deeper to community, country, to a sane world, and challenges us to remember their stand for what is right, their example to protect things that greed has no interest in protecting.

The Harper Family

LITTLE HUMBOLDT RANCH

Joe and Sam Harper

In 1872 I. V. Button bought the valley that would become the headquarters of the Little Humboldt Ranch for fifty dollars and two saddle horses. He fenced the meadow for a horse pasture, built willow corrals and a pole-saddling shed, and in the manner of the pioneer, he used an ancient means of cutting blocks from an outcropping on a nearby hillside for a stone root cellar. With a star bit he drilled down into the sedimentary rock, and in the winter he poured water down the drill holes. When the water froze, slabs split off like slices of bread. He sawed the slabs into blocks a foot and a half square and hauled them by wagon to the building site near the Little Humboldt River.

Over the next century and a half, buckaroo crews camped on the meadow and carved their names into those stone blocks of the root cellar, and the building became a historic record of the men who worked in the country around the Little Humboldt. Jay Harney was one of those buckaroos. At the age of twenty-six he hired on to learn the ways of northern Nevada's tough horses and tougher men. He scratched out a picture of a horse straight up in the bridle on a blank white stone of the building. Dates on other blocks told him his horse would last for the next hundred years. A cornerstone bore a drawing made by a man whose name was known around the world. His horse was carved bucking wild, legs in every direction, precisely the way it feels when it happens. A signature was not necessary. The explosive style was that of artist, writer, and Nevada buckaroo Will James. Hardly a day went by that Jay didn't think about that carving. It connected them, man to man, each loving the harsh country and stories of the buckaroo life, stars and sun, storm and sky; both tough enough to get the job done on horses that bucked like the one drawn with the blade of experience. Years later, a thief chiseled the block out of the building, leaving a hole like a missing tooth. If Will James had written the story, there would have been a fast chase and gunplay and the stone returned to hold up its corner of history.

An owner after I. V. Button improved the living conditions on the ranch to impress a woman of fine upbringing born in the San Francisco Bay Area. The new owner brought her by carriage on the dusty road into Paradise Valley, thirty-five miles up a long canyon, staying at night with neighboring ranchers along the way. Her first view of the Little Humboldt Ranch would have been of broad meadows and a barn fully one hundred feet long and sixty feet wide. From that turn he would have paused to present her first view of the grand house on the far side of the meadow sheltered in a stand of cottonwoods.

He designed a house like those in the city where they met and courted. Wagonloads of milled wood were hauled in for high ceilings and rooms large enough to dance in. The windows stood nearly floor to ceiling, and in the front parlor he paired two, drawing in southern light and warmth and displaying a pastoral scene of his cattle grazing on the meadow beyond teal floating on drainage ponds of irrigation water. Coming on it at close of day, lantern light on glass would have been festive and welcoming to guests. He separated off the parlor by ten-foot pocket doors that slid from within the walls, giving local ladies who came calling privacy from the activity of the men in his office and from the help in the kitchen. There was a library, several bedrooms, and a wide porch on the east side protected from winter winds.

His bride lasted two weeks. She refused to live in a house nearly one hundred miles from Winnemucca, a town of miners, sheepmen, cattlemen, railroad men, and little else. He put her on the train and in his disillusion lost interest in the ranch. Over the next half-century the barn burned to the ground and the house fell into disrepair. When Jay Harney camped there in the 1960s, all the doors were standing open. It took the men three days to clean out trash left by deer hunters and packrats so they could sleep inside. Jay mucked out the root cellar and put his bedroll there.

The house had been standing for nearly a century and neglected for most of it when the Harpers came to work for their friend, Charley Amos. The quality of the original construction was the only thing that had saved it. The windows were broken out, and packrats had returned. Jerry and Nancy camped outside while they worked to make it livable. When the dining room and kitchen were scrubbed down and painted, they moved inside and kept working through an endless list of repairs while tending Charley Amos's cattle and their own growing herd. The house is finally what it was meant to be: a home for a family building their lives, and a woman who is satisfied living there.

JERRY HARPER was born and raised far from Nevada's Paradise Valley, on the Pacific side of the Cascades. Looking back, his may have been a poor family, but to a boy, going barefoot all summer was freedom, not poverty. The kids got a pair of shoes when they started to school, and his mom sewed up trousers from burlap sacking for her boys. Jerry hated the scratchy pants and began saving nickels from his lunch money for a pair of Levis, because he wanted to be a cowboy. By the time he had saved enough he was told the price had gone up, so he saved more.

"There was a pretty good handful of us boys who wanted to be cowboys," Jerry said. "People probably wouldn't appreciate this, but we'd prowl around the country and find some horses turned out in pastures and ride them whether we were supposed to or not. We were like a bunch of bad dingo pups, always chasing something and getting into trouble."

When the boys' curiosity in riding horses bareback with no bridles was satisfied, they looked for other things to do—all but Jerry. "When I graduated from high school I left that country over there and drifted to Jordan Valley and went to work for Don McKay," Jerry said. "Up till then, I only knew how to stay on a horse. Don taught me everything I know about cattle. He was first class, good hand, good cowman, good cowboy. He raised nine kids on a two-hundred-fifty-cow outfit, and he stuck with me until I got so I could be some help."

NANCY'S FATHER worked for the Harney County road department and was transferred around Oregon. When Nancy was ten, her family lived in Frenchglen, in the heart of Oregon's buckaroo country. Spring and fall she could count on waking up to cattle being driven past the house, past the store and hotel, to and from summer grazing on Steens Mountain. From her bedroom window she watched buckaroos pushing cattle along, never dreaming that would be her life someday.

Nancy was in high school when the family moved to Burns and then to Juntura. After graduation, she worked in the cafés and got a part-time job helping Joe and Joyce McKay on their ranch across the valley. One day, she and Joe were checking on cattle at Skull Springs. As they rode over a hill Joe saw stray horses grazing in his pasture. He thought they belonged to an unneighborly neighbor and said, "Somebody's running horses in my field!"

When they got closer he recognized the horses of his uncle, Don McKay, and his friend Jerry Harper. Nancy said, "We crept over the crest of the hill and we could see them camped at the old barn, and Joe said, 'Let's just bust in on 'em!' So we galloped down the hill, and that's how I met Jerry, with a bang!"

Later, Jerry rode over to Joe's camp and the young people visited the day away. He followed her into Juntura. "We visited there, and then he went to Wyoming for a while," Nancy said. "But he came back in December and went to work for Joe. That's when we started courting."

Time came when the ice broke up on the two forks of the Malheur River circling Juntura in a bracelet of silvery water. Air coming up the canyon sweetened in the evening, and you would swear locust trees were blooming in Grand View down on the Snake. Spring was itching under everything. Meadowlarks were singing on fence posts. Cows left the feed ground to chase grass. Horses were shedding their winter hair. Joe and Jerry were getting the cavvyada shod up and the cattle classed up ready to move out of the valley for the summer.

After supper one evening, Nancy walked out to the feedlot with Jerry to help him throw some hay to the cattle. "Leaning up against a round bale

Jerry Harper

with all of Joe's calves looking at us, Jerry asked me to marry him," Nancy said in sweet remembrance.

THE RESOURCES that Nancy and Jerry brought to the marriage were not material. They offered optimism, energy, youth, and dreams in abundance. Sometimes dreams are what it takes to make the difference. Because they had no land of their own, they needed to find someone to work for who would allow a hired man to run his cows with the ranch herd. Then, Jerry told Nancy, they could build their herd one cow at a time. In time each cow's calf would reduce their initial investment. In a year or two, if the market was strong, the cost of the cow would be made back and profit from her remaining calves would buy another cow, and another.

With Joyce and Joe McKay standing up for them, Nancy and Jerry married in September, when the haying was done.

"I had never camped out a day in my life," Nancy said, "but when we got home from our honeymoon we lived in a tent for two months up at cow camp. One night I woke up cold, so I was going to start a fire. Jerry told me to wait a minute. He dressed and went out and swept two feet of snow off the tent. If I had lit the stove, that two feet of snow would have made quite a flood. I learned a lot our first year."

Dave Woolfolk, who leased the Creston place up near McKay's Shumway Ranch, offered to sell some of his cows to Jerry if he and Nancy would go to work for him. It was the chance they needed to get a start in the cow business. The newlyweds were on their way. Then another rancher, Jack Joyce, took over Woolfolk's lease on the Creston place, and they worked for Jack until it became clear that Jack didn't have enough hay to winter his cattle and theirs. "So we quit, hoping to find a place with winter feed," Nancy said. "The next day Jerry was riding a colt and it stampeded through a fence. Jerry's leg was broken into pieces."

Their good luck streak came to a halt in one day's time. They were out of a job and Jerry was laid up in the hospital. "Jack said we could stay up on the ranch until Jerry was able to find another job," Nancy said, "and he drove all the way from Juntura up to Creston every day to feed our little pet deer that we raised. Jack was a good friend."

Friendships will always have an important place in the Harpers' lives. Dave Woolfolk's operation expanded into Paradise Valley, Nevada, when he formed a partnership with Charley Amos.

"Dave was thinking about leasing part of the Little Humboldt Ranch, so we came with him," Nancy said. "The night we told my parents we were going to move here my dad had a massive heart attack and died. He was only fifty-two. He wanted us to move here, but leaving my mom freshly widowed was very hard for us. We moved down a month later. Our friend Leonard helped us, and when he went back he told my mom, 'They don't live at the end of the world, but if you go up on the hill, I think you can see it from there.' If we had had kids then, I don't know if we would have made this move."

The Little Humboldt Ranch had been badly used over the years. Some people who lease ranches are only interested in how to utilize the feed, and make do with the rest. But the Harpers were not short of ambition, and they wanted a place to be proud of. They cleaned up, fixed fence, and rebuilt the corrals and outbuildings. The place started looking alive again, like someone cared. At the same time they were learning the country and tending the cattle, putting up hay in the summer and feeding it out in the winter. The assets of the operation have grown under their care.

Paradise Valley is encircled by the Santa Rosa Mountains, nine thousand feet in elevation. Winters can be severe, but the Little Humboldt has range that stays open. "They feed more in Juntura than we do here even though we're at 4,800-feet elevation," Nancy said. "The cattle go on our winter country. If we get a bad storm and the cows want hay, they let us know."

A few years later, when Charley Amos went into partnership with Nevada First Corporation, owner of the Little Humboldt, he offered the lease on the Little Humboldt to Jerry and Nancy. The corporation owns the ranches on either side of the Harpers, and Charley manages the properties. He has split off the range of each ranch so the cattle don't mix, and the Harpers can ride out their back gate straight north about thirty miles before coming to a fence. Jerry and Nancy's cattle are branded with the Heart Hanging Two and run on their own allotment, giving Jerry and Nancy control of the bulls they use as sires and of the calving cycle—conditions that are sacrificed when cattle run in common with other ranches.

"Running on separate allotments cuts down on the work when it comes time to brand," Nancy said, "and that makes it easier for all us. But when there is work to do, we help our neighbors and they help us, especially Charley."

THE YOUNG COUPLE put all of their energy into building their cow-herd before they had time to think about children. "Nancy went with me every morning, no matter what time, no matter how long, no matter what weather," Jerry said. "I couldn't have done it without her. She is quite a woman."

Celebrating their seventh anniversary was a milestone of sorts. "We said we scratched the seven-year itch," Nancy said, "so we started our family."

Joe was born in January of 1992. It was one of those dry years when the road is dust all the way to the pavement. The highway is straighter than it was in the 1800s, but the last thirty-seven miles are still gravel. When the Harpers first moved to the Little Humboldt, they could count on four, maybe five, flat tires before they got to town. Jerry said that they had to have a flatbed truck just to carry the spares.

"Sam was born two years later, in July. We were in the middle of haying," Nancy said, "and I was in the house when my water broke." Nancy put Joe, her little toddler, in the ranch truck and drove down the field where Jerry was changing a tire on a wagon. He said, "Okay. Well, I've got to finish jacking this hay wagon up so it doesn't fall on anybody." She decided against reminding him how far it was to the doctor. He knew.

She drove back to the house, put her and Joe's overnight bag in the truck next to his car seat, and waited, all the while thinking about flat tires and giving birth in a pickup. "Jerry came in and said he had to shower," Nancy said, grimacing. "I was hoping he would hurry. When we got down in the canyon, we came on some cattle that weren't supposed to be there, so we had to stop

4-H advice, Joe and Nancy Harper

and he kicked them up the other way. Then he had a race with an antelope, and I thought, 'I don't know if I'm going to have this baby in the hospital.' But we made it, and my doctor delivered our new baby boy, Sam."

Joe and Sam know the outside world of ranching just as well as any kids, and probably better than most. They grew up riding in front of Nancy on her horse. Both of them cut their teeth on the big button on Nancy's rawhide reins. When Sam was born, he took the front seat and Joe became the backseat driver, a position that suited him perfectly.

"Joe would be waving his arms, telling Nancy all the things they had to do," Jerry said. "He'd get so busy, sometimes he forgot to hold on and he'd take a header. Maybe that's why he developed such good balance. Nancy worked cattle for several years to Joe's running commentary and advice."

Before Joe turned six, the Harpers had to face the dilemma of all ranch families living miles from town: what to do about school? The distance and isolation they prize so highly presented them with obstacles to overcome. To comply with state regulations, parents must provide their children with education. The details of time and travel are their responsibility to work out.

Some parents board their children out with relatives or friends in town and sacrifice family time together. Some opt to move the mother and kids into town for the duration of the school years. That solution leaves the father to do the driving, to stay alone during the week, or some combination of the two. Even that arrangement is complicated by after-school sports and activities. Some parents drive out to meet the school bus, and the children spend hours every day traveling to and from school, putting them home at night for dinner and their own beds. But many parents refuse to inflict that strain on their young children. However the problems are mitigated, the situation will continue until the youngest child graduates from high school. One-room schools are disappearing from the rural stretches of the West, leaving home schooling as an option some parents choose.

Homeschooling is guided by the state board of education. The parent/ teacher receives a series of daily plans. Scheduled testing checks the progress of each student, ensuring adherence to the curriculum. Homeschooling is not the answer for every family, but Jerry and Nancy feel it is worth the effort to maintain a normal family life.

The parlor became Joe's schoolroom in first grade. As an observer, Sam drew and played at his own desk for two years before lessons came in the mail addressed to him. The parlor looks like a schoolroom, with books, maps, and supplies. A generator provides the power for the house and the computer that connects them to the outside world.

Now that Joe is fourteen and Sam is twelve, Nancy assigns term papers with a practical rationale. She steers them away from using encyclopedias for reference by taking them to the Humboldt County Courthouse to research deeds, water rights, or well logs. Original documents bearing seals, signatures, and legal language are powerful symbols of authority and history, representing continuity and inescapable change. Descriptions of township and range are geometry, cartography, and topography, depicting the lay of the land in all of its relationships to elevations, the flow of water, and soils that harbor water, turn it, or in its porosity let it pass through. For an expanded perspective, they visit the newspaper archives and benefit from information on historical incidents by reading about them in the context of the time. A richness of information expands their thinking, making them aware of social order and law and how their rights on their ranch are affected. By understanding the resources available, they learn to use the system, gain self-assurance, and make their own decisions.

Three years ago, Nancy developed a challenging school project that went beyond the often-assigned essay titled "What I Did Over Summer Vacation." When she lived in Frenchglen, the school printed a student newspaper for the community. Based on that idea, Nancy and her sons launched *Desert Trails* as a modest monthly or bi-monthly newspaper. It now has a circulation of 330 and is mailed to subscribers in New York, Pennsylvania, Los Angeles, and England. There is no subscription fee; Nancy did not want the added bookwork. But people appreciate the news in the boys' paper enough to send from five dollars to one hundred, and write to express their interest and opinions. Joe and Sam include journal entries of their lives on the Little Humboldt, their work, animals, losses of family and friends, pleasantly interspersed with photographs. Nancy wants to let them write freely and edits only the most glaring errors. Subscribers correspond with the boys regularly.

"Whenever they get a little off base," Nancy said, "Jerry asks, 'Where are your facts? Show me the facts.' That makes them check their reference information. As they become more self-assured, I'll be more critical."

For now she is the advisor, photographer, typesetter, and runs the mailroom. They all lick stamps.

The January 2006 *Desert Trails* headline was, "Chrysler Saga Continues." In a series of articles that ran over several months, Sam and Joe took turns describing the numerous breakdowns of their 2004 Dodge pickup, including faulty rocker arms, a broken valve, a melted piston, clogged fuel filters, and plumes of smoke coming from the exhaust pipe. It was the injectors, it wasn't the injectors, the key wouldn't work, it refused to start, it started and died.

Joe related a conversation Jerry had with Chrysler District Manager Desarae Warner. Ignoring Jerry's mention of the 107 days the Dodge spent in the shop in the past year, Ms. Warner said that "Chrysler was not going to cover the pickup repairs. . . . We did not have a warranty since we use our pickup on a ranch . . . they replaced the first engine as a 'goodwill repair' . . . the rural technicians were not qualified to work on Chrysler vehicles . . . and the fuel system was not covered in the warranty."

On December 6 Joe wrote: "Dad told Mr. Billingsley, owner of the Dodge dealership, what Desarae Warner said about his mechanics and our warranty. Mr. Billingsley was not happy about that. Dad also told them exactly what he was going to tell people about our experience with Chrysler and the troubles we have had with our Dodge pickup. They started thinking of different people they could call."

The graphic accompanying the story is of their Dodge truck mounted on an oversized lemon.

"It is very disgusting," Sam wrote. "We have to pay our payments even when the pickup isn't running. . . . Mom is not very happy over this whole deal and it is a good thing she isn't writing this story."

Joe closed with this statement: "We feel that we were treated unfairly as customers of a Chrysler product. We hope in the future we will be treated in a more honorable way."

As it turns out, that was not the end of the story. Teague Motors, owner of one of the shops where the truck got stuck in a catch-22 repair line, is a subscriber to *Desert Trails*. Directly after the issue was mailed out, a courtesy pickup was delivered to the Little Humboldt Ranch and a deal was made with the Harpers for a brand-new flatbed Dodge.

Recently Dave Stoddart of Crooked Creek Ranch stopped in at Teague Motors to price a Dodge crew cab pickup, and the saleswoman asked why he came to Teague. He said, "Well, Joe and Sam said you stand by your word." She smiled and said, "You wouldn't believe how often we hear that." The power of the press.

In writing about their days growing up on the Little Humboldt, Joe and Sam are building their personal positions on the concerns of the day. Politics influences their ability to perform the work they do. Life and death is a part of every day on a ranch, and some issues the boys write about might not be considered PC, but they are part of *real life on the ranch.*

Three winters ago, Jerry started teaching the boys to trap because the coyotes were coming into the meadows and killing calves. They found eight coyotes eating on a dead cow. Coyotes have killed the boys' cats right in the front yard.

"We couldn't have that," Jerry said. "Trapping also gave me the chance to teach them gun safety."

"The first year we only had seven traps," Sam said. "We used the money we got from the hides to buy some more traps. We're up to fifty now."

All ranchers report seeing another predator that worries them more than coyotes. That includes Sam. "We've seen a decrease in the deer population and an increase in the cougar population. If people saw coyotes kill their pet dog or cat or calf, I bet they would be for trapping. God said in the Bible, 'Man has dominion over the earth.' That's that."

The week before the fair the boys were washing and grooming their steers. The Harpers don't pamper their cattle. The boys choose their 4-H steers from the cattle that come in from the desert on their mothers wearing Sam and Joe's iron, the Double Square. The steers haven't seen a human since they were branded and turned out in the spring. After they choose their project steers, gentling them down begins. The process taking them from weaners to show steers for the fair takes over three and a half months. Every day is spent in their company: feeding, halter breaking and leading, washing, grooming, and gentling the animals that will go from the six-hundred-pound range to nearly twelve hundred pounds. The boys heap

Sam reclines on his Limousin

affection on the steers as they do their horses. They can't help it; it's how they see the world. Cynicism has no berth on the Little Humboldt.

Last year, Joe won Reserve Grand Champion Showmanship at the fair on Labor Day weekend, and his steer took a fourth in his weight class. This year, Joe's steer Gilhooley will become belligerent and try to drag Joe back to the barn, ruining his chance for a repeat in the Championship division. Joe will still be disappointed in Gilhooley at sale time and find it easier to lead him into the auction ring.

Sam reclines on top of his shining black steer Jackson, as if the sky looks bluer from up there. Or maybe he can see the future from there, because when the delicate issue of selling the steers comes up, he slips down. This year, Jackson will win Reserve Grand Champion, and he will take fourth in the heavyweight division. Although Sam will be thankful that Les Schwab will pay three dollars a pound for Jackson, when Jackson stands in the sale ring licking Sam's hand, he will cry but he won't be ashamed of his tears.

For now, the fair is a month off, and Joe is explaining the difference in their philosophies on their breeding programs. "This is my fourth year with the 4-H beef program," he said. "I should have gotten started a year earlier. It was simple mortal ignorance that I didn't, not knowing how to go about it. I'm on it now." He combed Gilhooley's black hair into waves, then ran his hand down the steer's long hip. "I like Angus-Limousin cross. Sam's the purebred Limousin guy. The Angus has a tendency to more marbling, their shoulders are bigger, and they have a deep body. The Limousin has the broader back and a bigger rib eye and a better rump. They're long, but they can support their weight because they're thick in the back. Working with Angus and Limousin, you kind of get a feel for the two, and I wonder if you couldn't combine the two to get a better animal."

THERE ARE distinct signs of maturity in Joe's and Sam's *Desert Trails* stories. They easily accept more responsibility than the majority of children their age, and to write about their work and play they have to think about *what they think*. Except for the occasional school report, most children are never asked to examine their motives and actions, to describe where they live, or how they contribute to the family. Value judgments are present in every excerpt.

> *Ice Skating, by Sam Harper*
> Joe and I got ice skates for Christmas and February 20th we finally got to try them out. It was 7 below zero and the pond froze up. We had a lot of fun. We are getting really good and can even do figure eights. I am better at turning and Joe is better at stopping. We have ice skated for two days. It is warming up again so we probably won't be skating much longer. I hope our skates still fit next year.

> *Anger Management Class, Taught by "Mucho High Loping Lady," by Joe Harper*
> Never get mad while you are on a young horse. It may lead to unpleasant cir-

cumstances. May 16th I was trying to get my filly across a creek and instead of taking it easy I started to kick her a little. Then my dog took off and I got mad; I kicked my horse and pulled on her at the same time. She dumped me into a bed of dried mud and kept bucking across the lot. Soon she stopped and my anger went out of me as I limped up to her and caught her again. She looked at me as if to say, 'I'm sorry, you were mad so I got mad too!' She didn't buck after that.

Tom's Vests, by Sam Harper
When Dad and Mom went to McDermitt . . . they stopped to see Honorine Pedroli. She gave Joe and me some vests that were Tom's and also some nice neck scarves. They are very special to us and I am almost afraid to use them. I still miss Tom a lot. Thank you, Honorine.

Another friend's passing is remembered by Joe Harper.

C. M. "Mort" Bishop
(January 24, 1925–July 11, 2007)

C. M. 'Mort' Bishop was a gentleman that I never met, but through correspondence I knew. He was friends with my grandfather and I came to 'meet' him through Grandpa.

Mr. Bishop's family owned Pendleton Woolen Mills. He also owned a Limousin cow/calf operation in Washington; we would correspond about cattle. He always encouraged and supported us with our newspaper. His birthday was the same month and day as mine but he was born about 60 years before I was. Mr. Bishop traveled quite a bit and sent back information on the countries he was visiting. It was amazing to me that he thought of us in his travels. One of the neatest things he sent was a map of the history of Scotland. He also sent us many stamps for our stamp and foreign money collection. Just a couple of weeks before his death he and his granddaughter, Whitney White, sent us a Pendleton Round Up poster. It was signed by all the rodeo court; Whitney is the queen. Mr. Bishop was Grand Marshall of the Pendleton Round Up several years ago. I was impressed that Mr. Bishop had been in the Pacific theater and fought on Guam. I can't help but to think of the limited acquaintance with this man and not wish that I could have met him. Perhaps I will some far away day.

This year Sam stacked most of the hay. He also did most of the raking. He writes about the work and a new equipment purchase for the ranch:

Dad bought a new rotary mower from Buddy at Ford New Holland. It really paid this year because we were able to put up more of the swamp field. The swather would always get stuck but this mower just plows right through it. John Welch brought the Kuhn representative out and he was even impressed with how well it cut that thick hay on wet ground!!! It was sure good for us because we needed every bit of hay we could get. We didn't put up much in the Button or House Fields (due to the drought).

Joe ran the rotary mower part of the time and baled part of the time. The wiring caught on fire in the old white tractor one day when he was baling. He had a fire extinguisher and got it put out.

On a snowy spring day Joe writes about working cattle:

May 11th: On a cloudy afternoon Dad, Sam and I went out to work some cattle off the first and second calf heifers. We gathered them up and put them into the fence corner. Then we worked off the cattle that didn't have calves. After being off Sassoon for a while it sure felt nice to ride her. Once while we were working she unfortunately slipped on the snowy ground and we fell like a rock. Scared her more than it scared me! After she stood up I mounted up again . . . Where we fell it looked like a snow angel!! Well that is an interesting way to make one. I think Sassoon made an awful big snow angel!!

Sam's heifer Buttercup calves:

March 23rd: We checked Buttercup. Mom shined the flashlight over at her and we saw that she was calving. There were two feet sticking out of her, then she pushed and the head came out, she pushed again and the shoulders came out. She pushed two more times and the calf came out. A little part of the sack was still on the calf's head so I pulled it off of its head so it wouldn't suffocate. It was a healthy bull calf. Mom and I were going back to the house when Dad came over the hill. Joe was putting Dad's horse up and finishing up with chores. Mom helped Joe finish chores while I ran down the driveway to meet Dad and tell him that Buttercup calved. Ross

(Zimmerman, the veterinarian) was only 2 days off when he pregged her last fall and gave me a due date."

Joe goes out deer hunting with Sam, his dad, and his grandfather, Jerry Harper Sr.:

October 23rd: Grandpa came and stayed with us . . . Grandpa, Dad, Sam and I went hunting about six miles west of the Bullhead. Grandpa and I walked one side of a canyon and found nothing. Only lots of lion sign.

October 27th: We hunted behind the North Fork. Grandpa and I walked stealthily along in the wet grass. After going over many rocks we jumped some deer but they left the country with grandpa and I trying to stop them in a gap. We must have been a sight dashing down the slick rocks to the gap. We couldn't stop them but we had fun doing it. As we rode back we talked and joked about it.

Nov. 1st: Dad and I went up a ridge behind the ranch. It was a beautiful place as the sun rose throwing crimson color on the pale rock. As we circled down we came across a buck chasing a doe. Dad said, "There he is, take him." So I drew a bead and took him in the right spot exactly! He was a 3 × 4 but one tip was broken off. We took him home to butcher him. The next day we cut the meat up. It sure is good venison and a pleasant hunting experience behind it.

THE HARPERS are concerned about the future of ranching. In the last ten years, the things they value about living in Paradise Valley are being picked away like golden leaves in the wind. Strangers are moving into the valley from big towns in Nevada and California. They are parents looking for a better place to raise their kids away from overcrowded schools, out of the line of fire of the dangers and drugs prevalent in the suburbs. But instead of absorbing the simple lifestyle of the ranchers, they bring their city attitudes with them. Road rudeness makes a shocking appearance in the country where people slow down for elderly drivers or tractors pulling equipment rather than zooming past. Impatience shows up in the local grocery store and post office. People don't make eye contact, don't stop to visit, perpetuating an air of *them and us*. To parents who work hard to teach their children good manners and to protect them from bad influences, the change feels like an invasion.

"They want what we have, but they'll never get it," Jerry said, "because they don't even know what it is. They're not ranch kids, they're city kids. They dress like city kids and listen to their rap music. They bring their drugs and gangs with them.

"Even if we lived where the boys could go to public school, I'd be tempted to homeschool," Jerry said. "Joe and Sam have a lot of opportunity to socialize with kids their age at 4-H and church and with our friends' kids. They get their schoolwork done and we have time to spend together. They're self-sufficient and secure in who they are when they come up against kids who are using dope. I told my boys, 'If you want to drink beer, I can't say don't do it because I did it when I was young. But if you do, I'd like to buy you the first one. Give me that honor.'"

Jerry and Nancy feel fortunate that the boys have lived in one place all their lives. Ranching operations are susceptible to change, especially lease properties owned by absentee owners. They have been assured that the Little Humboldt will be their home for as long as they want, but they are aware that situations change and contracts can be broken. Over the years they've been able to build a herd that they own free and clear. If they had to liquidate, the equipment could go, but the cows belong to the family. Decisions about production and expansion are made as if their place on the Little Humboldt will last forever, with the flexibility to move if it doesn't.

Lessons in the schoolroom occupy the morning. In the afternoon the boys join their dad in his work. It isn't recess, but they do have fun together. They might work with the young horses, sort cattle, scatter salt, fix fence, or learn mechanics or blacksmithing or welding in the shop. Working with combustible gasses and hot metal can be dangerous, and Jerry is emphatic about safety. Ranchers save time and money by welding their own broken equipment. Blacksmithing is the art of bending or joining iron heated to white hot in a forge, using coal and forced air. For the Harpers, blacksmithing is how they shape a horseshoe to fit a horse's hoof. Either process lends itself to ornamental uses and artwork. The boys have learned to make coat hooks and hat racks. Sam also makes and sells cinches for extra money.

All of their lessons are subjects of exploration in *Desert Trails*. The September 2006 issue focused on the dangers of lightning fires on the range, something they have experienced firsthand. This fire was different. It was dangerous, like all lightning strike fires on the range, but the handling of the fire brought into question the policies of the Bureau of Land Management.

On the evening of July 24, 2006, a lighting storm lashed across the valley just at bedtime and started a fire south of the Harpers' headquarters. The glow was visible from the front porch. Immediately, the Harpers jumped into the truck and drove down the road to where the smoke was lifting skyward. The fire already had a good start. Jerry called the BLM on his cell phone and got authorization to fight the fire. Permission was given because the BLM fire crews were busy with other fires. Then Jerry called their neighbor Jess at the Bull Head Ranch and asked him to walk the Cat up toward the fire. While they waited for Jess, they all got busy with shovels throwing dirt on flames, beating out fires in the brush. When Jess got there, Jerry got on the Cat and started cutting breaks on the perimeter of the fire. Sam and Joe worked along the road putting out hot spots and tried to keep safe, like their dad told them. They fought the fire all through the night and all the next day, trying to stay ahead of it, cutting it off when they could. Wind whipped the summer-dry brush into a blaze, making it difficult to control. The county road crew came along. They built some road crossings for the fire crew while Jerry rested. Before long he was back on the Cat, going around the line. Nancy kept cooking and bringing out food and water. She manned the telephone, keeping Charley Amos and the other neighbors apprised of their progress.

Two weeks later, Jerry was still wearing dark glasses to ease the damage done by the heat and smoke of the fire. He said, "I ran the Cat and they mopped up behind me. We just had it contained when we saw a plume of smoke over to the southeast over the Snow Storms. The BLM gave me permission to walk the Cat up to the second fire. I headed over that way and got up there at eight o'clock that evening. Charley came along and he took over the Cat to fix a crossing so the BLM could get the equipment and fire crews across. Just as he finished, Heidi Hopkins, the wild horse specialist from the Winnemucca BLM office came driving up. She said, 'It's getting dark and this is a wilderness study area and we're not going to do anything until morning. We've got to get a decision whether we can put equipment on that wilderness study area or not.'

"So they had their meeting at ten o'clock the next morning. Meanwhile the fire, named the Winters fire, was burning out of control across their wilderness study area. About 11:00 AM, when the wind came up, the BLM Elko Field manager got word from Heidi Hopkins to order us not to take any equipment on the wilderness study area. The fire burned like that for two days; it just ran to the north and the east and burned into so many fingers that it would have been impossible to stop it then. They didn't even try to flank it. They could have and saved a lot of that country."

"We watched good productive land burn," Sam said.

Jeff Fedrizzi, BLM fire management officer, Winnemucca office, said, "You have to think of the BLM chain of command as if it's the military. Helen Hankins is the person who gave Heidi Hopkins that order. That decision was made according to the guidelines of the resource management plan, about three levels above Helen Hankins. She was the messenger."

By Friday, July 28, the fire had been running for three days. The *Elko Daily Free Press* gave it the headline WINTERS FIRE GOES SUPER NOVA: "The Winters Fire, which is threatening the town of Midas, has grown from 19,000 acres to 106,224 acres in 24 hours . . . burning about 10 miles northeast of Midas . . . is 5% contained. A Type II Fire Management Team assumed control of the fire today. More than 200 firefighters are assigned to the blaze."

"The economy of that country is grass. It always will be," Jerry said. "The federal government will either put it through cattle to raise beef, or burn it. Raising beef to feed the people of this country is doing something honorable with it; burning it is a waste."

More than a waste, the resource is gone. Property is lost; land and livestock are adversely impacted. The cost, like flames and smoke, goes sky high. When summer and winter feed are destroyed, supplementary feed must be purchased and fed, or livestock must be moved off to rented pastures, if they can be found and leased. Freight costs are high owing to the hike in fuel costs. Expenses such as these are unexpected and staggering on the scale of the Winters fire. Ranchers are the ones who bear the financial burden. BLM employees and fire crews get paid regardless.

Commonly, "grazing allotments are given a two years' rest after a fire, or, until the objectives are met" to reduce pressure on the resource, further interrupting the rancher's ability to manage his operation in a normal fashion, and adding on expense, if auxiliary feed can be located.

The determination by the BLM of when "the objectives are met" has become subjective.

"In '94 when Babbitt forced through the range reform," Jerry said, "the biggest objection that anybody had when it came down to public comment was that it gave arbitrary and capricious powers to the officers in the individual agencies. So the standards and guidelines that we live by today can be twisted and turned to be used by some manager who has a personal agenda, and it opens up these decisions to whim, and an abuse of power."

Airplanes carrying retardant flew the Winters fire early on the second day. Jerry was operating the Cat again at the request of the BLM. At one point when he was out of sight of Nancy and the boys, they heard him call for air support on the radio. The BLM dispatcher told him air support was coming, but it never did. The tankers had been pulled out of Humboldt County to fight a fire near Elko. No one, neither the men on the ground nor Jerry on the Cat cutting breaks in the path of the Winter's fire, was notified.

If the BLM's chain of command is like that of the military, it is logical to assume that three levels above Helen Hankins it was known that air support would be limited to areas where fires threatened homes, as in Elko. And it's safe to assume that Helen Hankins and Heidi Hopkins knew there was no air support coming to save the wilderness study area when Jerry Harper was told that he was not to drop a blade on it, a sector of land under the protection of the U.S. Congress. The obvious question then is, *Wouldn't it have made sense to cut a fire trail across a wilderness study area to confine the fire, even at the expense of a few acres rather than allow the whole wilderness study area to be incinerated?*

"That's a fair question," said BLM Fire Management Officer Jeff Fedrizzi. But he had no answer.

A neighboring rancher who has fought many lightning strikes shares the Harpers' frustration with BLM's reluctance to allow chemical retardant to be dropped on a fire that reaches a wilderness study area. Water can be dropped, but water is less effective. "I told them, it's a matter of having a little red spot or a big black spot," he said. "But they don't listen."

"If the BLM hadn't shown up that night, it's likely we would have put that fire out before morning," Jerry Harper said. "Now, the BLM won't admit to that, but I was there. As it was, it took them ten days to get the fire out. In the meantime, it burned about 240,000 acres of range.

"It would be interesting to know how much wildlife was killed out there. That fire was moving fast enough to kill birds and small animals, and when it started running up hills into that steeper country, it likely killed deer, too. It will take years for the economy of these counties to recover. Money generated on these fires goes somewhere else, not into the local communities. You hear the stories of the BLM renting pieces of equipment from operators who get paid $2,500 to $3,000 a day for standby. A lot of money is wasted while they wait for an expert to arrive and tell the firefighters what to do."

Russ Mason, game bureau chief for the Nevada Department of Wildlife said, "These fires are an environmental disaster for the state of Nevada. That is not an overstatement."

Preston Wright, past president of the Nevada Cattleman's Association, heard the story of the Winter's fire. "I think that's a true story," Preston said. "I think that every fire we had in Nevada this year had a similar story. Most of them could have been put out at some point, and they continued to burn acreage and scared everybody. Unfortunately I think that's where we are right now, culturally I mean. Fire suppression is a huge industry. *They're not paid to put fires out; they're paid by time on fires, not by minimum acreages burned.*"

Preston is frustrated with how fire management works, but feels that in reality ranchers got the structure that grew up out of their own needs. "In the old days everybody used to quit haying and go out and fight fires," he said. Once we had a taxpayer-funded firefighting force that was good, we didn't ever have to stop haying. Well, now we've got to put the fires out because they're not going to because they make money being *on fires* rather than on call. But we hope that with these extreme fires we've had this year that we can keep a little momentum for moving some of that money into more controlled burns that are a little easier to manage."

Through the months of July and August wildfires raged across Humboldt and Elko counties, carried by dead sagebrush not cleared out by controlled burns or small fires. After the Charleston fire they found twenty-three buck deer in one pile, four hundred head of cows and calves driven by fire into a fence corner and burned to death. Ranch houses were lost along with barns and corrals, and hundreds of thousands of acres of grazing land were destroyed in the "super nova."

"I'm not sure they had a good understanding of how bad these fires would be in the heat of the day with the wind blowing," Preston said. "Certainly, I didn't. The way fires are managed they're mandated for firefighter safety. That's only going to be compounded because they've got a person in Idaho who's up on criminal charges and could go to jail because he was a team leader and he let a couple of people get burned up. The family members or the state or the county or somebody decided to prosecute this person, and the federal government has not stood by him. As a consequence, he may have to spend some time in jail or may end up on a manslaughter charge, or civil liability. Because of that, these people that run these fires are even more cautious about risking any firefighters. So it's all kind of a big mess."

Many fire managers have said that if the Idaho team leader is convicted, they are going to quit. Where does that leave us? Will we be a country without fire protection because we cannot distinguish between a case of egregious neglect and a situation that a trained professional didn't count on? Already there is a suspicion that lawyers and lawsuits are determining policy, and that firefighters are kept from working at night because workman's compensation insurance reports that more common injuries—such as twisted ankles and sprained knees—occur in the dark.

"We've come full circle," Preston said. "We need to be prepared to put out our own fires, and to do that nowadays, you need to have some training. My concern is that they keep that training accessible to us and not raise the qualifications to the point that we cannot put the fires out ourselves."

THE RESPONSIBILITY for the loss of millions of acres of feed, the death of untold numbers of wildlife and domestic animals, the loss in millions of dollars of private and public property, in addition to the cost of fighting the fires that raged throughout the summer of 2006, belongs to the BLM, and the taxpayer foots the bill.

Joe and Sam saw their father's fatigue after twenty-four hours of pushing brush out of the teeth of the fire. They fought at his side. And just when they saw him getting it to a point near control, they heard the BLM employee give an order to let it go.

"And," Jerry said, "those BLM fire suppression guys had the nerve to say to my boys, 'Say, you're not making any money out here in this desert. When you turn eighteen, you come see me and you'll make *big* money.'

"I just tell them, 'You can do that, but whatever you choose, I hope you're honorable about what you do.'

"I saw nothing honorable about the way that fire was handled."

Planning for Succession

HANDING IT OVER

The sentiment of a generation of Americans for land is easily understood. In these times of change and world unrest, a lifetime commitment to anything is to be respected. Devotion to land and to the production
of food has ensured the health of our people and the strength of our country. The transfer of that land to the next generation is as important as the
original effort of building the business. Planning, and the commitment to
seeing the process to the end, are essential if family-owned ranches are to
be maintained as viable operations beyond the current generation.

The information contained herein may serve as a guide to those setting
out to protect their land and their family's interest. Laws controlling the
elements of succession will vary according to each state. It is important that
those laws are understood and adhered to. Surprises are never appropriate
in business or law.

Some of the families in this book have struggled with the loss of their
home ranches; others are determined not to. It is to them, and succeeding
generations, that this chapter is dedicated.

THE STODDARTS, having moved back to Crooked Creek Ranch, are currently working with the family corporation to ensure that they will have a
voice in the management of the home ranch, and to solve the transition of
property to the younger generation amicably.

The Tyson family resolved their issues of legacy in a unique way, but
even as carefully as the arrangement was designed, there are changing laws
they must be cognizant of.

The Hammond family lost their generations-old ranch because there was no structured plan to save it from a forced sale. Dorothy and Carl are taking an active role in determining their future.

The McKays recently discovered that there are family members who don't fully support the adoption of their children and intend to block the transfer of the family ranch to them. Years of work for expansion may be sacrificed to unanticipated family differences.

The Harper family knew going in that they were on a lease program at the Little Humboldt. They have built a rental property into a family ranch that is their home. It would not be to their liking, but if the lease were no longer available, their assets are all on four hooves and can be moved on a moment's notice.

The Walkers' title to the land is secure. Their people have been there for 15,000 years; they hope to be there for 15,000 more.

IT MAY seem a generalization, but surveys prove out that rural families are ill prepared for succession. Parents who watched their parents "drop in the harness" expect the same may happen to them, and when their turn comes, their heirs will likely go on working just as they did. If the transition of land and assets is left to chance, and if there is no change in the inheritance laws, their kids will be lucky to end up with the pink slip on the feed truck, when it's all said and done.

The Trigg Ranch
"THE LAST FAMILY RANCH LEFT STANDING"

"'Gaaaawwd-daaaammn, let 'em fight over it when I'm gone.' That was my Uncle Steve's estate planning," Linda Decker said of the last operator of the historic Trigg Ranch.

"Someone counted the number of Dad's *Gaaaawwd-daaaammns* in every sentence," said Steve Trigg's daughter Sally, "and it was more than four and five and tended to slow down a conversation."

The Trigg Ranch, situated in northeastern New Mexico, has been under the control of an eclectic parade of land barons: iguanodon dinosaurs,

Jicarilla Apaches, Comanches, and Spanish explorers. In 1824, it was established as a land grant ranch by the king of Spain. Fifty years later, it was a route for Charles Goodnight when he trailed cattle to Kansas. It was bought by a developer in the 1880s. Graves and rock ruins of homestead claims abandoned during the Great Depression were absorbed into the 750,000 acres of the Bell Ranch in the 1890s and bought by Tuck Trigg and his children in 1917. History.

Today, three generations later, the Trigg Ranch is owned and operated by Trigg descendants, but only because it was their determined dream.

Sally Trigg was in the title business for thirty years, and during those years she saw the sales agreements of big ranches come across her desk.

"It just tears at your heart," Sally said, "because I could see how these ranches were put together: 160 acres there, 1,500 here, and you know those old ranchers put these 50,000- and 80,000-acre ranches together by just working so damned hard and not spending any money. And once they died, it didn't take very long for it to fall apart."

An attempt at estate planning took place in the mid-1970s, with accountants and lawyers and the principal partners, but, because of a lack of support by their children, it was never finalized.

The seven children of Steve and his two sisters, Adaline and Louise, met in 1995 at a family funeral.

One of the cousins, Linda Decker, said, "Well, I guess it's too late to keep the ranch together."

"Oh, I don't think so," Sally said.

Steve said openly what they'd all been thinking privately, "I don't want a piece of the ranch. What I want is for it to keep on being a ranch and I want to come out here."

Thus began the intricate process of keeping Trigg Ranch together. Sally and her siblings decided what they wanted to happen, and, because Sally has a law degree, she took on the job of gathering information and hiring an outside lawyer to handle the paperwork.

"I interviewed a lot of lawyers, big firms in New Mexico and Texas, but I was getting the same answer, 'It can't be done.' People have to remember that those lawyers are supposed to be working for you. If they can't find a way to make your wishes a reality, get another one."

They finally found a lawyer who was intrigued by their vision to give up any right to financial gain in order to ensure that Trigg Ranch would endure for all of time. Linda Decker puts the terms that were signed in 2001 into perspective for us:

"The heirs of the Trigg Ranch would form a trust into which all ownership interest would be surrendered to the trust. The trust would own all the shares of Trigg Cattle Company and a family limited partnership; Trigg Cattle Company as general partner would continue to operate the cattle business. All profits would stay in the trust to benefit the ranch; no Trigg heir would have any right to receive any income, except as an employee. The ranch could only be sold if 85 percent of the heirs agreed. In return, every Trigg descendant, who becomes a beneficiary of the trust at birth, shares the right of access to the ranch."

The trust document, renamed the Steve and Bess Trigg Trust, in honor of their grandparents, became even more complex. In order to avoid death duties upon the passing of each heir, which would quickly crush the ranch, a number of separate "Crummey trusts" had to be established to separate out each heir's ownership.

Sally kept track of all the trusts and all the gifting, with documents of acceptance to be signed by each of the twenty-one beneficiaries.

Both Adaline and Louise passed on during the process, but Steve gifted his own ownership into the trust. At the time of his death in 2002, the trust was complete, and his estate owed no "death tax." By the end of 2004, all beneficiaries had signed over their ownership to the trust and a new kind of history was made. After nine years, a sizable sum of money (most of which was provided by the trust), and the unfailing commitment of family members who had all gone their separate ways, the dream of a Trigg Ranch forever was assured.

When Steve Trigg passed away in 2002 at the age of eighty-five, he knew Trigg Ranch would survive. Linda Decker recorded the day:

"A memorial was held under the cottonwoods in the Creek Pasture. A procession led by Steve's beloved D6 Caterpillar carrying his ashes was followed by a bagpiper—his only request—and then by granddaughter Hilary driving the skid loader with Jack Daniels and ice in its bucket. There was a final toast as three Cessnas (his two sons are pilots) took off to scatter Steve's ashes on Alamosa. Their "missing man" formation as they came over the point of Alamosa made his absence all too vivid. Suddenly the third generation was in charge."

There are many fascinating details of the trust and its disposition over the ensuing years as an active cattle ranch, made possible by grazing innovations and generations of accumulated knowledge and hard work. There are details of keeping everyone involved by participation in boards of directors and subcommittees. The annual Work Week and Kids Play Week keep them physically close. Their motto is: "Grumbling gets little sympathy."

The Trigg family trust document opens with a poem by a lifelong friend, the late Buck Ramsey. His poem, "Anthem," articulates the intention and passion of their commitment. The family provides the sound structure of an ideal that ties them eternally to the care of the land. Art gives it meaning.

Anthem
And in the morning I was riding
Out through the breaks of that long plain,
And leather creaking in the quieting
Would sound with trot and trot again.
I lived in time with horse hoof falling;
I listened well and heard the calling
The earth, my mother, bade to me,
Though I would still ride wild and free.
And as I flew out on the morning,
Before the bird, before the dawn,
I was the poem, I was the song.
My heart would beat the world a warning—
Those horsemen now rode all with me,
And we were good, and we were free.

. . .

We were not told, but ours the knowing
We were the native strangers there
Among the things the land was growing—
To know this gave us more the care
To let the grass keep at its growing
And let the streams keep at their flowing.
We knew the land would not be ours,
That no one has the awful pow'rs
To claim the vast and common nesting,
To own the life that gave him birth,
Much less to rape his mother earth
And ask her for a mother's blessing
And ever live in peace with her,
And, dying, come to rest with her.

Oh, we would ride and we would listen
And hear the message on the wind.
The grass in morning dew would glisten
Until the sun would dry and blend
The grass to ground and air to skying.
We'd know by bird or insect flying
Or by their mood or by their song
If time and moon were right or wrong
For fitting works and rounds to weather.
The critter coats and leaves of trees
Might flash some signal with a breeze—
Or wind and sun on flow'r or feather.
We knew our way from dawn to dawn,
And far beyond, and far beyond.

It was the old ones with me riding
Out through the fog fall of the dawn,
And they would press me to deciding
If we were right or we were wrong.
For time came we were punching cattle
For men who knew not spur or saddle,

Who came with locusts in their purse
To scatter loose upon the earth.
The savage had not found this prairie
Till some who hired us came this way
To make the grasses pay and pay
For some raw greed no wise or wary
Regard for grass could satisfy.
The old ones wept, and so did I.

Do you remember? We'd come jogging
To town with jingle in our jeans,
And in the wild night we'd be bogging
Up to our hats in last month's dreams.
It seemed the night could barely hold us
With all those spirits to embold' us
While, horses waiting on three legs,
We'd drain the night down to the dregs.
And just before beyond redemption
We'd gather back to what we were.
We'd leave the money left us there
And head our horses for the wagon.
But in the ruckus, in the whirl,
We were the wolves of all the world.

The grass was growing scarce for grazing,
Would soon turn sod or soon turn bare.
The money men set to replacing
The good and true in spirit there.
We could not say, there was no knowing,
How ill the future winds were blowing.
Some cowboys even shunned the ways
Of cowboys in the trail herd days
(But where's the gift not turned for plunder?),
Forgot that we are what we do
And not the stuff we lay claim to.
I dream the spell that we were under;

I throw in with a cowboy band
And go out horseback through the land.

So mornings now I'll go out riding
Through pastures of my solemn plain,
And leather creaking in the quieting
Will sound with trot and trot again.
I'll live in time with horse hoof falling;
I'll listen well and hear the calling
The earth, my mother, bids to me,
Though I will still ride wild and free.
And as I ride out on the morning
Before the bird, before the dawn,
I'll be this poem, I'll be this song.
My heart will beat the world a warning—
Those horsemen will ride all with me,
And we'll be good, and we'll be free.

from "And as I Rode Out on the Morning"

The most important business decision we face is this one. It may be our final opportunity to assert our personal, spiritual, and political beliefs: Our essential statement on the value of untrammeled nature, on the importance of agriculture to our society, on the preservation of cultural individuality, on water conservation, whatever core beliefs our lives have grown around.

"Anthem" suggests that this is our singular opportunity to protect Mother Earth from the greed of all comers. Trigg Ranch teaches us that only we can take the first step toward securing the future of our children and our investment. These are facts we need to seriously consider:

1. The largest transfer of wealth in world history is currently under way. In excess of $26 trillion is in the process of changing hands. "And to further complicate this massive shift, the baby boomers inheriting this property are looking toward retirement."

2. "Nationally, the number of family farmers sixty-five or older has risen sharply since 1989. Statistics also show that as small farmers and ranch-

ers near retirement, they're not transferring their property to younger operators."

3. Our agricultural land base is in peril. If specific plans to transfer those assets to succeeding generations are not implemented, not only will the families and their histories on the land be lost, but the ground as well, as it is put to uses other than agriculture.

4. It is reported that 82 percent of farmers have no exit strategy, nor do they have plans to develop one. Astonishingly, 88 percent "planned to rely on the government or the grace of God to ensure the transfer of assets and the continuation of the family farming business."[1]

The royal rule of continuity, "The King is dead; long live the King," is meant as a guarantee that the kingdom will continue to function regardless of who occupies the throne. The land is the only thing that will surely survive. But we are realizing another truth: *The legacy of the land may not survive, if we are not prepared.*

The process of successfully passing the ranch on to the next generation can be daunting: complicated, time consuming, and expensive. The more assets there are, the more it costs to disburse them. *Any effort will be better than none.*

The *good news* is that there are many professionals with agricultural knowledge and experience who can explain the options and guide our decisions. In all probability, there is at least one suitable option for each situation, from the small family operation to the multifaceted one.

A stumbling block often lies in our children's reluctance to face our mortality or to make us face it, or for them to appear to be "taking over." All parents want to be fair in the disbursement of assets. But part and parcel with the development of a business is a strategy ensuring its continuation beyond us: to be responsibly prepared for the future, like parents who set up a college fund the day their child is born. Otherwise, those in line to inherit will be unable to protect the assets from being lost to taxes and/or attorneys. *Experts warn us: Start early. Start now.*

The following examples of failures and successes provide perspective and/or options:

1. For one family, the structure of a complex agreement came apart over which sibling would inherit a certain family ring. The ring's only real value was sentiment, but it ended up costing them all dearly. From this family we learn that *personal items should be dealt with separately from the business arrangement.*

2. One family corporation wrote a clause into their articles restricting the sale of shares. If any stockholder proposed selling their shares outside the family, their stock was automatically forfeited. For the founders of that corporation, the ranch was to continue as a working landscape.

3. Another family corporation allowed no woman to hold shares because of a difficult aunt several generations back who made life miserable for the men of her family. All women of the ensuing generations have been discouraged from taking an active interest in the operation.

4. In another case, the current working generation has agreed that when the children of the next generation come of age, all shares of the senior generation will be forfeited over to them, with the senior members of the family staying in place as advisors and teachers and receiving compensation for their work. But control, within guidelines written into the language of the original mission, is transferred forward when the junior members step into their shoes. Fully indoctrinated into the philosophy of the operation, care of the land is absolute. Once again, it is continuity the family strives for, and the children are raised as future kings might be.

5. One owner who succeeded in keeping both operation and family together said it can't be done in one meeting. It takes time to build the structure, to work through issues that arise, and to meet the challenge of developing a team with one goal. Those who have moved away come back for an annual retreat to reacquaint themselves with the operation, and renew their respect for the effort it takes to keep it running smoothly. The new generation of children spend as much of each summer as they can learning the work and developing a sense of participation in something important and lasting, strengthening their sense of loyalty to the land and to each other. Sibling differences and conflicts are avoided through communication and by respecting each other's commitment. All the family members are deter-

mined to stay on track, with an eye to the intent of the parents, *even if it becomes necessary to hire a professional facilitator to give unbiased opinions or negotiate differences.*

If the value of the land is high, the parents may be able to hire highly qualified consultants and facilitators for advice. In that case, they hold a golden carrot out to their children and grandchildren, making it in their best interest to attend the retreats, continue their participation, and strengthen their loyalty to the values the ranch was built upon.

The complexities of conveyance require a concentrated effort. But it will turn out worse—in logarithms—if attended to after death.

A recent law exempts a husband and wife in the amount of $2 million apiece from their taxable estate.

Something to remember: *In a case of death without planning, if the husband dies (for example), the wife inherits his $2 million, making her taxable estate valued at $4 million. She will be taxed on his $2 million. Planning can avoid that.*

All important projects, from spring cleaning to building a new set of corrals, should be tackled with an overview and a segmented work plan. You and your spouse would do well to focus on each segment and continue working forward.

The Plan
STEP ONE

1. Discuss and decide what you want for yourselves when you retire: freedom to travel; money enough to see you through your dotage; to live —— (where?).

2. Decide what you want for your land: for the ranch operation to continue; to be set aside for wildlife habitat; to be taken over by family; to be sold at the children's discretion.

3. Independent of any other family occasion: Call the children together and begin talking about your plans to enter into the process of disposing

of the family business. It may be your dream that the kids will all gather around you, loving all the things you love about the ranch, and that they will want that, too, for their children. That may be their answer exactly.

But they may have their life invested elsewhere and, without wanting to disappoint you, ask you to sell the ranch and give them their inheritance in cash. Be prepared for that answer.

If there are a number of children, they may be split—some who have moved away and made their lives around another family or career; some who have spent their life working beside their parents—and the impetus to continue ranching may be very different. In that case, the sibling(s) who live at a distance from the everyday operation might regard the one(s) who stayed as self-serving. To those who stayed, the desire of the other(s) to sell out and collect the inheritance might be construed as disloyalty to the parents' working life. This is where patience and openness are essential to compromise. There are ways to make everyone happy.

One of the siblings or a spouse may be qualified to help you with a plan. Even so, *it is wise to seek advice outside the family to ensure fairness and family harmony.*

4. Everyone needs to be honest. The commitment the children have to returning may have a direct relationship to the assets of the ranch and the return on the crops produced. Raising cattle in Monterey County, California, will provide a different income base than sagebrush and salt grass country in the Great Basin. It is an unusual situation when a ranch can support a family in the kind of lifestyle they would have to give up to come home. More often, there is just not enough to go around.

5. For most people with two, three, or four kids, it may be impossible for a family ranch to offer a living plus living quarters, impossible to divvy up the cows and cropland to suit their needs, and in many counties with strict zoning laws, it might be out of the question entirely.

Each ranch/farm will have its own configuration with specific benefits to assign or problems to work out. Legal advice is imperative to ensure a democratic result.

Make an appointment with an attorney who specializes in estate planning. You may be able to get a referral from your accountant, your state cattlemen's association, the local farm bureau representative, or your banker.

1. *Estate Planning* and *Succession Planning* differ:

a. *Estate planning* is developed around reducing estate tax liability. It is a generic term that just means sitting down and discussing the situation, who's involved, who owns it, how old are they, what's their life expectancy, who are the beneficiaries—that sort of thing.

b. *Succession planning* is in essence "passing it on" so that the business will continue after the retirement or death of the owner(s).

2. The *Will*: Guidelines for writing a simple will are available at the library or online. *However, guidelines offer no advice or explanation for complex situations, which are bound to arise.* An attorney can set up wills and help you understand the legal issues of land splits, sales, and/or transfer of ownership.

3. The *Living Trust*: A fiduciary (a person to whom property or power is entrusted for the benefit of another) relationship is one in which one person (the trustee) holds the title to property (the trust estate or trust property) for the benefit of another (the beneficiary).

4. The *Living Trust* and the *Will*: The execution of the combination of these legal documents helps your property avoid probate, which is *an expensive nuisance on the death of the first spouse.* On the death of the second, *it is time consuming and expensive.*

If you and your spouse have a living trust, you probably own property as joint tenants. That is a benefit. In the event that one spouse dies, the remaining spouse inherits and *there is no probate.*

If you have property valued over $100,000, you will have probate *unless you have a living trust.*

5. The *Second-to-Die Policy*: In this case, a life insurance policy is taken out on the parents, naming as the beneficiaries the logical person(s) who is/

are going to take over the ranch. A life insurance trust is set up for the parents in the form of the "second-to-die policy." It pays off when the second person dies, whether it's the husband or wife. These policies are available at a fairly low cost because it is basically a policy on the life of two people. The money goes to the beneficiaries *tax free,* giving them the ability to buy the property out of the estate. For this to be effective, it must be started as soon as possible to build the amount invested to a point of potential worth.

In the case of several children inheriting: The one(s) most likely to stay with the ranch is/are named as the beneficiary(s), providing the money to buy the ranch from their other siblings. If you can get everyone to agree in advance, you can put the terms in an agreement, and the one who wants to stay can buy the others out. It doesn't cover all the bases, but it covers them pretty well and it is the cleanest tax way to handle the disbursement.

An appraisal at the time of the death of the second party is necessary for tax purposes. You can't do the appraisal in advance. You just estimate the amount needed to secure the buyout. The estate tax laws change all the time; hopefully the limit will be raised to favor the beneficiaries.

Of course, on the death of the first spouse, if the husband dies first, his share of the community property goes to the wife with no estate consequences in what is called the "marital deduction." When the wife passes away, the ranch is appraised for estate tax purposes, assuming there are estate taxes. Then the child who wants to continue the ranching operation has the money available to buy the ranch from his/her sibling(s).

6. The *Conservation Easement*: A conservation easement is an optional tool in the transfer of land. The motivation may be to have up-front money to settle the family's claims and to secure peace for all concerned and/or to ensure that the land remains wholly an agricultural operation. (The Hyde family in the later chapter titled "The Hope and the Promise" used this option to their advantage.)

A conservation easement gives you a bundle of rights *and one irrevocable condition.* If you enter into a conservation easement, you are selling the right to develop the property into perpetuity. The legal definition of perpetuity reads: "*An* interest under which property is less than completely alien-able (capable of being sold or transferred) for longer than the law allows." *The land can never be developed. Never.*

Conservation easements are administered by a land trust that serves as an agent to secure the funding needed to purchase the rights from the land-owner, for example: Fish and Wildlife, Cal Trans, Audubon Society. But not every site appeals to them. These organizations look for wildlife and water, but if there is a property that they want for some other reason, they will work to find a buyer. Those transactions happen all the time. A word of cau-tion is that some agencies or organizations that purchase easements word their contract so that no one else can develop *except* them.

A conservancy agreement can protect the resources forever. For exam-ple: the contract can be written to prohibit the sale or transfer of ground-water from the property so the water can never be sold and pumped off of the land and transferred to some distant city. By virtue of the conservancy agreement, no other federal or state agency can override that contract.

The price is set by an appraiser first in a full value, *as-is* condition, and secondly in the *after* condition. For all intents and purposes, the value of the land does not change. But it does put a cap on the value of the property and restricts future options: it cannot be subdivided. For estate tax purposes, the value of the property is reduced. The rancher stays in possession and con-tinues to ranch. What he or she is selling is the right to subdivide or change the nature of the property.

Generally, the trust offers a "boiler plate" contract and the right to enter into negotiations. This step can be time consuming but allows the owner input into the design of the agreement. It is advisable for the landowner to seek advice from the attorney, the accountant, and the appraiser prior to settling on the final terms.

The trust, the group purchasing the conservation agreement, will have no say over who inherits the land, but it may set a number of *conditions* that, once agreed to, the owner must observe. The trust may want to schedule activities at the site, or visits to check on the condition of the land. It may restrict how much firewood is removed, or what kinds of buildings are constructed. *These terms are negotiable prior to signing.*

The title company will state the holder of the agreement and issue a deed and a present conditions report after the closing.

Remember, *the land can never be developed,* even if in one hundred years Disneyland goes in next door and an international airport is built across the street. You are selling the *promise to preserve* wildlife and botanical values. So it must not be entered into lightly. *Your decision will affect generations to come.* But, if it is your wish that your ranch never be developed, it may be a vehicle to secure your dream.

A conservation easement is a good way to get some cash now and allow you to stay on the ranch as long as you want. When you are gone, if the ranch is sold, the selling price will probably be less than it would have been if you hadn't sold the conservation easement. It is a way to avoid being land poor while everything is tied up in the ranch operation.

You will want to work with your accountant in finalizing the agreement because, hopefully, you will sell the easement for a substantial amount of money and there will be tax consequences, either capital gains or income tax due on the sale. The capital gains tax is only 15 percent at the time of this writing.

As with all legal contracts, the devil is in the details. Your attorney, who now understands your wishes, can advise you before you sign the contract.

Remember that the trust that purchases your conservation easement will have on staff more powerful and experienced attorneys than the common person can afford to hire. Control of the property could slip right out of your hands, and someone else would wind up calling the shots.

Ranchers might be better off dealing with a local conservancy in their home county. They may realize less for the easement but be more secure in the contract that they set up for themselves.

STEP THREE: THE ACCOUNTANT

An accountant will ensure observance of tax laws, financial accountability, and estate tax.

1. The accountant is part of the team and should be privy to all arrangements you make.

2. The person who does your tax returns may, through long-term knowledge of the operation, be in a better position to advise you.

3. The accountant will know the basis of your property and be able to offer advice as to the best way to proceed on property sales, to balance any expenses that have accrued over the years, and how to develop a strategy based on past procedures.

STEP FOUR: THE APPRAISER

An appraiser sets the taxable estate value and offers invaluable information.

ARMED WITH THE FINANCIAL ADVICE described above and knowing the wishes of your children, you need to make a decision and move forward. It is your property, and the decisions rest with you—with the advice from your attorney, accountant, and appraiser—to draw up a trust, will, limited liability partnership, corporation, charitable foundation, or to sell your property. It is important to protect family harmony.

In the end, it will be done. Your children and your land will be protected, and the effort will be among the most important expressions of *mothering* that you will ever do.

NOTE

1. "$26 Trillion at Stake: Passing on Assets Requires Good Planning," *Ag Alert*, June 7, 2006; http://www.cfbf.com/agalert/sidebar/handingdown001.cfm.

The Walker Family

Tillie, Ira, Cristi, Erla, Kyon, Fern, and Tammy Walker

W heeler Mountain and McAfee Peak in northern Nevada is where the waters of the region divide: the Humboldt River flows south into the heart of the Great Basin; the Owyhee River runs north through the Shoshone-Paiute reservation in Duck Valley and joins the Snake River on the breaks of the Columbia Plateau before merging with the Columbia River.

The Duck Valley Reservation is 453 square miles and represents at least three bioregions: the Owyhee River valley, the sloping steppes of the high desert at fifty-two hundred feet elevation, and the rim rock plateaus and mountains peaks at nine thousand feet. The state line between Nevada and Idaho splits the tribal land almost exactly in half. The Shoshone and the Northern Paiute People trace their presence in the area back over fifteen thousand years. Owyhee, the only community on the reservation, is near the southern border of the Nevada side. It offers housing, medical care, school K–12, stores, restaurant, post office, and is the center for the tribal administration offices. Agriculture, livestock grazing of cattle and horses, and some farming are the economic bases of Duck Valley.

The town of Owyhee has a look of impermanence, like a military town that lacks long-term pride. Except for the banners and tidy appearance of the school, there are few signs of civic projects that draw a community together.

That impression ends at the city limits sign. It is in the ranches dotting Duck Valley and running its length and breadth that history is deep and unity is evident. Abandoned and trashed cars common on reservation lands are missing from this landscape. Some tribes elsewhere have sold off reservation property to non-Indian interests, but not at Duck Valley, and the result is a marked appearance of democratic pride. Trucks and stock trailers, tractors and feedwagons, stackyards full of hay, cattle and horses scattered across open meadows are signs of hard work and prosperity. Trees mark ranch headquarters; barns and corral complexes are located down roads lined with wild rose bushes and willows that delineate fence lines. Irrigation ditches spill water across the meadows. There is a sense that the ranchers are the warriors of another time, the ones whose songs are sung. In building a business from the land to make their children's future more stable financially, they also give them culture and tradition.

THE NAME "Owyhee" originated from an incident that took place during the Donald Mackenzie expedition of 1818. Mackenzie led a group of men up from the Columbia River to explore the rivers on the high tablelands that feed the Columbia. At a fork in the river, three Hawaiians who were among the crew were sent to scout up one fork for beaver, find the headwaters, and determine if the river was navigable. They did not return. One source reports that the body of one of the Hawaiians was found, which led to the theory that they were the victims of an Indian attack. However, other historians doubt that conclusion, pointing out that the rest of the expedition traveled the country in safety. The mystery held the interest of many, and in the 1830s the river and surrounding area was named Owyhee, in honor of the Hawaiians. The phonetic spelling and pronunciation of their home country, Hawaii, has endured to the present day.

The Shoshone and Paiute People were hunter-gatherers of prehistoric times who roamed in seasonal harvests of antelope, rabbits, fish, seeds, fruits, and nuts. Salmon was the mainstay of their diet, both fresh and sun dried for winter storage. They relied upon each other and maintained close family ties. Leaders grew up within the ranks, to be chosen for physical abilities, wisdom, and pragmatic decision-making for the benefit of the people as a whole.

It is thought that the horses the conquistadors brought to the New World on sailing ships from Spain in the 1400s came into the hands of the Shoshone and Paiute People sometime after the 1803–6 Lewis and Clark expedition to the Pacific. The People became skilled horsemen and later livestock men and ropers. These are traditions that continue today despite the social pressures of the modern world on the Duck Valley people. Some have fallen victim to unemployment (currently at 40 percent on the reservation), and drugs and alcohol, the downfall of all cultures, lure some into dependency. Serious health issues such as diabetes continue to plague them. Their strength remains their horse culture.

Arnold Rojas writes with respect for the Indian buckaroo in his book *The Vaquero*. Rojas, himself a mix of Spanish and Indian, chronicled the lives of men and women who, like him, were horsemen—vaqueros.

> When a vaquero was especially skilled, and he was asked how he had reached such a degree of proficiency, his answer would invariably be: "Me crie entre los Indios"—"I was raised among the Indians . . ." Or when some vaquero had performed his work with great skill, the other men would look at each other, smile approvingly, and say, "Se crio entre los Indios pues"— "Well, he was brought up among the Indians." . . . The Indian vaquero was sparing in speech and serene under all circumstances. He was pithy in all his expressions and often spoke in metaphor or ironically. One would have to be well acquainted with him to know his meanings. He had a knack for giving names that never failed to correspond to something visible in their owners."

Rojas might have been writing about the Walker family.

George Walker met Maggie at a rodeo in Battle Mountain, Nevada, in the early 1960s. After they married, he brought Maggie to Duck Valley, to his family's ranch at Paradise Point where the Owyhee River breaks away from the road to Elko and opens into the great expanse of Duck Valley. Just below the road, poplars and cottonwoods, golden with fall's frost, mark the homestead of John Paradise, George's grandfather. True to the tradition of the Shoshone, George was born in a seclusion tent set back from the house. The house is vacant now and the yard gate is closed.

"That big hill up to the right," said Ira, George and Maggie's eldest son, "is where our great-grandmother Grace Toy used to ride to go hunting. I'm not sure where she originated, but I remember Dad telling me stories of her. They'd hook the horses to a wagon and go up into the hills to hunt sage grouse. That would be lunch. Then they'd go deer hunting. When she got older, they went up in a truck. At age eighty-five she could pick a buck out of a set of trees as they were going by. She was just sharp. I can remember going up to see her and she'd have pies."

The word "pies" was echoed by Ira's sisters, Fern and Cristi, and they all laughed, remembering being little kids at grandma's house. "I don't know when she had time to make those pies because she was always working outside," Ira said. "But they'd have the fireplace going and we'd sit in front of it eating pie."

GEORGE GREW UP ranching on his family land, as his father had and his father before him. After he and Maggie returned to Duck Valley, they picked up where he left off. The Walkers have always raised and ridden good horses, and they tend cattle that are descendants of those early generations of cattle. The vaquero tradition remains the core of the Walker family and is a source of pride.

George and Maggie began in a small house on a knoll beside a sweet spring. The newlyweds had little need of spacious rooms until a child came into their lives. They took in one of George's nephews, Clint, when his mother became ill and, later, died. Maggie took Clint with her on horseback when helping George with the cattle. After Ira was born, Clint rode alone on his own horse, and Ira was strapped in his cradleboard on Maggie's back. If he got tired, she put him in the shade where she could see him and continued her work. Each of the children were part of their workday in this way. As soon as the children could ride on their own, George had their horse and saddle ready. Maggie remembers Ira roping horses when he was six years old. He never stopped.

Several years Clint's junior, Ira said, "Clint has always been part of our family. He and his wife, Erla, and their daughter Lacy built a house on the same land where our grandfather lived. Clint may be a cousin, but he's more like a brother to us."

Five children made the walls of the little cabin seem to draw in when the family went inside at night. They said it was almost as if they pulled the house over their heads like a blanket. A second house was started, and the whole family pitched in to make it large enough for the growing Walker family. The uncles did the rock-work on the entryway and built a big, open fireplace. Even the little ones helped paint. From construction to finish work, the family built the house. Trees were planted around the yard and near the barn and corrals. The swing in the tree out front is there for other generations.

In 2007, four of George and Maggie's five children—Clint, Ira, Fern, who is two years younger than Ira, and Cristi, the youngest—were gathered around the dining room table of their homeplace talking about the reservation land where they were born. Only their brother Jon was not present. Cristi moved back from a job in Reno when her father became seriously ill with diabetes. After he passed away a few years ago, Maggie retired from teaching at the reservation school and moved to Sparks, Nevada, where she lives with Jon, his wife, Diana, and Adia, their year-old daughter.

In the Walker house, the round oak dining room table is a symbol of the unity of the family. Maggie rarely used the center leaf to make it larger. When the center leaf is added for company, it stands out, perfect and unmarred between the ones tracked by years of bowls and platters passed hand to hand in daily use. She kept the table small, preferring the closeness of shoulders and knees touching, eliminating any distance between her children. Busy schedules, homework, deadlines, and term projects were set aside when it was time to gather for breakfast or supper. "Even if we weren't hungry," Fern said, "Mom and Dad asked us to come and sit with the family here at the table. We joined in conversations. This was where they kept us close."

Ira, Fern, and Clint went to the College of South Idaho, while Jon graduated from the University of Nevada, Reno (UNR), where he also played rugby. After two years at college, Fern was offered a job with a cutting horse trainer in California, and later worked for D-M, a saddle shop in Reno. Now, she has a position at the health clinic on the Pyramid Lake Reservation, north of Reno. "That's where our grandpa was from," Fern said, "but when he came to Duck Valley, the people here took him in. I like working with the elders at Pyramid Lake. They are his people."

"Mom's kitchen is so small," Cristi said, "especially now that appliances are so big. But that's where we always were, getting in each other's way, all of us. Mom had to weave through us to get to the stove and back to the sink. But she never chased us out."

Cristi also left college early for a job in Reno, but she rediscovered her buckaroo roots when she moved home to the family ranch. Being with her father at the end of his life had many rewards. Living near and working with family, having a daily presence in the lives of Tammy and Ira's children, Shantell, called Tilly by her family, and Kyon, and Clint's daughter Lacy, has become more important than she would have guessed.

Cristi has her own cattle and supplements her income doing daywork for a neighboring rancher. When she needs help, Ira, Tammy, and the kids lend a hand. She does the same for them. Fern comes up as often as her job allows, timing her days off with cattle work, as does Ira and Tammy's oldest son, Rusty, a senior at UNR.

Clint works at the hospital in Owyhee and has cattle of his own. He, Erla, and Lacy help out on the weekends and summer evenings until dark.

After George died and Maggie moved to Sparks, Cristi stayed on in the family home, the house they all grew up in. Outside and in, George and Maggie are felt everywhere. A pair of chaps and the bits and bridles George used in his daily work hang in the living room. His boots with his silver spurs on the heels sit on the hearth. One of the two trophy saddles made for him when he won the Big Loop Horse Roping contest in Jordan Valley in 1976 and 1977 is on a saddle rack. Before George died, he told his children, "It all stays here with Maggie. If you want to use something, ask your mother so she knows where it is. Then bring it back."

Bedrooms are cozy with quilts and weavings Maggie has made. She has earned respect for her handwork. In 2006, she and her four sisters were invited to take part in a seminar at the National Museum of the American Indian in Washington DC. They spent three weeks consulting with other artists on weaving and design techniques. Maggie enjoyed the trip, the museum, sightseeing, and the people she met but sorely missed her desert country home.

During the years the Walker children attended school in Owyhee, Maggie worked as an aide at the school, and began taking correspondence courses in education. In 1985 she enrolled at UNR and graduated in 1987 with a BS degree in education. Maggie's first teaching position was in Carlin, Nevada, before she returned to Owyhee to teach in the Elko County School District. She retired in 2005. Cristi kept the home fires burning while Maggie was away, and George fought the loneliness of a nearly empty house by filling it up again.

"He took in three nieces and a boy that needed a home," Cristi said. "Dad got himself another boy he could take to rodeos and rope with. He just liked having kids around, and he was always a good cook. Even when Mom came back home from college, he made breakfast every morning and had dinner waiting when she came home at night."

Tammy was also born on the reservation and went to school with all of the Walker kids. She and Fern were classmates and friends, but she and Ira didn't take much notice of each other. They bumped around like two foals from different mare bands, territorial, perhaps, keeping their distance until they met again in college and started to date.

"I don't think we thought it would be a serious relationship at the time," Tammy said. "But as the days went by, and the months, it became something serious. We had to grow on each other."

Ira teases that as a traditional man, it cost him twenty horses to gain Tammy's hand in marriage. And when he wants to make her smile, he says, "I'm gonna go get my horses back if you don't straighten up."

"They're old and spavined and toothless and lame by now," she laughs.

Their first child, Rusty, was two years old when Ira got a job in Reno working for the Palomino Valley Wild Horse Center, a facility where horses taken off the government lands are processed and held in pens until they are adopted out.

"I worked there a year to the day," Ira said. "We had an apartment in town, and Rusty wasn't even able to go outside and play because of being in the city."

All parents who live in highly populated areas fear for their children's safety. Tammy and Ira had the added anxiety of being from a small rural community where everyone knows everyone and has for generations. Rusty was raised to be a happy, friendly little boy. But newspaper stories of kidnappings made Ira and Tammy extremely cautious and protective.

"I always had to be with him," Tammy said. "When we came home to visit, he had freedom here that he didn't have in Reno. He just dreaded going back."

"Dancing with the mop was Rusty's biggest deal when he was a little boy," Ira said. "We lived in town maybe eight or nine months, and then we moved out to Sutcliffe on the reservation at Pyramid Lake. We rented a trailer house that had a little yard. One day Rusty's mop was gone. He didn't know what happened to it. His mom had used it and she had it outside drying. He came in the door from out in the yard and he said, 'Mom! She's back! She's come back! My dancing partner.'

"Those cows there at Sutcliffe are so skinny," Ira said. "One would actually come over the cattle guard every day to eat in the yards at Sutcliffe. So, Rusty's deal was to watch that cow come over the cattle guard and eat and leave, every day." The tension around Ira's eyes when he talked of that year away released when he said, "I had to get out of there. I moved back home with my little family. I never, ever want to leave again. But, you know, I had to get away to see the beauty of this place."

AFTER RETURNING TO OWYHEE, Tammy got a job with the tribe. Their weekends are split between working with the cattle and traveling to rodeos and jackpot ropings. Tammy and Ira both work hard to make ends meet and to save money for their kids' education. The cattle bring in a part of their

Ready to sort, Tammy and Fern

income, but their day jobs provide fixed and consistent salaries they depend on. Tammy works in the tribal office, and Ira works in the rodeo arena.

At the age of eight, Ira began competing in junior rodeos, continued to rodeo in junior high and high school, and was on the college rodeo team. He has competed at the local, state, and national levels in both roping and rough stock events. After Rusty was born, Ira concentrated on roping and quickly earned a reputation as one of the best in the Great Basin. George, Clint, and Ira are widely known for their ability with a rope. Some people say that's how they avoided the alcoholism and drug addiction so prevalent on the reservation today. One of Ira's competitors spoke of the Walkers respectfully: "They don't drink; they don't do drugs. They rope. And they rope tough!"

Ira's decision to eliminate alcohol from his life came like most things that structure his life, the influence of family.

"One year we were going to a rodeo and Rusty was probably five or six years old and he knew what drinking does to people. He'd seen it. We stopped at a store and Rusty saw me buy a beer for the road. As we drove up the highway I reached for the beer. Rusty turned his head and looked right into my face. So I put the beer down. Then I reached for it again; Rusty looked up at me again. The third time it happened, I just threw the beer out the window. And his face broke into the biggest old smile I've ever seen. That was in the eighties."

Recently, while visiting the cemetery above the town of Owyhee, Ira walked through the area where his family is buried, and, looking at the headstones, he began to notice the ages of the men in the family buried there. "They were forty years old," he said, counting them off on his fingers, "thirty-five years old, nineteen years old, and all because of alcohol." Now, he spoke quietly and his palm cupped up as if he held their misery. "I never thought about it until this year."

Tammy and Ira are concerned about Shantell and Kyon growing up in a generation exposed to dangerous influences.

"Peer pressure is frightening in its power over young people," Tammy said. "Our only defense is open discussion."

AS A CHAMPION ROPER, Ira commands respect from boys and young men he comes in contact with at rodeos. In Shoshone terms, he is an elder. His stature and poise contribute to that position. Within the community, others defer to him. With his siblings, he is the head of the family.

"I do a lot of talking to my kids about drugs, too," Ira said. "I was not an angel when I was a kid. But when I'm around kids in general situations who aren't related to me, I talk about what drugs or alcohol do to people. I know for a fact what alcohol does to you. I tell them, 'Stop and think before you do anything. Look at the people it's affecting. What people could have been able to do with their lives, talented people—it has hurt them."

Tilly was born a few years after Rusty, and then Kyon. "We had a really nice woman who would come into our home while I was at work," Tammy said." When she got hired into the day-care center, we just didn't trust anyone else, so they went to day care with her."

Tammy's job in the reservation's human resources office puts her in a position to receive criticism from the community. "I have to work with the community, employees, committees, and the business council. I try to avoid the politics. I dread going to work at times. Right now, it's something I have to do. But I can't bring any of it home because it's confidential and the issues are sensitive. Ira tells me to leave the problems at work. Tillie and Kyon know when I've had a tough day at work. They avoid me for a while. Kyon tells me, 'Mom, you need a time-out.'"

Many rural communities are helpless when it comes to controlling drugs in their midst. Official drug control departments are often underfunded and overworked in rural counties, giving the dealers free rein. Police are spread too thin over vast distances to the point that drug use is epidemic on many reservations.

"The people know who is bringing the drugs in, but the cops will not stop them until they violate the law in some form or other, or a person signs a complaint," Tammy said. "Drug dealers are not going to run a stop sign or speed. It's just a bad deal. Sometimes when Ira comes in at night and says, 'Gee, I had to count to ten today,' I say, 'Yeah? How many times?' His work is nothing compared to what I have to deal with. Getting on my horse and going riding blows all that away."

The young couple keeps a close eye on their kids, they stay involved in their activities, and they know their friends. Never before has the strength of family been more important to them. They set a good example for the children by working hard for everything they have, and they involve the kids in their projects, but it takes more than that. Tammy and Ira make it a point to constantly talk to Tilly and Kyon about good values to build their lives on.

In 1998, the home adjacent to the ranch came up for sale. It was in bad shape and Ira was not in favor of buying it. He worried that it would turn into a money pit.

"But I told him we'd have it paid off faster than he would believe," Tammy said. "It was a lot of work. I'll never forget what my son, Rusty, told me: 'Mom, I think that when we get this house ready for us to move in, we'll appreciate it because we've worked hard for this house.' Every one of us pitched in. The water wasn't very good; there were holes in the walls; there were no solid windows; so we practically had to rebuild it. It was fun. We lifted up the tile and put down new flooring and painted. Rusty was right: we all appreciated it when it was finished."

GEORGE AND MAGGIE started out branding calves for each of the kids every year so they would have a herd of their own cattle. Ira's parents did that for him, and Tammy's parents gave them a few heifers to get them started.

"We are really grateful for that," Tammy said, "and we've done the same for our children."

"A couple of times a year, Rusty will ask me how many calves he had this year," Ira said. "I keep a count for him of all his cattle, and I tell him how many calves we branded with his iron. It seems to make him feel content to know his herd is growing."

Ira may tease Tammy about being a traditional man, but he is exactly that. As a role model, Ira gave Rusty what he could. Rusty's Uncle Jon became an influence when he graduated from UNR with a degree in geography. Today Jon is a GIS specialist and works for Eco:Logic, a company that designs water infrastructure all over the West. But when George was ill, Jon came back to Owyhee for two years and worked for the tribe, to be close. He has always been a good cowboy, but it's not enough for him. His wife, Diana, is a coordinator of English as a Second Language for the Washoe County School District. They are happy living in the city. Jon's move from the reservation and his success may have given Rusty the courage to go on his own. Still, he calls to ask his dad about his herd of cattle.

Rusty's cattle are only one herd of seven that belong to the Walker family members. Each owner's cattle are identified by separate brands. The Walker Ranch cattle run together as one herd on the reservation range all summer, and winter on the home ranch meadows. When spring comes, they start the cattle west across the valley toward the desert. The cows feed in the lower country at 5,500 feet until the first of June, when the ranchers gather the desert, separate out the strays, and everyone brands their calves born since turnout. Each ranch drives their cattle up over the rim to spread out across the miles of high desert until the middle of June. Then they drive them down off the desert. The ranchers separate their cattle again and take their herds to different branding pens. When the cattle are branded up, they are pushed across the valley floor and up onto the mountains on the east side of the valley for the rest of the summer. In all, the cows travel more than sixty miles from spring to fall.

"In October we bring them down and they mix with everybody's on the reservation as a whole," Ira said. "Every family has their own set of cows. We take the res association bulls out in May, and they stay out of the cows until mid-October. But every ranching family has their own bulls too. Of course, in the winter we feed them the hay we take off the meadows during the summer here on the ranch. It works pretty well."

Rusty developed his ability with horses and cattle like his parents. He was considered "good help." It is a deceptively subtle compliment covering the gamut of talents and abilities required for ranching. Some people are better suited to one area of expertise than another. Rusty mastered all phases as a livestock manager and roper, and he has a natural ability with horses. College entrance exams gave no credit for his ranching history. When he enrolled at UNR, he felt unsure. He was interested in so many things. When he was considering studying art, he went home to talk with his parents.

"He changed majors three times," Tammy said. "He was really frustrated because he didn't even have a major. Kidding, I said, 'Well, Rusty, you've got some major problems here.'

"He said, 'Mom, I'm serious.'

"I said, 'Rusty, I'm serious, too. You are very lucky that you can pick up something that easy. You're willing to try. I think that you can adapt to anything you want to be and you're very capable of learning and I'm glad that you're not trying to limit yourself. There's so much out there for you.'"

As with anyone living in the confines of a small rural town, reservation life can blind a young person to the possibilities. Some feel intimidated by the system and the pace of big cities. The cocoon of home can be unhealthy if the young college student is not strong enough to develop goals and standards to guide his newly found freedom. Rusty was lucky. He had Jon and Maggie nearby in Reno and his parents' good advice. "Get your course subjects taken care of first," Tammy told Rusty, "then branch out to other interests."

"We told Rusty that we would support him in whatever he wants to do," Ira said. "He was relieved after that."

Work as a developing artist, perhaps designer, challenges Rusty. He's already comfortable with urban life, and his parents recognize that his future is not on the reservation. They have raised him to look beyond his own backyard, just as they are doing with Shantell and Kyon. They have given him the tools to succeed at any job, anywhere.

TILLY LIVES TRUE to the buckaroo tradition. Even as a little girl she was always interested in whatever could be done from the back of a horse, and yet she's very social.

"If we were working cattle or rodeared somewhere," Ira said, "Tilly wanted to go talk to everybody. And she's always been that way. She's had some little butt chewings for doing it. Not only from dad, but mom and uncle and aunties. You'd look up and Tilly was heading out to go see the guy over there. When I was a kid, I was never allowed to go and sit and visit with anybody when we were working cattle. Work comes first and visiting is for after.

"Today a lot of the kids, and grown-ups, if you offer them a job, they don't know where to begin," Ira said. "They don't know what to do, actually, until they are shown. Whereas with a kid raised on a ranch, regardless of what the job is, they'll get it started and work at getting it done, no matter what it takes. A lot of the kids here would rather watch TV or drive around the reservation all day. They don't want to work. So, I try to keep Tilly lined out a little bit, but she still sneaks off and finds somebody who wants to visit."

Art class, Rusty Walker

Most of Tilly's favorite friends are buckaroos who rope or are learning to be buckaroos. For all her socializing, Tilly is developing a keen sense of observation. She watches her dad's eyes when he rides through the rodear to determine which animal he's after. With seven different irons on the ranch, and perhaps a hundred when they separate cattle belonging to the Reservation Association in the fall, it is very important that riders pay attention. The rider cutting out the cattle may have a cow and calf that won't stay together. The relationship of cow and calf may be detected only as a glance across the herd. By slow, careful work, the rider can edge the pair toward the outside of the rodear, but being herd animals, they often resist being pushed away from the other cattle. If the rider looks up and sees that the others holding herd know which animals he is after and are prepared to help him out, it is a moment of unity of purpose. "I think it's pretty neat when that happens with Tilly," Ira said. "She's getting to be pretty good help. I don't know what she'll do in her life, but I'm pretty sure it will be on the reservation.

"Most mornings Tilly knows I'm going to go somewhere with my horses, and it's, 'Dad, what are you going to do today?' And I'll tell her.

"She'll say, 'Oh! I wish I could go.'

"And I say, 'Well, you've got to go to school first.'

"'Yeah, I know. But could you come and get me?' she'll ask.

"I say, 'No, you've got to finish all day.'

But I have taken her out to brandings and to do other work different places than just with our cattle, and she's gotten where she's good help. I can tell her different ways to throw her loop, place her horse, and it's made a big difference in her ability to rope. And once she figured it out, that it was that easy, it was hard to keep her away from it. Now she wants to ride all of my horses."

At age seven, Kyon is more interested in dinosaurs and rocks than he is in cattle. Last June, the family drove a herd of cattle off the desert side of the mountain. It was nearly noon and the drive had been a long one.

"The cattle were getting pretty hot," Ira said, "and we had to corral them. Kyon and I were in the back and Tammy and Shantell were up in the lead.

I said, 'We've got to get going.' He says, 'Oh, wait, wait. Look at here, Dad!' And he's looking at a rock.

"I said, 'No, son. We've got to go. We'll come back up after.' We hurried down and helped get the cattle corralled. When we went back up afterward, we couldn't find the rock, so I was in trouble."

Ira keeps the old stories he heard as a child alive for his kids. Even if they are just stories, he thinks they teach Tilly and Kyon to keep their eyes open. For instance, there is the story a friend of George's told Ira about gathering horses on the Owyhee desert.

"Down along the rim they could see these horses traveling all in a line," Ira told Kyon and Tilly, "ten head of them. He wanted to get to the lead, so he went out and around to get where he knew they would be coming out. When he got there, no horses. Nothing. So he followed back. No horse tracks." He paused and enjoyed the interest in his children's eyes. "The older people say that the people of that time are still there. I don't know whether it's truth or just stories that have been here forever."

BEFORE THE ANTIQUITIES ACT was signed into law, collecting arrowheads was a hobby for many people who wandered the desert country. For most, it was a fascination with all things ancient and a respect for the artistic nature of the weapons of primitive cultures that roamed this earth before modern times. For some, it was touching those lives, connecting with a time before the sorrow and wrong that befell the native peoples.

"We treasure arrow points," Ira said. "Our father had a couple. I've seen them when I'm riding, but I never touch them. I can go out and see them when I want to. They'll be there. Our people were here a long time. I took a fella out to see the writings on the rocks, and he told me the Indians only drew what they saw. I got to looking and there are pine trees and bear prints. So at one time this desert might have been a forest."

Again, Ira's children watched their father's face enrapt as he passed the story into their idea of what is possible.

Kyon and Tilly find their own way through imagination and observation, through being in touch with the world around them. For many children in the city, soccer, ballet, baseball must all feel like work with no payoff at the end, as activities that develop from the outside of a child. Unstructured play builds from the inside. In self-invented play out of doors, nature is both playmate and teacher. The only boundaries are those set by the parents with safety in mind.

Recently, Tammy went to Arizona, and Kyon asked her to bring him some sand. "But I couldn't find any sand," she said. "The whole city was either apartments or parking lots or pavement."

"I'M EIGHT ON APRIL 7," Kyon said. "My horse's name is Kid. I like to ride. I'm learning to rope. I like school. I'm in second grade, so I'm learning to divide and subtract. I like rocks and I'm going to grow up to be a geologist. I like to take the rocks to school and show the whole class. They're what the earth is made of. My favorite rock is the one with little sprinkles of gold on it. My favorite part of science is the part about dinosaurs. I think birds are related to dinosaurs."

When George was in the hospital for a short time, Kyon was sitting on the floor beside his bed looking at a dinosaur book when the doctor came in. George said, "Dr. Myers, I'd like to introduce you to my grandson, Kyon. Kyon, this is Dr. Myers."

Kyon glanced up and saw Dr. Myers's long legs in khaki pants and said, "No, he's the Jurassic Park man."

TILLY IS THIRTEEN and in the eighth grade. She is a little apprehensive about her immediate future despite her recent accomplishment in the Powder Puff football game when she kicked the football fifty-three yards.

"I'm not excited," she said. "There are two hundred and fifty kids in high school. Too many."

Something else is troubling Tilly. The ground beneath her feet is not as solid as it once was. She was deeply affected by her grandfather's illness, and his death. Now, there's someone else she's fond of who is worrying her.

Tillie and Kyon

"I like math because we have a cool teacher," Tilly said. "But he's kind of sick right now. He has MS, so that put him down for a couple of months. He's our basketball coach, too, and he said he'll be back for basketball season."

"Tilly has been riding since she was just a little thing," Ira said. "She used to ride with Grandpa. We had an old mare that was gentle, and one time we were riding and she was showing me the things her Grandpa showed her. He was always teaching her something, and she doesn't forget."

Her grandpa left her things of intrinsic worth that she constructs her life around. He also left her something physical that she can lay her cheek against and feel a heart beating, and remember him by—one of his horses.

"She's a Paint," Tilly said. "Black, white, and a light bay color, and she's going to have a colt in the spring. I like riding up on the desert. It's nice and open and you can do just about anything up there. I used to be scared that I would mess up when we were driving the cattle up there, but then, I figure that my grandpa is with me all the time, so I don't worry about it."

IRA DOESN'T WORRY EITHER. The family is strong, all of them. They rope. That's how they stay focused. And often, they win. At the Labor Day Fair in Elko, Nevada, Ira and other members of the Mountain Ranch Team, entered the team branding event. It is a timed event that represents everyday ranch work. Each team ropes and paint-brands four head of big calves. The fastest team that strictly adheres to the rules wins. The whole Walker family was in the Elko County grandstands to support the team, because they're proud of them, and they love to watch them rope. The team won the event for the third consecutive year and retired the trophy.

The Mountain Ranch team has a reputation for being fast, efficient ropers. That they are tough, fair competitors is an unstated verification for their way of living and working. Roping and family are Ira's commitment to being a worthy parent to his children and a worthy elder to the children he befriends. Ira and Tammy do not strive to be role models for others; they strive to uphold the traditions and values their parents lived by, to respect their heritage, and to pass it on intact.

MAGGIE'S ROLE in her children's lives, and her grandchildren's lives, is equally as strong as George's. Maggie is a woman who felt that gathering her family around a small table made them a close family, and she has learned that mothering never ends. Right now, living with Jon and Diana, she has time to strengthen her relationship with Adia, the first of the Walker family to be born off the reservation. At the age of one year, Adia takes the book from Maggie's hands and reads to herself. Her steady eyes follow the lines, and suddenly she laughs. She turns her pages and laughs. Then she looks up at Maggie and says a word in Shoshone. Maggie responds in Shoshone. They smile at each other and touch foreheads. Adia turns the page.

The Hope and the Promise

> As opportunities to expand water supplies dwindle, competition over
> existing supplies is mounting. How this competition plays out is about
> much more than whether rich investors get richer. It is about food
> security, social stability, the health of rural communities, the plight of
> the world's poor, and the ability of the aquatic environment to continue
> supporting a diversity of life.
>
> —SANDRA POSTEL, *PILLAR OF SAND*

Rick Woodley

The evidence of a water deficit in the West is obvious on any map. Where
there is scant precipitation, the population is also scattered. In the Klamath
Basin of south-central Oregon, lava and juniper dominate the southeast
corner, a region called the Devil's Garden. An hour north of Klamath Falls
the snowy peaks of the Cascade Range string the length of the state, breaking off at Crater Lake. The exact range of their influence is plain to see.
Moisture gathers in narrow skirts of green at their feet, soaking first into
the forest and woodlands, then dwindles where the earth turns gray and
tan. Springs run out onto the blotter of dry land as far as they are able.
Some join into creeks and reach the valleys, streams to rivers, lakes, reservoirs, always moving toward the sea. Water is king in a dry and parched
kingdom. This has become especially true in the Tulelake Basin.

In February 2001, the Klamath Basin was put on notice when a Ninth
District federal court judge ruled that all irrigation water for agricultural
production on the Upper Klamath watershed was to be shut off for violation
of the Endangered Species Act (ESA).

To say the reaction in the basin was explosive is an understatement.
More than two thousand ranchers and farmers—landowners and holders
of water rights as legitimate, as enduring, as indisputable as any other on
the Upper Klamath watershed—were singled out as responsible parties in

a suit brought in support of the decline of sucker fish in Upper Klamath Lake and wildlife habitat, and the death of 300,000 salmon in downstream Klamath River. They alone were asked to compensate for the shortage. No irrigation for fields of potatoes, wheat, or alfalfa meant financial disaster. It couldn't have come at a worse time. In 2001, the basin was in the grip of a severe drought.

These were farmers and ranchers who had already been through the 1980s economic depression. Those who survived did so by cutting expenses, working harder, and testing every method and decision for efficiency. They were tougher, smarter, or simply lucky. Over the years they paid their bills, downsized maybe, but got back on their feet financially just in time to take on challenging marketing issues and rising equipment and fuel costs. Then the court pulled the plug: no more water until further notice. Not a reduction, not sharing the loss as in a power rolling brownout, but a total cessation of water rights.

MOST of the basin farmers and ranchers held water rights tied to the 1917 U.S. Reclamation Service project. Such projects were designed to drain and reclaim tillable land, "to make the desert bloom." In the Tulelake Basin just south of Klamath Falls, many landowners around the rim of the basin held titles extending back to the late 1800s. In the center of the basin lay an ephemeral lake, sometimes swamp, sometimes baked mud playa. It was noticed that when the area dried, it was extremely fertile. The Reclamation Service began an ambitious plan to drain water collected there into canals and send it toward a wildlife refuge to improve habitat for migratory birds and to open the reclaimed land to agriculture. The reclaimed land was offered in the form of a lottery draw to servicemen and women returning from the war. In the end, 2,577 applicants were given title to eighty-acre tracts, totaling 210,000 acres, which included homestead rights and land and water rights. On staggered squares of green, brown, and gold crop and pasturelands, the lottery winners went to work farming and ranching, building homes and a community centered around Tulelake, but economically influencing every town on the perimeter of the newly productive land.

AGRICULTURE has title to the largest chunk of water rights of all claims on the Upper Klamath watershed, and as such, offered the easiest solution to the problem addressed in the lawsuit. It will always be so. Growing demands have the potential to stress the Klamath system with shortages. One surety is, it will happen again. Another is, promises to agriculture will be broken again and irrigation headgates will be screwed shut.

This issue is not new in the world. Sandra Postel, author of *Pillar of Sand: Can the Irrigation Miracle Last?* has made a study of the collapse of ancient cultures and found that when agriculture and societies clash over declining water levels, agriculture is the first to be sacrificed, *leaving a society without food*. A society that looks to another to supply the essentials of life becomes dependent and loses control of its future. It cannot be maintained without food; the collapse is inevitable and certain. In her book she warns against allowing the process to be repeated.

THE KLAMATH BASIN'S annual precipitation level of 4–12 inches has conditioned farmers and ranchers to depend on the irrigation system designed by the Reclamation Service for production on their crop and pasturelands. Following the 2001 court-ordered shutdown, the estimated financial loss was between $134 million and $250 million. But that is just the dollar figure.

"I don't even know how you statistically quantify the disruption of an entire irrigation project," said Rick Woodley, a third-generation rancher in the basin, now district manager of the Klamath Basin Soil Conservation Service (SCS), "I don't even know how you statistically quantify the loss of property, the loss of income, the loss of equipment, and the mental health of farmers and ranchers. I don't know how you do that."

In 2002, Secretary of the Interior Gail Norton convened a panel of seven academics, scientists esteemed in their field, drawn from across the country. The panel was asked to review the data that led to the controversial closure of the irrigation headgates and to report on their findings. The Ninth District federal court decision came under review because in one hundred years there was no recorded breakdown in the system. The panel's conclusion was that the 2001 ruling was unfounded and that denying irrigation water to the project was an "injustice."

Population in the Klamath Basin has doubled since 1950 and continues to grow. Periods of low precipitation will occur in the Upper Klamath watershed, bringing the viability of the system into question again. There are too many straws in the glass, about 700, and the rights overlap in 5,600 places. One hydrological study reports that, considering the increasing burden on the system, it will be in a shortfall seven years out of ten.

What began as a workable system of water delivery, satisfying the needs of fish and wildlife, the rights of the area tribes, power, industry, city and residential growth, as well as agriculture, is coming up short, especially in years of low precipitation. It needs to be updated. The Department of Water Resources (DWR) of the state of Oregon is the agency of record. They can't make it rain, but it is their sworn duty to uphold the laws of their office, which includes the development of a workable plan to achieve a lawful and equitable distribution of the water available. The controversy occurs when the plan is opened to the scrutiny of special interest groups and lawsuits are filed. The result is that the DWR has been unable to determine the ladder of adjudication, top to bottom. "Duty" has been buried under twenty-six years of litigation.

Until the adjudication is completed, the DWR is sitting this dance out, leaving all of those seven hundred or so users perplexed and anxious over pending loss, and drawing everyone into disagreement over priority rights. The process is suffering at the hands of the state. Street-corner advice that farmers and ranchers dig wells to replace their shortfall is a quick-fix solution and irresponsible over the long term. Pumping 450,000 acre-feet per year, equal to the users' allocations, has the potential to tax the aquifer to the point of collapse, leaving no reserves for the future.

EVERYONE HAS AN OPINION. No one has a solution. But Rick Woodley and the SCS are running with an idea. Two and half years ago he spearheaded a movement to form the Klamath River Coalition of Conservation Districts (KRCCD). Under his leadership the SCS brought together all of the conservation districts from the headwaters to the ocean. The KRCCD is made up of Klamath Soil and Water Conservation districts, and includes five California districts and every district that is impacted or works on the Klamath River system and its tributaries in the entire watershed.

"Our boards of directors are made up of farmers and ranchers, not government employees. These landowners are elected, not appointed. The purpose is to work together in a unified group of citizens to do the best water quality and quantity projects that we can do on-farm," Woodley said, "to make sure that we're being the best stewards that we can be of our property that we own and farm and ranch while at the same time being very cognizant that the things we do can have impacts on fish and wildlife, and to minimize any adverse impacts that we might have but in all cases to improve fish and wildlife habitat at the same time."

The KRCCD uses the available resources and finds additional resources when needed to aid private landowners with projects. Some landowners have had their fill of "strings attached" government programs but will accept the technical expertise that the group can offer. The projects are wide ranging and perfectly simple: stream bank erosion, fish passages, a weir, a fish ladder, stabilizing a bank, opening up an oxbow that has been filled in with silt, riparian fencing, fish and water management. Some are Conservation Resource Project (CRP) programs where landowners take some land out of irrigation and make it available for cattle grazing. Juniper removal can free up old springs that have gone dry because of the encroachment of the weed-like trees that tax the near-surface water that short-rooted grasses require. They have cleared thousands of acres of juniper in the Klamath Basin, using some federal funds, some state funds, with some cleared at the expense of individual landowners. All of the programs are voluntary. Woodley claims that more than 65 percent of the landowners are involved. Approximately 75 percent of the landowners in the Klamath Basin have had assistance or technical advice on programs to improve their management for soil and water conservation.

"Many of these members did things way in advance of 2001 and still have not received credit for it," Woodley said. "Landowners have improved their irrigation efficiency so that they're applying only a net amount of water. They've come up with crops that are water efficient, and they run irrigation efficiency studies with the extension offices. There are so many things we're involved with to keep our basin whole. But the most important thing we do is get the word out about what is being done and what has been done. And that's probably the hardest thing to do."

The KRCCD is a small step but a positive one. Membership in and of itself puts the control back in the landowner's hands. This organization has documented studies of projects and the reasons for their success or failure. It is an entity that can take part in negotiations with the state of Oregon as it completes the adjudication of the Upper Klamath watershed. The KRC-CD's self-help projects invest the landowners in the partnership and make friends of neighbors. In short, it is a positive in a backwash of negatives.

Rick Woodley is making an impact one user at a time. Transformation does not happen overnight. It comes from diligent searching for answers and a concentrated sharing of ideas about what they all know to be a good and a necessary way of life.

Becky Hatfield Hyde

Becky Hatfield Hyde is a rancher and a mother of four small children. She and her husband, Taylor, ranch on the Sycan River in the Klamath Basin. Taylor, a son of Gerda Hyde, was raised on the Yamsi, the family ranch on the Williamson River, a tributary to the Klamath River. Both ranches are above Klamath Lake and the federal reclamation project where water was turned off to farmers in 2001.

Before Becky could begin our conversation about the Klamath Basin she needed to find her littlest person, Levi, age three. "We just got done with homeschool," she said. "We started working with another family, so we're still going through the 'they're coming, they're gone' stage."

In addition to being one of the many Klamath Basin citizens involved in finding resolution to the water issue, Becky was raised on a ranch in the high desert of eastern Oregon, and is the daughter of Connie and Doc

Hatfield, a couple well known for working on resource issues and the founders of Country Natural Beef. The family has been on the land in Oregon since the 1840s when ancestors settled on a claim that is still in the family. Becky's children represent the sixth generation on the land. Reaching a settlement between the various right holders on the Klamath River means a great deal to her. "It is brutal, absolutely brutal what this conflict has done to our rural ranching, farming, and tribal communities. It's taking a toll on people," she said.

All across the West, ranchers and rural communities are victims of environmental disputes just as real, just as devastating as the one on the Klamath River. Later in the week, Becky will be speaking with some ranchers in Malta, Montana, who are dealing with prairie dogs, and the Buffalo Commons, and the World Wildlife Fund. Serious issues, but merely three of many that are affecting the ability of ranchers to do business. Most result from bad decisions going back a hundred years: some made by ranchers, some made by capitalists, some made by the federal government. In many more cases than not, ranchers are the ones asked to mediate and mitigate.

Becky worries that these environmental issues are costly, time-consuming distractions. "I think there's something very precious here that is slipping through our hands," she said, "and when these ranches, these communities start to fragment, it's gone—really—fast. We need to tell that story of how fragmenting land and fragmenting these communities is environmental degradation. There have been some interesting studies done that show that when land gets sold out of ranch ownership—it's not the first owner that begins to subdivide, but the next, and the rural communities that keep these landscapes intact very rapidly disintegrate."

Ranchers are desperate to stop the trend and are frustrated when the rest of Americans aren't. It becomes obvious when a situation like the water issue comes to the forefront, as it is now. Ranchers are searching for solutions and make compromises that work for everyone so they can continue.

As we talked I could hear the sounds of children in the background. One of the little neighbor boys that has joined Becky's homeschool stayed to play. Levi came to tell his mom, "That the little boy is sad and lonesome. He needs some beans."

Laughing, she said, "They were all moving cows yesterday. They're doing really well. We have a couple of ancient ranch horses. Henry, our four-year-old, rides this old black horse that is perfect because he can't go very fast." She took the phone with her while she got them each a bowl of beans.

"The love of this life is transferring to our kids. Jack, our six-year-old, has his own goat herd, and he spends a lot of time out there roping and riding them. Lizzy is eight, and she's quite the little cowgirl. She was riding her horse, Robin, holding Levi in the front of her saddle and leading Henry's horse, C.D., all at the same time, and I thought, "That's pretty good.""

Henry chimed in saying, "I was holding the reins and a stick and the saddle horn. Three things all at the same time, Mom."

"That's good, buddy." And to me she said, "It's fun to talk about the horse stuff, but it's cows and grass that pay the bills here. My family is known for using motorcycles to move cattle, so I certainly don't want to come across as the last of the pure buckaroo culture."

Becky checked on all the kids before continuing about the challenges of reaching settlement.

"I believe we are closer than ever to some positive settlement in the Klamath Basin," she said. "In the state of Oregon, the Klamath is the guinea pig for adjudication. It's been a bumpy ride. And when the water was shut down in 2001, and then we had the fish die-off in 2002 in the lower river, coupled with ocean fisheries being curtailed this year, it's been hard to settle. What I think we're beginning to realize is that the rural people of this basin really need each other. A few years ago a rancher from Plush told me that the days when ranchers could grab their lawyers and their congressmen and thump somebody are gone. I think we've spent a lot of time—to our detriment—trying to do that here. I believe strongly that we need vibrant agricultural communities in this country, but to survive we'll have to adapt.

"Some people still want to fight. In the Klamath Basin people have spent hundreds of thousands of dollars in litigation with one another, and it is all for naught. It has been devastating. The farming community has litigated against the ranching community, and vice a versa. They've spent more money fighting each other than fighting the tribes. It's a pitiful story of what people do under stress," Becky said. "It's senseless confusion, really."

Changes have come over Becky in the course of sitting through eight years of meetings. She has gotten to a place where when she thinks of people on the land, she thinks of ranching, but she also thinks of the traditional tribal culture downriver where they're still harvesting salmon for their living. "There are many families on the Lower Klamath River taking the same path to the banks of the river to catch an eel or salmon for dinner that their ancestors walked," Becky said. "These people are hurting as well, and I can't look into their eyes and hear their stories and deny that truth."

This is not the back-to-the-land movement popular among former college students in the late sixties and seventies. It is multigenerational in nature, families who have always lived off the land.

"People don't believe that," she said. "They think the ranching culture is a subsistence culture. Urban people at the meetings are like, 'You've got to be kidding. They shoot a deer and put it in their freezer and they think that's living?' Well, actually, yeah. We put one in our freezer last fall. It's a big disconnect. But I think people also long for that connection to the land and to that subsistence culture and also to the ranching culture."

Again, it is a case of "Who has time to leave your work, your animals, to attend meetings that the government members, agency members, and representatives of environmental interests are paid to attend?" For ranchers, every expense, from a telephone call and letter-writing time, to gallons of high-priced fuel to get them to the meetings, to hiring someone to fill in doing their work while they are at the meetings is logged in red ink. Time away may mean the kids aren't seeing you, or a cow that is calving is on her own, or there's no one to change the irrigation water when the ditch rider turns it your way. "Who has the time?" Becky echoes. "I question that every other week. I don't have the time and I don't have the money. But if you don't get involved in the decision making, you won't be here tomorrow. It's the sad truth of where we are, at least in this place. And we're a lot more paranoid here than in other places. We have to show up to survive."

Gerda Hyde is indisputably the most generous-hearted, no-nonsense woman rancher in the basin. People wanted to know what she thinks about the water disputes. Years back when ranching went through difficult financial times, she started taking in fly fishermen to survive. They stay in the bunkhouse, stick their feet under her table at mealtime, and are guided by her son, John. He knows the Williamson like he knows cattle and horses. Fly-fishing on the Yamsi is considered world-class. But it's only a part of what the fishermen come for. They linger awhile with Gerda. They sit, but she is never still. The woman can build fifty pies while they're having their morning coffee. She's not Ma Kettle, but she is plain spoken and too busy for small talk. There's not a person in the county who doesn't know and respect her. Symbolically, she is the matriarch of the basin.

Year after year, the fishermen return to step back into the flowing infinity of the Williamson. They witness the growing up of Gerda's twenty-one grandchildren, and they notice how capable the kids are, even the little ones like Henry. Yamsi has been powered by kid labor for a long time. They have all been raised with the ranch as their classroom. Some have grown and gone, but when they're needed to brand or gather, they turn up. Recently, Taylor worked with a couple of nephews who came to pregnancy-test cows. "They're just such good help," he said. "They're the real deal: they know what to do and where to be, and they take it so seriously because they know it's our livelihood."

The California Science Museum is doing a documentary on the Klamath River. The crew visited with Gerda at Yamsi. In response to their questions about the conditions that led up to the 2001 court decision, she said, "I didn't even know we had an issue with water ten years ago."

That is how most landowners felt. They also agree that there is an issue with water quality. "Especially in Klamath Lake and below in the Klamath River," Becky said. "You don't have to be a scientist to go down there and look in the river and see the problem. I was at the mouth in February and it looked like pea soup."

Most of the problems the Klamath Basin is facing today have to do with federal decision-making that might have made sense at the time on paper but has proved to be woefully shortsighted, and certainly not equitable considering the disparity between ethnic and economic groups.

"It is the nightmare the government built," Becky said. "But I don't believe many of the decisions were made with ill intent. They have just added up to a tough story. We drained wetlands to create the Klamath Project to feed a hungry nation. Then in the fifties, the Army Corps of Engineers worked out here on the Sprague River valley. They ripped out the willows, they blasted the grasses and tules with some kind of herbicide that killed them all, and then they created this ditch system that basically drains this valley so you end up with all the sediment and phosphorus just dumping into Klamath Lake, which was the start of making it go bad with pollutants."

Prior to the Sprague River project, it was a perfect system because it used to naturally flood and cleanse itself. But now everybody runs big pumps to dump the high flows onto the floodplain, and they have power costs to do what nature did for free. "It was pretty darned good and beautiful before we 'fixed' it," she said. "On top of it, we've got the landowners being blamed. I went to a meeting recently and there was a guy from Bly named Butch Hadley, and he said, 'Hey, I was a part of this. I helped churn up the willows and do the work to change this because the government said it's what we should do, and now the government's coming back with their ESA regulations and the primary hydrologic problem here stems back to that diking and ditching.'

"There used to be a series of tremendous wetlands and grasslands along the Sprague River valley before we did that," Becky said. "The ecosystem and the habitat changed substantially, and now my argument is, we can grow riparian vegetation, we've got willows coming back, we can do a lot. But we cannot recover from that dike system, and we cannot hold landowners fully responsible. It was another Great Nation notion."

IT'S HENRY THIS TIME. He's got a brush and wants to fix Becky's hair like she braids Lizzie's hair. As Henry guides the hairbrush through Becky's brown hair, she now takes on a subject that wrenches her heart and yet is uplifting for the sake of the friendships that have come to her through the work she wishes she didn't have to do. If the truth were known, she would rather take the children down on the banks of the Sycan and show them the rushes and sedges coming back. But so would the mothers of the Klamath Tribes, if the truth were known.

THE TERMINATION of the Klamath Tribes Reservation in the 1950s is another of those government plans gone awry and is a sad commentary on our history of negotiations with native tribes. No one was looking out for the Indian community. The Klamath Indians had 800,000 acres of prime old-growth timber. They were a very prosperous tribe. Then came the federal idea called "termination." Before the deal was finalized, they needed the advice of someone who represented their interests to explain the long-term ramifications of the sale. No one did that. Nor did they have advice about how to invest for the future. Once again, an Indian community was tricked into a one-sided deal. The sale created problems with no solutions. Lives were affected. Many lives were lost. The Klamath Falls Cadillac dealer broke sales records that year, until the money was gone.

Today, only 6 percent of that old-growth timber is left after fifty years of it being Winema National Forest, and now the forest is a blast zone. Prior to the sale, the tribe harvested the timber on their land, but it was a selective harvest. "I have been told that after the reservation was 'sold,'" Becky said, "they cut more timber off of it in one year than in all the years of payments made to the tribal people. We're still reeling from that, and we'll continue to until we figure out how to manage that problem. It broke those people because up until that time a lot of them still had their Indian allotments of 160 acres and they ranched along the Sprague River. It's tough to make a living off 160 acres, but they were able to keep them intact because they also got a payment off their forestland, which was their reservation. Someone came up with an idea to terminate the reservation with a payoff. The result was that they didn't get their subsidy anymore, so they lost their allotment land. After that it was just violence, a horrid thing which comes back to today when the ag community is trying to get water and the tribes own the senior water rights. Well, it's their last treaty right, and they're going to hold onto it. Why wouldn't they?"

Then there was that federal decision, the Klamath Project, which included the dams on the Klamath River that are used for power. They are not agricultural dams, except for the one in Keno. "So you have the return flows out of the Klamath Project, and some of it is not really healthy," Becky said, "which I think could be fixed with just some wetland fringe before it hits the Klamath River again. But the bigger problem is that water sits behind those four Klamath dams and cooks, and they release this warm water whenever they want to downriver, and it makes that mess down there for the salmon and those lower basin tribal folks."

Some of the people in the Klamath agricultural community took a hard line against the tribes in the negotiations on the water rights, whereas the Hydes, who now have a pretty solid water settlement with the tribes, did not. They worked with them and listened to them.

"It's a sad story," Becky said. "And I know that tribes everywhere have a sad story, but what it points to, to me, is the devastation of separating people from land. I would rather die than not live on land. *I would rather die.* I cannot relate to what it would be like to live in town. And those people *did die.* They drank themselves to death, they had jealousies between families that were able to hold onto allotments and ones that weren't, and the murder that went on here is sickening. It was just a free-for-all of just horrible stuff of the human condition."

Becky has long been a part of the Yainix Partnership, a group that works with the four Klamath River tribes, the project irrigators, and the off-project irrigators. For the last eight years, they have focused specifically on settlement solutions. Yainix is a very quiet group. They don't talk outside. *Yainix* means "along the side of a butte." But Becky admits that sometimes it must feel like it means "in a deep crevasse."

"The lack of trust among these groups is phenomenal," she said. "If we can put aside the 'grab your lawyer, grab your congressman' path to solutions and compromise to the point of settlement, it would lead to a healing of some very old and deep wounds."

Recently Taylor and Becky sold a conservation easement on the property they bought on the Sprague River. That brought the value of the ranch down far enough for it to make sense to pay for the rest of it with the cows. "The way I look at ranching today is that one of the things in our bag to keep us on the land is to sell environmental services that we provide," Becky said. "The funding for the easement came in part from the Farm and Ranchland Protection group, and our easement is held in interim by the Klamath Tribes, which circles back to the whole needing to connect to them. Instead of having the tribes as the enemies, they're our partners, and they sanction what we do on the river here. Their scientists look at the river and look at the bugs and look at the fish and look at the grasses, and they're really happy with what we're doing and we turned that whole relationship around. And we're still here.

"I better go now. Henry is wanting to put lipstick on me," she laughs. "We try everything in this family to hang in here on the land with these kids."